SACREDSPACE
the prayer book 2008

from the website www.sacredspace.ie

Jesuit Communication Centre, Ireland

ave maria press  notre dame, indiana

acknowledgement

The publisher would like to thank Alan McGuckian, S.J., Gerry Bourke, S.J., and Piaras Jackson, S.J., for their kind assistance in making this book possible. Correspondence with the Sacred Space team can be directed to feedback@sacredspace.ie. Piaras Jackson, S.J., Gerry Bourke, S.J., Paul Andrews, S.J., and John McDermott welcome all comments on the material or on the site.

The Scripture quotations contained herein are from the New Revised Standard Version Bible, © Copyright 1989 by the Division of Christian Education of the National Council of Churches of Christ in the U.S.A. and are used with permission. All rights reserved.

First published in Australia 2007 by
Michelle Anderson Publishing Pty Ltd

Founded in 1865, Ave Maria Press is a ministry of the Indiana Province of Holy Cross.

www.avemariapress.com

ISBN-10 1-59471-138-0   ISBN-13 9781594711381

Cover and text design by K.H. Coney

Printed and bound in the United States of America.

SACREDSPACE

how to use this book

We invite you to make a sacred space in your day and spend ten minutes praying here and now, wherever you are, with the help of a prayer guide and scripture chosen specially for each day. Every place is a sacred space so you may wish to have this book in your desk at work or available to be picked up and read at any time of the day, whilst traveling or on your bedside table, a park bench . . . Remember that God is everywhere, all around us, constantly reaching out to us, even in the most unlikely situations. When we know this, and with a bit of practice, we can pray anywhere.

The following pages will guide you through a session of prayer stages.

Something to think and pray about each day this week
The Presence of God
Freedom
Consciousness
The Word (leads you to the daily scripture and provides help with the text)
Conversation
Conclusion

It is most important to come back to these pages each day of the week as they are an integral part of each day's prayer and lead to the scripture and inspiration points.

Although written in the first person the prayers are for "doing" rather than for reading out. Each stage is a kind of exercise or meditation aimed at helping you to get in touch with god and God's presence in your life.

We hope that you will join the many people around the world praying with us in our sacred space.

Teach Us, Lord

Gracious Jesus, as your disciples,
we ask you to teach us to pray.
Deep within our heart we have a great hunger
and need for your presence and guidance.
Teach us to pray; teach us to love; teach us to live.
This we ask in your name. Amen.

contents

december 2–8

Something to think and pray about each day this week:

Counting the Days

At this time of the year in many countries you can buy Advent calendars which allow you to count off the days of waiting and praying for Jesus' Coming—which is what Advent means. In many of the same countries, the Advent calendar you can buy may be not about religious events but about gifts you may want to buy or receive. In many countries the evening's television reminds us how many shopping days are left for us to complete our gift purchases.

Suppose for a moment that we take these advertisements as a call to pray rather than to purchase. I'll put myself in the mind of Mary and Joseph, focused on the expected baby, wondering what he will be like and how he will affect my life.

The Presence of God

Lord, help me to be fully alive to your holy presence.
Enfold me in your love.
Let my heart become one with yours.

Freedom

Many countries are at this moment suffering
the agonies of war.
I bow my head in thanksgiving for my freedom.
I pray for all prisoners and captives.

Consciousness

At this moment, Lord, I turn my thoughts to You.
I will leave aside my chores and preoccupations.
I will take rest and refreshment in your presence Lord.

The Word

The word of God comes down to us through the scriptures.
May the Holy Spirit enlighten my mind and my heart to respond to the gospel teachings. (Please turn to your scripture
on the following pages. Inspiration points are there should you
need them. When you are ready, return here to continue.)

Conversation

Sometimes I wonder what I might say
if I were to meet You in person, Lord.
I might say "Thank You, Lord" for always being there for me.
I know with certainty there were times when you carried me.
When through your strength I got through the dark times in
my life.

Conclusion

Glory be to the Father, and to the Son, and to the Holy Spirit,
As it was in the beginning, is now and ever shall be,
World without end. Amen

Sunday 2nd December,
First Sunday of Advent   Romans 13:11–12

Besides this, you know what time it is, how it is now the moment for you to wake from sleep. For salvation is nearer to us now than when we became believers; the night is far gone, the day is near. Let us then lay aside the works of darkness and put on the armor of light.

- "Salvation is nearer to us now than when we became believers." It is a powerful connection that Paul makes, between our belief in Jesus and a sense of urgency in how we live and what we do.
- Has my belief in Jesus really changed me? Have I allowed it to change me?
- Do I fend change off, moving it to "another day"?

Monday 3rd December,
St. Francis Xavier   Matthew 28:16–20

Now the eleven disciples went to Galilee, to the mountain to which Jesus had directed them. When they saw him, they worshipped him; but some doubted. And Jesus came and said to them, "All authority in heaven and on earth has been given to me. Go therefore and make disciples of all nations, baptizing them in the name of the Father and of the Son and of the Holy Spirit, and teaching them to obey everything that I have commanded you. And remember, I am with you always, to the end of the age."

- These are Jesus' last words, his final commission. The eleven fishermen, still shaken by Jesus' crucifixion, must have listened with astonishment. Make disciples of all nations! How?
- They started out from where they were, in Jerusalem. Francis Xavier, that globe-trotting missionary, also started out, not from a "special" place, but just from where he was.

- Lord, you are with me whenever I speak of you to others. Give me the courage for that.

Tuesday 4th December   Luke 10:22

At that same hour Jesus rejoiced in the Holy Spirit and said, "All things have been handed over to me by my Father; and no one knows who the Son is except the Father, or who the Father is except the Son and anyone to whom the Son chooses to reveal him."

- Jesus' mission flows entirely out of his relationship with the Father, and the same God-centered relationship is open to each of us. This is an immense, awe-inspiring privilege.
- Lord, may this knowledge sustain me when I falter, when the journey becomes difficult and I turn my face from you.

Wednesday 5th December   Isaiah 25:6–9

On this mountain the LORD of hosts will make for all peoples a feast of rich food, a feast of well-aged wines, of rich food filled with marrow, of well-aged wines strained clear. And he will destroy on this mountain the shroud that is cast over all peoples, the sheet that is spread over all nations; he will swallow up death forever. Then the Lord GOD will wipe away the tears from all faces, and the disgrace of his people he will take away from all the earth, for the LORD has spoken. It will be said on that day, Lo, this is our God; we have waited for him, so that he might save us. This is the LORD for whom we have waited; let us be glad and rejoice in his salvation.

- "He will swallow up death forever." This text of Isaiah, with its luscious imagery of fine food and wines, and of the dynamic power of the Lord wiping away our tears at the end of days, is also read at funeral liturgies.

- Our waiting for the birth of Jesus and for the joy of salvation are the same waiting—for the Lord who conquers death forever. Let us rejoice and be glad.

Thursday 6th December   Matthew 7:21

Jesus said to his disciples, "Not everyone who says to me, 'Lord, Lord,' will enter the kingdom of heaven, but only the one who does the will of my Father in heaven."

- Lord—there I go again, calling you Lord—look at my life and my actions, not my speeches.
- I do not expect to be judged on pious words, but on the love and justice evident in my life.

Friday 7th December   Matthew 9:27–30a

As Jesus went on his way, two blind men followed him, crying loudly, "Have mercy on us, Son of David!" When he entered the house, the blind men came to him; and Jesus said to them, "Do you believe that I am able to do this?" They said to him, "Yes, Lord." Then he touched their eyes and said, "According to your faith let it be done to you." And their eyes were opened.

- From among the crowd the blind men shout out to Jesus using a formal title, Son of David, as though he was a powerful messianic figure dispensing health to crowds. But Jesus waits until he can meet these men in person, in the quiet of the house where he can test and reveal their faith.
- Lord, you do not meet me as one among many, but face to face, on my own, where you can test the truth of my words, free from the illusions of mass emotion.

Saturday 8th December, The Immaculate
Conception of the Blessed Virgin Mary   Luke 1:26–38

In the sixth month the angel Gabriel was sent by God to a town in Galilee called Nazareth, to a virgin engaged to a man whose name was Joseph, of the house of David. The virgin's name was Mary. And he came to her and said, "Greetings, favored one! The Lord is with you." But she was much perplexed by his words and pondered what sort of greeting this might be. The angel said to her, "Do not be afraid, Mary, for you have found favor with God. And now, you will conceive in your womb and bear a son, and you will name him Jesus. He will be great, and will be called the Son of the Most High, and the Lord God will give to him the throne of his ancestor David. He will reign over the house of Jacob forever, and of his kingdom there will be no end." Mary said to the angel, "How can this be, since I am a virgin?" The angel said to her, "The Holy Spirit will come upon you, and the power of the Most High will overshadow you; therefore the child to be born will be holy; he will be called Son of God. And now, your relative Elizabeth in her old age has also conceived a son; and this is the sixth month for her who was said to be barren. For nothing will be impossible with God." Then Mary said, "Here am I, the servant of the Lord; let it be with me according to your word." Then the angel departed from her.

- When a woman in the crowd cried to Jesus: "Blessed is the womb that bore you," he replied, "Blessed are they who hear the word of God and keep it." First of these was his mother, who said, "Let it be with me according to your word."

- Lord, this is not an easy prayer to make. You prayed it yourself in Gethsemane in a sweat of blood: "Not my will but yours be done."

- Help me to make it the pattern of my life. What issues of surrender and trust does it raise for me?

Something to think and pray about each day this week:

Blessed Expectation

In the last month of pregnancy, a young mother becomes more and more preoccupied with the child she carries. In Ireland she may hear the old blessing: "God be with you both." She is more careful of herself, of her food and drink, her habits, and the daily hazards of living. She feels the movement of the child in her, exploring its comfortable ambiance, and starting to listen to the sounds of the womb, the mother's heart-beat and the music and noises that penetrate to her womb. So it was in Nazareth, as Mary kept house and lived in expectation. This was how the Lord was entering our world, as Alice Meynell wrote:

> No sudden thing of glory and fear
> Was the Lord's coming; but the dear
> Slow Nature's days followed each other
> To form the Saviour from His Mother
> —One of the children of the year.

The Presence of God
God is with me, but more,
God is within me, giving me existence.
Let me dwell for a moment on God's life-giving presence
in my body, my mind, my heart
and in the whole of my life.

Freedom
God is not foreign to my freedom.
Instead the Spirit breathes life into my most intimate desires,
gently nudging me towards all that is good.
I ask for the grace to let myself be enfolded by the Spirit.

Consciousness
Help me, Lord, to be more conscious of your presence.
Teach me to recognize your presence in others.
Fill my heart with gratitude for the times your love
has been shown to me through the care of others.

The Word
I read the Word of God slowly, a few times over, and I listen to
what God is saying to me. (Please turn to your scripture on the
following pages. Inspiration points are there should you need
them. When you are ready, return here to continue.)

Conversation
How has God's Word moved me? Has it left me cold?
Has it consoled me or moved me to act in a new way?
I imagine Jesus standing or sitting beside me,
I turn and share my feelings with him.

Conclusion
Glory be to the Father, and to the Son, and to the Holy Spirit,
As it was in the beginning, is now and ever shall be,
World without end. Amen

Sunday 9th December,
Second Sunday of Advent   Matthew 3:1–6

In those days John the Baptist appeared in the wilderness of Judea, proclaiming, "Repent, for the kingdom of heaven has come near." This is the one of whom the prophet Isaiah spoke when he said, "The voice of one crying out in the wilderness: 'Prepare the way of the Lord, make his paths straight.'" Now John wore clothing of camel's hair with a leather belt around his waist, and his food was locusts and wild honey. Then the people of Jerusalem and all Judea were going out to him, and all the region along the Jordan, and they were baptized by him in the river Jordan, confessing their sins.

- Extraordinary how a mortified man draws people. They admire one whose needs are minimal, who is the master of his own appetites, who has a deep interior freedom. John the Baptist, with minimal clothes and minimal food, was a magnet. People trusted him because clearly he could not be bought.
- Where are the chains on me, the appetites which I have not mastered, and that pull me in ways I do not want? Help me towards a freer heart and body, Lord.

Monday 10th December   Isaiah 35:1–4

The wilderness and the dry land shall be glad, the desert shall rejoice and blossom; like the crocus it shall blossom abundantly, and rejoice with joy and singing. The glory of Lebanon shall be given to it, the majesty of Carmel and Sharon. They shall see the glory of the LORD, the majesty of our God. Strengthen the weak hands, and make firm the feeble knees. Say to those who are of a fearful heart, "Be strong, do not fear! Here is your God. He will come with vengeance, with terrible recompense. He will come and save you."

- During Advent the passages from Isaiah often bring us to the experiences of parched and lifeless wilderness.
- Can I bring to prayer a part of me that feels dry and withered?

Tuesday 11th December   Isaiah 40:3–5

A voice cries out: "In the wilderness prepare the way of the LORD, make straight in the desert a highway for our God. Every valley shall be lifted up, and every mountain and hill be made low; the uneven ground shall become level, and the rough places a plain. Then the glory of the LORD shall be revealed, and all people shall see it together, for the mouth of the LORD has spoken."

- Lord, I make this prayer in Advent. My days may be short and cold, or long and hot; but I really struggle when my heart is arid and dark.
- What I pray for is not the tinsel and giddiness of Christmas, but a strengthening of my weak hands, firming of my feeble knees. I pray to be strong and to leave my fears in your hands.

Wednesday 12th December   Isaiah 40:28–31

Have you not known? Have you not heard? The Lord is the everlasting God, the Creator of the ends of the earth. He does not faint or grow weary; his understanding is unsearchable. He gives power to the faint, and strengthens the powerless. Even youths will faint and be weary, and the young will fall exhausted; but those who wait for the Lord shall renew their strength, they shall mount up with wings like eagles, they shall run and not be weary, they shall walk and not faint.

- The words of the Lord are like the eagles' wings, words that soar, words that cut through, words of great power and strength.

- Can I deepen my hope in God by giving more attention and time to these words? Can these words become part of my very being?

Thursday 13th December — Matthew 11:11–15

Truly I tell you, among those born of women no one has arisen greater than John the Baptist; yet the least in the kingdom of heaven is greater than he. From the days of John the Baptist until now the kingdom of heaven has suffered violence, and the violent take it by force. For all the prophets and the law prophesied until John came; and if you are willing to accept it, he is Elijah who is to come. Let anyone with ears listen!

- How are we to understand what Jesus says to us here? On the one hand, John is a great man; there is none greater. On the other hand, he ranks below the very least who are in the kingdom.
- Can I focus on this kingdom John speaks of? Or am I distracted by what is around me? Am I really listening to Jesus' message?

Friday 14th December — Matthew 11:16–19

Jesus spoke to the crowds, "But to what will I compare this generation? It is like children sitting in the marketplaces and calling to one another, 'We played the flute for you, and you did not dance; we wailed, and you did not mourn.' For John came neither eating nor drinking, and they say, 'He has a demon'; the Son of Man came eating and drinking, and they say, 'Look, a glutton and a drunkard, a friend of tax collectors and sinners!' Yet wisdom is vindicated by her deeds."

- In this frustrated comment of Jesus, we have some sense of how people saw him. In contrast to John the Baptist, he ate and drank like the common man, and his friends were considered disreputable. From the beginning of his public life, those who did not believe in Jesus' preaching or his miracles discerned nothing of the divine in his features. He was too ordinary.

- Lord, I take comfort in your ordinariness. May I find you in what is workaday, ordinary and routine.

Saturday 15th December   Matthew 17:10–13

And the disciples asked him, "Why, then, do the scribes say that Elijah must come first?" He replied, "Elijah is indeed coming and will restore all things; but I tell you that Elijah has already come, and they did not recognize him, but they did to him whatever they pleased. So also the Son of Man is about to suffer at their hands." Then the disciples understood that he was speaking to them about John the Baptist.

- God's messengers tend to be rejected. This is a bitter truth about our human condition in the midst of our Advent journey. Advent still calls us to a fulfillment promised and guaranteed by God.
- In my prayer can I hold together both the promise and the shadow?

december 16–22

Something to think and pray about each day this week:

God's Refugees

Like any young couple planning together, Mary and Joseph would have given thought to the coming birth in Nazareth: what friend or neighbor would be the midwife, and how they would prepare the room and the house. But in the weeks before the birth, menacing rumors reached them of a census that would force them away from home. Quiet, imperturbable Joseph had to make travel plans. We think of him walking, with his pregnant wife on a donkey, up the ninety miles to Jerusalem and Bethlehem. The last part of the journey was a climb into the hills of Judea. But more stressful than the journey was the uncertainty. Where will we sleep? How can I care for Mary in her condition? What does God mean by putting us through this? He and Mary and her child were in the condition of refugees the world over. In that winter season it was a question not of shopping but of survival. In this season we try to open our hearts to the refugees of our time.

The Presence of God

What is present to me is what has a hold on my becoming.
I reflect on the presence of God always there in love,
amidst the many things that have a hold on me.
I pause and pray that I may let God
affect my becoming in this precise moment.

Freedom

There are very few people
who realize what God would make of them
if they abandoned themselves into his hands,
and let themselves be formed by his grace. (St Ignatius)
I ask for the grace to trust myself totally to God's love.

Consciousness

In the presence of my loving Creator,
I look honestly at my feelings over the last day,
the highs, the lows and the level ground.
Can I see where the Lord has been present?

The Word

God speaks to each one of us individually. I need to listen to
hear what he is saying to me. Read the text a few times, then
listen. (Please turn to your scripture on the following pages. Inspiration points are there should you need them. When you are
ready, return here to continue.)

Conversation

What is stirring in me as I pray?
Am I consoled, troubled, left cold?
I imagine Jesus himself standing or sitting at my side,
and share my feelings with him.

Conclusion

Glory be to the Father, and to the Son, and to the Holy Spirit,
As it was in the beginning, is now and ever shall be,
World without end. Amen

Sunday 16th December,
Third Sunday of Advent   Matthew 11:2–11

When John heard in prison what the Messiah was doing, he sent word by his disciples and said to him, "Are you the one who is to come, or are we to wait for another?" Jesus answered them, "Go and tell John what you hear and see: the blind receive their sight, the lame walk, the lepers are cleansed, the deaf hear, the dead are raised, and the poor have good news brought to them. And blessed is anyone who takes no offense at me." As they went away, Jesus began to speak to the crowds about John: "What did you go out into the wilderness to look at? A reed shaken by the wind? What then did you go out to see? Someone dressed in soft robes? Look, those who wear soft robes are in royal palaces. What then did you go out to see? A prophet? Yes, I tell you, and more than a prophet. This is the one about whom it is written, 'See, I am sending my messenger ahead of you, who will prepare your way before you.' Truly I tell you, among those born of women no one has arisen greater than John the Baptist; yet the least in the kingdom of heaven is greater than he."

- There is real comfort in this story. John the Baptist, the powerful, austere man who held such a sway among the Jews, still had his moments of darkness. Imprisoned in Herod's dungeon, he wondered: Am I a fool? Is this all there is? Was I wrong about Jesus?
- John does not just brood on the question. He acts; he sends messengers to Jesus. And Jesus does not send back reassurances; he just asks the messengers to open their eyes and see the evidence of Jesus' life.
- Lord, in my moments of doubt and darkness, may I fill my eyes with you.

Monday 17th December   **Matthew 1:1–11**

An account of the genealogy of Jesus the Messiah, the son of David, the son of Abraham. Abraham was the father of Isaac, and Isaac the father of Jacob, and Jacob the father of Judah and his brothers, and Judah the father of Perez and Zerah by Tamar, and Perez the father of Hezron, and Hezron the father of Aram, and Aram the father of Aminadab, and Aminadab the father of Nahshon, and Nahshon the father of Salmon, and Salmon the father of Boaz by Rahab, and Boaz the father of Obed by Ruth, and Obed the father of Jesse, and Jesse the father of King David. And David was the father of Solomon by the wife of Uriah, and Solomon the father of Rehoboam, and Rehoboam the father of Abijah, and Abijah the father of Asaph, and Asaph the father of Jehoshaphat, and Jehoshaphat the father of Joram, and Joram the father of Uzziah, and Uzziah the father of Jotham, and Jotham the father of Ahaz, and Ahaz the father of Hezekiah, and Hezekiah the father of Manasseh, and Manasseh the father of Amos, and Amos the father of Josiah, and Josiah the father of Jechoniah and his brothers, at the time of the deportation to Babylon.

- This is more than a list of biblical names: Matthew is rattling skeletons in the cupboard of Jesus' ancestry. He includes four controversial mothers with his list of fathers. Tamar dressed as a prostitute and bore twins to her father-in-law. Rahab betrayed her city. Ruth was a gentile. Solomon was the child of David's adulterous affair with Bathsheba.

- There is no airbrushing of Jesus' pedigree: he comes to us laden with all the disreputable past of his race, and shows how each birth is a fresh beginning.

- How do I regard the "wayward" ones in my family tree or treat the embarrassing relatives I have? Lord, teach me to accept my humanity, my genes, my relatives, as you did.

Tuesday 18th December   Jeremiah 23:5–6

The days are surely coming, says the Lord, when I will raise up for David a righteous Branch, and he shall reign as king and deal wisely, and shall execute justice and righteousness in the land. In his days Judah will be saved and Israel will live in safety. And this is the name by which he will be called: "The Lord is our righteousness."

- When speaking about the future of Israel, the prophets remind us of God's great works in the past.
- By looking back in meditation I can look forward in expectation; by holding on to the memory of Jesus' birth, I can progress towards the kingdom.
- During this Advent, Lord, lead me to deepen my memory of God's great deeds for his people so I look forward with courage.

Wednesday 19th December   Judges 13:2–7, 24–25

There was a certain man of Zorah, of the tribe of the Danites, whose name was Manoah. His wife was barren, having borne no children. And the angel of the LORD appeared to the woman and said to her, "Although you are barren, having borne no children, you shall conceive and bear a son. Now be careful not to drink wine or strong drink, or to eat anything unclean, for you shall conceive and bear a son. No razor is to come on his head, for the boy shall be a nazirite to God from birth. It is he who shall begin to deliver Israel from the hand of the Philistines." Then the woman came and told her husband, "A man of God came to me, and his appearance was like that of an angel of God, most awe-inspiring; I did not ask him where he came from, and he did not tell me his name; but he said to me, 'You shall conceive and bear a son. So then drink no wine or strong drink, and eat nothing unclean, for the boy shall be a nazirite to God from birth to the day of his death.'" The woman bore a son, and named him Samson. The boy grew, and the LORD blessed him. The spirit of the LORD began to stir him in Mahaneh-dan, between Zorah and Eshtaol.

- The readings this week are about fertility and birth, often against the odds. New-born children can seem a miracle to their parents, who marvel at the power of new life which has flowed through them.
- Lord, open me to the new life which you promise at Christmas. Are there areas of "barrenness" in my life where I might be open to being surprised?

Thursday 20th December   Isaiah 7:10–14

Again the LORD spoke to Ahaz, saying, "Ask a sign of the LORD your God; let it be deep as Sheol or high as heaven." But Ahaz said, "I will not ask, and I will not put the LORD to the test." Then Isaiah said: "Hear then, O house of David! Is it too little for you to weary mortals, that you weary my God also? Therefore the Lord himself will give you a sign. Look, the young woman is with child and shall bear a son, and shall name him Immanuel."

- The sign which God promises is not mountainous or powerful, but tiny and fragile, alive with promise, a mother with child.
- "Immanuel" means God is with us. How is that true for me?

Friday 21st December   Luke 1:39–45

In those days Mary set out and went with haste to a Judean town in the hill country, where she entered the house of Zechariah and greeted Elizabeth. When Elizabeth heard Mary's greeting, the child leaped in her womb. And Elizabeth was filled with the Holy Spirit and exclaimed with a loud cry, "Blessed are you among women, and blessed is the fruit of your womb. And why has this happened to me, that the mother of my Lord comes to me? For as soon as I heard the sound of your greeting, the child in my womb leaped for joy. And blessed is she who believed that there would be a fulfillment of what was spoken to her by the Lord."

- How profound are the instincts and insight of mothers! While husband Zechariah is baffled and struck dumb, and foster-father Joseph has misgivings, it is a woman, Elizabeth, herself pregnant, who recognizes the action of the Lord in her young cousin.
- This is a special gift given to Elizabeth, the intimate appreciation of what is happening and who is really present.
- Do I always appreciate what is happening and who is really present? Am I open to God's gifts?

Saturday 22nd December   Luke 1:46–56

And Mary said, "My soul magnifies the Lord, and my spirit rejoices in God my Savior, for he has looked with favor on the lowliness of his servant. Surely, from now on all generations will call me blessed; for the Mighty One has done great things for me, and holy is his name. His mercy is for those who fear him from generation to generation. He has shown strength with his arm; he has scattered the proud in the thoughts of their hearts. He has brought down the powerful from their thrones, and lifted up the lowly; he has filled the hungry with good things, and sent the rich away empty. He has helped his servant Israel, in remembrance of his mercy, according to the promise he made to our ancestors, to Abraham and to his descendants forever." And Mary remained with Elizabeth about three months and then returned to her home.

- The Magnificat, as we call Mary's prayer, has become our traditional hymn of gratitude and joy. This is a moment of ecstatic fulfillment, when Mary looks back on all the promises of the Old Testament, and begins to sense and relish her own role in the Lord's plan.
- Can I pray the Magnificat in gratitude for God's goodness to me?

Something to think and pray about each day this week:

The Little One

As Mary's time drew near, the situation grew more baffling and distressing. Even the shelters which Joseph had budgeted for, the wayside inns, turned them away: no vacancies. In children's Christmas plays, the inn-keeper is played variously as cruel and uncaring, or as concerned but unable to help, other than by offering a stable. It is there that we have one of the most familiar and loved scenes in human history, the manger in Bethlehem, as Sartre pictured it:

> The Virgin is pale, and she looks at the baby. What I would paint on her face is an anxious wonderment, such as has never before been seen on a human face. For Christ is her baby, flesh of her flesh, and the fruit of her womb. She has carried him for nine months, and she will give him her breast, and her milk will become the blood of God. There are moments when the temptation is so strong that she forgets that he is God. She folds him in her arms and says: My little one.

The Presence of God
God is with me, but more, God is within me.
Let me dwell for a moment on God's life-giving presence
in my body, in my mind, in my heart,
as I sit here, right now.

Freedom
A thick and shapeless tree-trunk would never believe
that it could become a statue, admired as a miracle of sculpture,
and would never submit itself to the chisel of the sculptor,
who sees by her genius what she can make of it. (St Ignatius)
I ask for the grace to let myself be shaped by my loving Creator.

Consciousness
Knowing that God loves me unconditionally,
I can afford to be honest about how I am.
How has the last day been, and how do I feel now?
I share my feelings openly with the Lord.

The Word
I read the Word of God slowly, a few times over, and I listen to
what God is saying to me. (Please turn to your scripture on the
following pages. Inspiration points are there should you need
them. When you are ready, return here to continue.)

Conversation
Do I notice myself reacting as I pray with the Word of God?
Do I feel challenged, comforted, angry?
Imagining Jesus sitting or standing by me,
I speak out my feelings, as one trusted friend to another.

Conclusion
Glory be to the Father, and to the Son, and to the Holy Spirit,
As it was in the beginning, is now and ever shall be,
World without end. Amen

Sunday 23rd December,
Fourth Sunday of Advent   Matthew 1:18–24

Now the birth of Jesus the Messiah took place in this way. When his mother Mary had been engaged to Joseph, but before they lived together, she was found to be with child from the Holy Spirit. Her husband Joseph, being a righteous man and unwilling to expose her to public disgrace, planned to dismiss her quietly. But just when he had resolved to do this, an angel of the Lord appeared to him in a dream and said, "Joseph, son of David, do not be afraid to take Mary as your wife, for the child conceived in her is from the Holy Spirit. She will bear a son, and you are to name him Jesus, for he will save his people from their sins." All this took place to fulfill what had been spoken by the Lord through the prophet: "Look, the virgin shall conceive and bear a son, and they shall name him Emmanuel," which means, "God is with us." When Joseph awoke from sleep, he did as the angel of the Lord commanded him; he took her as his wife.

- Joseph had lived his life as a good man, an upright person. But now this is something else again, for God has burst in on his life and on his family, and tipped everything upside down. How is he to respond to all this?
- The Christian life has little to do with "doing the right thing" but everything to do with giving our way over to God's way, with falling into unconditional love. Like Joseph, can we spend our life learning this.

Monday 24th December   Luke 1:67–79

Then his father Zechariah was filled with the Holy Spirit and spoke this prophecy: "Blessed be the Lord God of Israel, for he has looked favorably on his people and redeemed them. He has raised up a mighty savior for us in the house of his servant

David, as he spoke through the mouth of his holy prophets from of old, that we would be saved from our enemies and from the hand of all who hate us. Thus he has shown the mercy promised to our ancestors, and has remembered his holy covenant, the oath that he swore to our ancestor Abraham, to grant us that we, being rescued from the hands of our enemies, might serve him without fear, in holiness and righteousness before him all our days. And you, child, will be called the prophet of the Most High; for you will go before the Lord to prepare his ways, to give knowledge of salvation to his people by the forgiveness of their sins. By the tender mercy of our God, the dawn from on high will break upon us, to give light to those who sit in darkness and in the shadow of death, to guide our feet into the way of peace."

- "By the tender mercy of our God." Our God has such a long history of "tender mercy" towards his people, a constant invitation to each of us, culminating in the gift of an infant Son.
- Am I ready this Christmas to invite Jesus into my heart and my home, giving all that I have over to him?

Tuesday 25th December,
Feast of the Nativity of the Lord   John 1:1–5

In the beginning was the Word, and the Word was with God, and the Word was God. He was in the beginning with God. All things came into being through him, and without him not one thing came into being. What has come into being in him was life, and the life was the light of all people. The light shines in the darkness, and the darkness did not overcome it.

- The light shines in the darkness, and the darkness did not overcome it. Despair, loneliness, and evil do not take a holiday at Christmas. We work hard to keep depression at bay by lights and music but many suffer deep pain.

- This is our faith: that the light of love from Bethlehem's Baby was strong enough to withstand the darkness around it; and that it continues to shine through the darkness, which can never extinguish it.

Wednesday 26th December,
St. Stephen, the first martyr   Matthew 10:17–22

Jesus said to his apostles, "Beware of them, for they will hand you over to councils and flog you in their synagogues; and you will be dragged before governors and kings because of me, as a testimony to them and the Gentiles. When they hand you over, do not worry about how you are to speak or what you are to say; for what you are to say will be given to you at that time; for it is not you who speak, but the Spirit of your Father speaking through you. Brother will betray brother to death, and a father his child, and children will rise against parents and have them put to death; and you will be hated by all because of my name. But the one who endures to the end will be saved."

- Pope John Paul II wrote that the best word to describe *agape*, or perfect Christian love, is "solidarity"—a word for hanging in, despite brokenness in ourselves and others, for letting love lead us where it will, even to being willing to pay the price.
- Lord, when I close my eyes for the last time, may I have purged all my resentments and forgiven any enemies; and may I see your face.

Thursday 27th December,
St. John, Apostle and Evangelist   John 20:2–8

So Mary Magdalene ran and went to Simon Peter and the other disciple, the one whom Jesus loved, and said to them, "They have taken the Lord out of the tomb, and we do not know where they have laid him." Then Peter and the other disciple set out and went toward the tomb. The two were running together, but the other disciple outran Peter and reached the tomb first. He bent down to look in and saw the linen wrappings lying there, but he did not go in. Then Simon Peter came, following him, and went into the tomb. He saw the linen wrappings lying there, and the cloth that had been on Jesus' head, not lying with the linen wrappings but rolled up in a place by itself. Then the other disciple, who reached the tomb first, also went in, and he saw and believed.

- This gospel for St John's feast refers to him only as the other disciple, the one whom Jesus loved. It is a moment of unalloyed joy, as John and Peter grapple with the fact of Jesus risen from the dead. They move from concern with burial cloths and an empty tomb, to a realization that death had met its master; the one whom they loved was with them for ever.
- How does this affect me, today? Can I move beyond my immediate concerns, towards what is really important?

Friday 28th December,
Feast of the Holy Innocents   Matthew 2:13–18

Now after the wise men had left, an angel of the Lord appeared to Joseph in a dream and said, "Get up, take the child and his mother, and flee to Egypt, and remain there until I tell you; for Herod is about to search for the child, to destroy him." Then Joseph got up, took the child and his mother by night, and went to Egypt, and remained there until the death of Herod. This was to fulfill what had been spoken by the Lord through the prophet, "Out of Egypt I have called my son." When Herod saw that he had been tricked by the wise men, he was infuriated, and he sent and killed all the children in and around Bethlehem who were two years old or under, according to the time that he had learned from the wise men. Then was fulfilled what had been spoken through the prophet Jeremiah: "A voice was heard in Ramah, wailing and loud lamentation, Rachel weeping for her children; she refused to be consoled, because they are no more."

- Another sad feast, remembering Herod's bloodthirsty massacre and the heartbreak of the babies' mothers. As we recover from Christmas, other parts of the world—perhaps even in our own country—are suffering bombs, bloodshed, bereavements.
- Lord, keep my heart open to the grief and tragedies that confront me.

Saturday 29th December   Luke 2:33–35

And the child's father and mother were amazed at what was being said about him. Then Simeon blessed them and said to his mother Mary, "This child is destined for the falling and the rising of many in Israel, and to be a sign that will be opposed so that the inner thoughts of many will be revealed—and a sword will pierce your own soul too."

- Simeon, one of a group of people known as the Quiet in the Land, waited for the Messiah, not as a conquering warlord, but as God breaking into human history in his own way. Simeon lived a life of constant prayer and quiet watchfulness, and here we have the blessed moment of recognition, as he embraces the baby.
- Lord give me that grace of quiet prayer, and of recognizing you when you show yourself to me.

december 30–january 5

Something to think and pray about each day this week:

Endings and Beginnings
As my year draws to a close, I look back at its mixture of joyful and sorrowful episodes, some times that were boring, others exciting or deeply moving. Where was the love in my life this year? Has the year 2007 left me with any unresolved angers or resentments? How can I go into 2008 with a peaceful and clean heart? Where was God in all the personal experiences which leap into my memory? Did I recognize him in them at the time? Can I work through them now in my prayer?

May the favor of God be upon me in 2008.

The Presence of God
As I sit here, the beating of my heart,
the ebb and flow of my breathing, the movements of my mind
are all signs of God's ongoing creation of me.
I pause for a moment, and become aware
of this presence of God within me.

Freedom
I ask for the grace
to let go of my own concerns
and be open to what God is asking of me,
to let myself be guided and formed by my loving Creator.

Consciousness
In the presence of my loving Creator,
I look honestly at my feelings over the last day,
the highs, the lows and the level ground.
Can I see where the Lord has been present?

The Word
I take my time to read the Word of God, slowly, a few times, allowing myself to dwell on anything that strikes me. (Please turn to your scripture on the following pages. Inspiration points are there should you need them. When you are ready, return here to continue.)

Conversation
Remembering that I am still in God's presence,
I imagine Jesus himself standing or sitting beside me,
and I say whatever is on my mind, whatever is in my heart,
speaking as one friend to another.

Conclusion
Glory be to the Father, and to the Son, and to the Holy Spirit,
As it was in the beginning, is now and ever shall be,
World without end. Amen

Sunday 30th December, Holy Family   Colossians 3:12–15

As God's chosen ones, holy and beloved, clothe yourselves with compassion, kindness, humility, meekness, and patience. Bear with one another and, if anyone has a complaint against another, forgive each other; just as the Lord has forgiven you, so you also must forgive. Above all, clothe yourselves with love, which binds everything together in perfect harmony. And let the peace of Christ rule in your hearts, to which indeed you were called in the one body. And be thankful.

- "Bear with one another . . . forgive each other." We can focus on all the "holy" words that Paul uses here—"compassion; kindness; humility; meekness; perfect harmony"—but what often troubles us in our daily lives is putting up with each other. We can feel deep failure in our relationships with those who are close to us.

- At the core of each marriage and strong relationship is the union: we are together. Don't question that; God certainly doesn't. We can fall out along the way but we are always welcomed back into this union.

- This is a wonderful and powerful image of the way God loves us: God just won't let go of us. Let us give thanks, and forgive one another.

Monday 31st December   John 1:14–18

And the Word became flesh and lived among us, and we have seen his glory, the glory as of a father's only son, full of grace and truth. (John testified to him and cried out, "This was he of whom I said, 'He who comes after me ranks ahead of me because he was before me.'") From his fullness we have all received, grace upon grace. The law indeed was given through Moses; grace and truth came through Jesus Christ. No one has ever seen God. It is God the only Son, who is close to the Father's heart, who has made him known.

- This is the truth round which the Fourth Gospel was written: that in Jesus, God has broken his immemorial silence. His Word, the perfect reflection of his Godhead, has become flesh.
- We look at Jesus and wonder at the grace and truth that shine in and through him. Lord, let me continue to receive from your fullness.

Tuesday 1st January,
Solemnity of Mary, Mother of God   Luke 2:15–21

When the angels had left them and gone into heaven, the shepherds said to one another, "Let us go now to Bethlehem and see this thing that has taken place, which the Lord has made known to us." So they went with haste and found Mary and Joseph, and the child lying in the manger. When they saw this, they made known what had been told them about this child; and all who heard it were amazed at what the shepherds told them. But Mary treasured all these words and pondered them in her heart. The shepherds returned, glorifying and praising God for all they had heard and seen, as it had been told them. After eight days had passed, it was time to circumcise the child; and he was called Jesus, the name given by the angel before he was conceived in the womb.

- For centuries Christians tried to put words on Mary's relationship with God, and with the Council of Ephesus they affirmed that she can rightly be called Mother of God, the feast that is celebrated today. We may still struggle to find the right words to describe this mystery, but more easily contemplate Mary at the crib, as described by Sartre in his Christmas play, *Barjona*:

There are rapid, fleeting moments when Mary realizes at once that Christ is her son, her very own baby, and that he is God. She looks at him and thinks: "This God is my baby. This divine flesh is my flesh. He is made from me. He has my eyes, and the curve of his mouth is the curve of mine. He is like me. He is God and he is like me."

Wednesday 2nd January   John 1:19–28

This is the testimony given by John when the Jews sent priests and Levites from Jerusalem to ask him, "Who are you?" He confessed and did not deny it, but confessed, "I am not the Messiah." And they asked him, "What then? Are you Elijah?" He said, "I am not." "Are you the prophet?" He answered, "No." Then they said to him, "Who are you? Let us have an answer for those who sent us. What do you say about yourself?" He said, "I am the voice of one crying out in the wilderness, 'Make straight the way of the Lord,'" as the prophet Isaiah said. Now they had been sent from the Pharisees. They asked him, "Why then are you baptizing if you are neither the Messiah, nor Elijah, nor the prophet?" John answered them, "I baptize with water. Among you stands one whom you do not know, the one who is coming after me; I am not worthy to untie the thong of his sandal." This took place in Bethany across the Jordan where John was baptizing.

- There is a question for me: "Who are you? . . . What do you say about yourself?"
- Lord, I think of you beside me, seeing the good and the promise in me. This is what I want to say about myself: I am called into being by God, who loves me.

Thursday 3rd January   John 1:29–34

The next day John saw Jesus coming toward him and declared, "Here is the Lamb of God who takes away the sin of the world! This is he of whom I said, 'After me comes a man who ranks ahead of me because he was before me.' I myself did not know him; but I came baptizing with water for this reason, that he might be revealed to Israel." And John testified, "I saw the Spirit descending from heaven like a dove, and it remained on him. I myself did not know him, but the one who sent me to baptize with water said to me, 'He on whom you see the Spirit descend and remain is the one who baptizes with the Holy Spirit.' And I myself have seen and have testified that this is the Son of God."

- "Lamb of God" stirs biblical images in us: of the Passover lamb, and of the Suffering Servant in Isaiah, led like a lamb to the slaughter, bearing our sins.

- Lord, whenever I hear of atrocious barbarism committed by one of our race, and of the injustice and pain which people suffer through others' wickedness, I remember that this is the same world you entered, the burden you took on yourself. You had a strong back to carry the evil that is in the world.

Friday 4th January   John 1:35–42

The next day John again was standing with two of his disciples, and as he watched Jesus walk by, he exclaimed, "Look, here is the Lamb of God!" The two disciples heard him say this, and they followed Jesus. When Jesus turned and saw them following, he said to them, "What are you looking for?" They said to him, "Rabbi" (which translated means Teacher), "where are you staying?" He said to them, "Come and see." They came and saw where he was staying, and they remained with him that day. It was about four o'clock in the afternoon. One of the two who heard John speak and followed him was Andrew, Simon Peter's brother. He first found his brother Simon and said to him, "We have found the Messiah" (which is translated Anointed). He brought Simon to Jesus, who looked at him and said, "You are Simon son of John. You are to be called Cephas" (which is translated Peter).

- There is a lovely moment here, which the two disciples remember with a dart of pleasure. They are watching Jesus with curiosity, following him from a distance.
- But I cannot be merely a spectator with Jesus. He involves me. I could not begin to look for God unless God had already found me. Jesus says: Come and see where I am staying. And remain there.
- Lord, show me how to stay with you and learn your spirit.

Saturday 5th January   John 1:43–51

The next day Jesus decided to go to Galilee. He found Philip and said to him, "Follow me." Now Philip was from Bethsaida, the city of Andrew and Peter. Philip found Nathanael and said to him, "We have found him about whom Moses in the law and also the prophets wrote, Jesus son of Joseph from Nazareth." Nathanael said to him, "Can anything good come out of Nazareth?" Philip said to him, "Come and see." When Jesus saw Nathanael coming towards him, he said of him, "Here is truly an Israelite in whom there is no deceit!" Nathanael asked him, "Where did you come to know me?" Jesus answered, "I saw you under the fig tree before Philip called you." Nathanael replied, "Rabbi, you are the Son of God! You are the King of Israel!" Jesus answered, "Do you believe because I told you that I saw you under the fig tree? You will see greater things than these." And he said to him, "Very truly, I tell you, you will see heaven opened and the angels of God ascending and descending upon the Son of Man."

- Nathanael may be the same person as the apostle Bartholomew, who is always mentioned with Philip. Jesus' vision of him sitting under his fig-tree evokes the Jewish ideal of peace: somebody meditating under the leafy shade of his own vine or fig-tree.
- Lord, may *Sacred Space* be my fig-tree, the place where I can meditate in peace, for however brief a time, and feel your loving eyes on me.

january 6–12

Something to think and pray about each day this week:

God's Revelations

The word "epiphany" originates from the Greek language and it means a "showing" or "manifestation." The feast of the Epiphany of our Lord is linked closely to Christmas as both are feasts of God's manifestations: the first in the form of a helpless, newly-born infant born homeless and in poverty; the second celebrates the same recently born baby in similar circumstances but the material and social surroundings are hardly touched on. On the feast of Epiphany the emphasis is quite different. Here are strangers, foreigners, total outsiders coming to give royal homage to this tiny child. This will be the theme of Matthew's Gospel during the coming year: "Go, therefore, make disciples of all nations." We celebrate a third manifestation, the Baptism of Jesus, next Sunday to close the Christmas celebration of the Incarnation.

Each feast reminds us that Jesus is the revelation of God's unconditional and unending love for each one of us, in every age—not because we "deserve" it in some way but because God is a God of love.

The Presence of God

I pause for a moment
and reflect on God's life-giving presence
in every part of my body, in everything around me,
in the whole of my life.

Freedom

Many countries are at this moment suffering
the agonies of war.
I bow my head in thanksgiving for my freedom.
I pray for all prisoners and captives.

Consciousness

Knowing that God loves me unconditionally,
I look honestly over the last day, its events and my feelings.
Do I have something to be grateful for? Then I give thanks.
Is there something I am sorry for? Then I ask forgiveness.

The Word

God speaks to each one of us individually. I need to listen to
hear what he is saying to me. Read the text a few times, then
listen. (Please turn to your scripture on the following pages. Inspiration points are there should you need them. When you are
ready, return here to continue.)

Conversation

How has God's Word moved me? Has it left me cold?
Has it consoled me or moved me to act in a new way?
I imagine Jesus standing or sitting beside me,
I turn and share my feelings with him.

Conclusion

Glory be to the Father, and to the Son, and to the Holy Spirit,
As it was in the beginning, is now and ever shall be,
World without end. Amen

Sunday 6th January,
The Epiphany of the Lord   Matthew 2:1–12

In the time of King Herod, after Jesus was born in Bethlehem of Judea, wise men from the East came to Jerusalem, asking, "Where is the child who has been born king of the Jews? For we observed his star at its rising, and have come to pay him homage." When King Herod heard this, he was frightened, and all Jerusalem with him; and calling together all the chief priests and scribes of the people, he inquired of them where the Messiah was to be born. They told him, "In Bethlehem of Judea; for so it has been written by the prophet: 'And you, Bethlehem, in the land of Judah, are by no means least among the rulers of Judah; for from you shall come a ruler who is to shepherd my people Israel.'" Then Herod secretly called for the wise men and learned from them the exact time when the star had appeared. Then he sent them to Bethlehem, saying, "Go and search diligently for the child; and when you have found him, bring me word so that I may also go and pay him homage." When they had heard the king, they set out; and there, ahead of them, went the star that they had seen at its rising, until it stopped over the place where the child was. When they saw that the star had stopped, they were overwhelmed with joy. On entering the house, they saw the child with Mary his mother; and they knelt down and paid him homage. Then, opening their treasure chests, they offered him gifts of gold, frankincense, and myrrh. And having been warned in a dream not to return to Herod, they left for their own country by another road.

- As Jesus' life begins to unfold for us, the gospel writers underline that Jesus was excluded: born "outside," in a stable; acclaimed as a king but immediately under threat from those who held the political power.

- The three wise men are also outsiders; they are our spiritual forebears; through them we are invited to approach the Messiah.
- Lord, teach me to recognize God's children, and welcome them.

Monday 7th January   1 John 3:22–4:6

And we receive from him whatever we ask, because we obey his commandments and do what pleases him. And this is his commandment, that we should believe in the name of his Son Jesus Christ and love one another, just as he has commanded us. All who obey his commandments abide in him, and he abides in them. And by this we know that he abides in us, by the Spirit that he has given us. Beloved, do not believe every spirit, but test the spirits to see whether they are from God; for many false prophets have gone out into the world. By this you know the Spirit of God: every spirit that confesses that Jesus Christ has come in the flesh is from God, and every spirit that does not confess Jesus is not from God. And this is the spirit of the antichrist, of which you have heard that it is coming; and now it is already in the world. Little children, you are from God, and have conquered them; for the one who is in you is greater than the one who is in the world. We are from God. Whoever knows God listens to us, and whoever is not from God does not listen to us. From this we know the spirit of truth and the spirit of error.

- "Do not believe every spirit, but test the spirits to see whether they are of God; for many false prophets have gone out into the world." St Ignatius wrote: "It is characteristic of the good spirit to give courage, strength, consolations, inspirations and peace. He does this by making all easy, by removing all obstacles, so that the soul goes forward in doing good."
- Jesus said: "By their fruits you shall know them." A sound way of assessing would-be gurus is the integrity and goodness of their lives.

Tuesday 8th January   1 John 4:7–10

Beloved, let us love one another, because love is from God; everyone who loves is born of God and knows God. Whoever does not love does not know God, for God is love. God's love was revealed among us in this way: God sent his only Son into the world so that we might live through him. In this is love, not that we loved God but that he loved us and sent his Son to be the atoning sacrifice for our sins.

- "In this is love, not that we loved God but that he loved us and sent his Son." It is God who takes the initiative, and we try to respond. When God forgives our sin, he is not changing his mind about us; the change is in our mind about God, who does not change. Our sorrow for sin is the forgiveness of God working within us.
- Lord, as I reach towards you in prayer, it is your Spirit in me that is working. When I feel weary and godless, I am happy that it is your saving action, not my effort, that really counts.

Wednesday 9th January   1 John 4:11–16

Beloved, since God loved us so much, we also ought to love one another. No one has ever seen God; if we love one another, God lives in us, and his love is perfected in us. By this we know that we abide in him and he in us, because he has given us of his Spirit. And we have seen and do testify that the Father has sent his Son as the Savior of the world. God abides in those who confess that Jesus is the Son of God, and they abide in God. So we have known and believe the love that God has for us. God is love, and those who abide in love abide in God, and God abides in them.

- "God abides in those who confess that Jesus is the Son of God." Behind these words there is a deep understanding of the links between God's love, our relationships with each other, and the way we "confess" Jesus in how we live.

- Can I spend some time thinking about how I confess Jesus in my words and actions? Are there things I can change here?

Thursday 10th January   Luke 4:16–21

When Jesus came to Nazareth, where he had been brought up, he went to the synagogue on the sabbath day, as was his custom. He stood up to read, and the scroll of the prophet Isaiah was given to him. He unrolled the scroll and found the place where it was written: "The Spirit of the Lord is upon me, because he has anointed me to bring good news to the poor. He has sent me to proclaim release to the captives and recovery of sight to the blind, to let the oppressed go free, to proclaim the year of the Lord's favor." And he rolled up the scroll, gave it back to the attendant, and sat down. The eyes of all in the synagogue were fixed on him. Then he began to say to them, "Today this scripture has been fulfilled in your hearing."

- "Today this scripture has been fulfilled in your hearing." Imagine for a few moments how this scene appeared to those who had known Jesus and his family for years. How did they respond?
- Jesus had a mission, and he announced it first among those who knew him best.

Friday 11th January   Luke 5:12–16

Once, when Jesus was in one of the cities, there was a man covered with leprosy. When he saw Jesus, he bowed with his face to the ground and begged him, "Lord, if you choose, you can make me clean." Then Jesus stretched out his hand, touched him, and said, "I do choose. Be made clean." Immediately the leprosy left him. And he ordered him to tell no one. "Go," he said, "and show yourself to the priest, and, as Moses commanded, make an offering for your cleansing, for a testimony to them." But now more than ever the word about Jesus spread abroad;

many crowds would gather to hear him and to be cured of their diseases. But he would withdraw to deserted places and pray.

- This man was beyond all accepted boundaries—covered in ugly leprosy, daring to come among those who were clean, and begging Jesus for healing without hesitation. He was beyond caring; he was desperate.
- Jesus' healing gesture is remarkable. But as he heals, so also he insists that the Law be followed: "Show yourself to the priest . . . as Moses commanded."
- Jesus responded in prayer. How do I respond?

Saturday 12th January   **John 3:22–30**

After this Jesus and his disciples went into the Judean countryside, and he spent some time there with them and baptized. John also was baptizing at Aenon near Salim because water was abundant there; and people kept coming and were being baptized—John, of course, had not yet been thrown into prison. Now a discussion about purification arose between John's disciples and a Jew. They came to John and said to him, "Rabbi, the one who was with you across the Jordan, to whom you testified, here he is baptizing, and all are going to him." John answered, "No one can receive anything except what has been given from heaven. You yourselves are my witnesses that I said, 'I am not the Messiah, but I have been sent ahead of him.' He who has the bride is the bridegroom. The friend of the bridegroom, who stands and hears him, rejoices greatly at the bridegroom's voice. For this reason my joy has been fulfilled. He must increase, but I must decrease."

- John's disciples view Jesus' rise in popularity as a threat to their master, but John himself does not seem disturbed.

- "He must increase, but I must decrease." How do we account for John's response? What is the source of his joy?

Something to think and pray about each day this week:

Jesus and the Jordan

This is the third of three manifestations celebrated in the Church's calendar. While Christmas and the Epiphany, the first two, are linked with the birth of Jesus, this event comes at a much later date, at the moment when Jesus is about to begin his public life.

We might very well wonder, along with John the Baptist, why Jesus needed to be baptized. "It is I who need baptism from you," John said to Jesus, "and yet you come to me!" All those being baptized by John in the Jordan were doing so as a sign of repentance for their sins. How could Jesus, the Son of God, be part of this? One answer to this is that Jesus was expressing his total solidarity with us, not as a sinner but as a fellow human being. The expression of that solidarity is a much higher priority for him than any social status he might lose by being seen in the close company of confessed sinners. This solidarity will have its final dramatic expression as Jesus dies on a cross, executed with and like two convicted criminals.

The Presence of God
The world is charged with the grandeur of God
    (Gerard Manley Hopkins).
I dwell for a moment on the presence of God
around me, in every part of my body,
and deep within my being.

Freedom
"In these days, God taught me
as a schoolteacher teaches a pupil" (St. Ignatius).
I remind myself that there are things God has to teach me yet,
and ask for the grace to hear them and let them change me.

Consciousness
How do I find myself today?
Where am I with God? With others?
Do I have something to be grateful for? Then I give thanks.
Is there something I am sorry for? Then I ask forgiveness.

The Word
I read the Word of God slowly, a few times over, and I listen to
what God is saying to me. (Please turn to your scripture on the
following pages. Inspiration points are there should you need
them. When you are ready, return here to continue.)

Conversation
Sometimes I wonder what I might say
if I were to meet You in person, Lord.
I might say "Thank You, Lord" for always being there for me.
I know with certainty there were times when you carried me.
When through your strength I got through the dark times in my life.

Conclusion
Glory be to the Father, and to the Son, and to the Holy Spirit,
As it was in the beginning, is now and ever shall be,
World without end. Amen

Sunday 13th January,
The Baptism of the Lord   Matthew 3:13–17

Then Jesus came from Galilee to John at the Jordan, to be baptized by him. John would have prevented him, saying, "I need to be baptized by you, and do you come to me?" But Jesus answered him, "Let it be so now; for it is proper for us in this way to fulfill all righteousness." Then he consented. And when Jesus had been baptized, just as he came up from the water, suddenly the heavens were opened to him and he saw the Spirit of God descending like a dove and alighting on him. And a voice from heaven said, "This is my Son, the Beloved, with whom I am well pleased."

- The meaning of Jesus' baptism is not so much in cleansing as in rebirth. The water of baptism recalls the other waters in which we begin our lives, in our mother's womb. Birth, new life: signaled by the breaking of the waters, the amniotic fluid, and emergence into a less protected life outside mother's body.
- When Jesus came out of the water, a voice from heaven was heard: "This is my beloved Son." The Spirit came down on him. This symbolism of rebirth as a child of God is central in our own christenings.
- Thank you, Lord, for being my brother. Of me too the Father could say: "This is my beloved child."

Monday 14th January   Mark 1:14–20

Now after John was arrested, Jesus came to Galilee, proclaiming the good news of God, and saying, "The time is fulfilled, and the kingdom of God has come near; repent, and believe in the good news." As Jesus passed along the Sea of Galilee, he saw Simon and his brother Andrew casting a net into the sea—for they were fishermen. And Jesus said to them, "Follow me and I will make you fish for people." And immediately they left their nets and followed him. As he went a little farther, he saw James son of Zebedee and his brother John, who were in their boat mending the nets. Immediately he called them; and they left their father Zebedee in the boat with the hired men, and followed him.

- "The time is fulfilled." Mark tells this story with some urgency, as Jesus moves towards these men, inviting them to follow him. They responded "immediately."
- How am I called? How do I respond?

Tuesday 15th January   Mark 1:21–28

Jesus entered the synagogue and taught. They were astounded at his teaching, for he taught them as one having authority, and not as the scribes. Just then there was in their synagogue a man with an unclean spirit, and he cried out, "What have you to do with us, Jesus of Nazareth? Have you come to destroy us? I know who you are, the Holy One of God." But Jesus rebuked him, saying, "Be silent, and come out of him!" And the unclean spirit, convulsing him and crying with a loud voice, came out of him. They were all amazed, and they kept on asking one another, "What is this? A new teaching—with authority! He commands even the unclean spirits, and they obey him." At once his fame began to spread throughout the surrounding region of Galilee.

- I imagine myself entering the synagogue and listening to Jesus. He does not shout, nor appear remarkable, yet people listen with astonishment, astounded.
- What is it that gives him such authority in his speech? Like the afflicted man, I recognize Jesus as the Holy One of God.

Wednesday 16th January   Mark 1:35–39

In the morning, while it was still very dark, he got up and went out to a deserted place, and there he prayed. And Simon and his companions hunted for him. When they found him, they said to him, "Everyone is searching for you." He answered, "Let us go on to the neighboring towns, so that I may proclaim the message there also; for that is what I came out to do." And he went throughout Galilee, proclaiming the message in their synagogues and casting out demons.

- When Jesus prays, it gives him strength and guidance for his mission. He rises from prayer to go out to others.
- How about my prayer? Does it make me energetic and outgoing, or is it sometimes a cocoon, insulating me from the real world?

Thursday 17th January   Mark 1:40–45

A leper came to Jesus begging him, and kneeling he said to him, "If you choose, you can make me clean." Moved with pity, Jesus stretched out his hand and touched him, and said to him, "I do choose. Be made clean!" Immediately the leprosy left him, and he was made clean. After sternly warning him he sent him away at once, saying to him, "See that you say nothing to anyone; but go, show yourself to the priest, and offer for your cleansing what Moses commanded, as a testimony to them." But he went out and began to proclaim it freely, and to spread the word, so that Jesus could no longer go into a town openly, but stayed out in the country; and people came to him from every quarter.

- In several passages of Mark's Gospel, Jesus warns people not to talk about him as the Messiah; he did not want to be stereotyped as the military hero saving Israel from the Romans. He was shy of acquiring what we call an "image," a public mask. Jean Vanier said:

When you become important, it is easy to fall from a true prophet into a false one.

- Lord, save me from worrying about my image. I am better without one. What matters is how you know me, looking into my heart with the eye of a lover.

Friday 18th January   Mark 2:1–5

When Jesus returned to Capernaum after some days, it was reported that he was at home. So many gathered around that there was no longer room for them, not even in front of the door; and he was speaking the word to them. Then some people came, bringing to him a paralyzed man, carried by four of them. And when they could not bring him to Jesus because of the crowd, they removed the roof above him; and after having dug through it, they let down the mat on which the paralytic lay. When Jesus saw their faith, he said to the paralytic, "Son, your sins are forgiven."

- The friends of the paralytic take endless trouble in looking for a cure. Instead Jesus seeks the cause of the paralysis, in some old hurt that binds up the man's strength. It is often our past that cripples us: guilt, unforgiven wrongs, rankling resentments.
- You did not come, Lord, to judge me, but to seek what is lost, and to save me when my heart accuses me. Take me as I am here with all that sinful past of the world.

Saturday 19th January   Mark 2:13–17

Jesus went out again beside the sea; the whole crowd gathered around him, and he taught them. As he was walking along, he saw Levi son of Alphaeus sitting at the tax booth, and he said to him, "Follow me." And he got up and followed him. And as he sat at dinner in Levi's house, many tax collectors and sinners were also sitting with Jesus and his disciples—for there were many who followed him. When the scribes of the Pharisees saw that he was eating with sinners and tax collectors, they said to his disciples, "Why does he eat with tax collectors and sinners?" When Jesus heard this, he said to them, "Those who are well have no need of a physician, but those who are sick; I have come to call not the righteous but sinners."

- In his early ministry Jesus was invited to speak in the synagogue, but quite soon the rulers of the synagogue grew uneasy with him, and he was forced out to speak wherever he could, on the roads and the lakeside. He had been marginalized by his own people, and the marginalized were drawn to him, justifiably unpopular people like tax-collectors.
- Lord, it is when I feel on the edge that I need you, and you are there for me.

january 20–26

Something to think and pray about each day this week:

One in the Lord

This week sees the start of the Octave of prayer for church unity.
It has taken us centuries of misunderstandings to reach the point
where Christian churches can dare to do that most obvious thing:
pray together. Images like those of John Paul II praying in Can-
terbury with its Archbishop, or gathering the faith-leaders of the
world in Assisi, have taught us so much. When we come close to
those of other traditions, and know something of their riches, we
can be grateful for the extraordinary fullness of Catholic tradition, and at the same time marvel at the uprightness of Presbyte-
rians, the Friends' passion for peace, the openness of Hindus, the
devotion of Moslems. This is the week when we ask our God to
warm our hearts to take in all his children. If the chance arises,
it is the week when we should pray with strangers, remembering
St. Peter's words (Acts 10:14): "The truth I have come to realize is
that God does not have favorites, but that anyone of any nationality who does what is right and fears God is acceptable to him."

The Presence of God

As I sit here, God is present,
breathing life into me and into everything around me.
For a few moments, I sit silently,
and become aware of God's loving presence.

Freedom

If God were trying to tell me something, would I know?
If God were reassuring me or challenging me, would I notice?
I ask for the grace to be free of my own preoccupations
and open to what God may be saying to me.

Consciousness

In God's loving presence I unwind the past day,
starting from now and looking back, moment by moment.
I gather in all the goodness and light, in gratitude.
I attend to the shadows and what they say to me,
seeking healing, courage, forgiveness.

The Word

I take my time to read the Word of God, slowly, a few times, allowing myself to dwell on anything that strikes me. (Please turn to your scripture on the following pages. Inspiration points are there should you need them. When you are ready, return here to continue.)

Conversation

What is stirring in me as I pray?
Am I consoled, troubled, left cold?
I imagine Jesus himself standing or sitting at my side,
and share my feelings with him.

Conclusion

Glory be to the Father, and to the Son, and to the Holy Spirit,
As it was in the beginning, is now and ever shall be,
World without end. Amen

Sunday 20th January,
Second Sunday in Ordinary Time   Isaiah 49:3, 5–6

And he said to me, "You are my servant, Israel, in whom I will be glorified." And now the LORD says, who formed me in the womb to be his servant, to bring Jacob back to him, and that Israel might be gathered to him, for I am honored in the sight of the LORD, and my God has become my strength—he says, "It is too light a thing that you should be my servant to raise up the tribes of Jacob and to restore the survivors of Israel; I will give you as a light to the nations, that my salvation may reach to the end of the earth."

- "I will give you as a light to the nations, that my salvation may reach to the ends of the earth." Is it fanciful to speak of the *Sacred Space* website in this way?
- What thanks we owe to the legions of scientists, technologists and computer buffs who have made it possible to reach round the world in this way. Inspired by a vision of a worldwide web, they created the means by which we can fulfill what Isaiah barely glimpsed.

Monday 21st January   Mark 2:18–22

Now John's disciples and the Pharisees were fasting; and people came and said to him, "Why do John's disciples and the disciples of the Pharisees fast, but your disciples do not fast?" Jesus said to them, "The wedding-guests cannot fast while the bridegroom is with them, can they? As long as they have the bridegroom with them, they cannot fast. The days will come when the bridegroom is taken away from them, and then they will fast on that day. "No one sews a piece of unshrunk cloth on an old cloak; otherwise, the patch pulls away from it, the new from the old, and a worse tear is made. And no one puts new wine into old wineskins; otherwise, the wine will burst the skins, and the wine is lost, and so are the skins; but one puts new wine into fresh wineskins."

- People noticed the contrast between two sorts of religion: the Pharisees' preoccupation with law and regulation, and Jesus' love of celebrations and feasts. In his parables the kingdom of heaven is often a banquet, a wedding, a party: venues for untrammeled joy, not of tight rules.
- It is so easy for us to reduce the interior life, and the freedom and flame of the Gospels, to a set of pieties and regulations. Jesus would measure our religiousness not in laws but in love. His images here are of freshness: new clothes, new wine.
- Things are different now that he is among us. A new era has begun.

Tuesday 22nd January   Mark 2:23–28

One sabbath Jesus was going through the grainfields; and as they made their way his disciples began to pluck heads of grain. The Pharisees said to him, "Look, why are they doing what is not lawful on the sabbath?" And he said to them, "Have you never read what David did when he and his companions were hungry and in need of food? He entered the house of God, when Abiathar was high priest, and ate the bread of the Presence, which it is not lawful for any but the priests to eat, and he gave some to his companions." Then he said to them, "The sabbath was made for humankind, and not humankind for the sabbath; so the Son of Man is lord even of the sabbath."

- Observance of the sabbath was a distinguishing mark of the dutiful Jew. Jesus pushes us to see what the sabbath truly means: finding time and space for God—as St. Benedict's rule phrases it beautifully in Latin: *vacare Deo*.

- The Pharisees had reduced it to detailed regulations about what could be done and how far you could travel on the sabbath, as we sometimes reduce it to "getting to church" or "making it to mass."
- Lord, I beg for this grace for the community I live in: that the sabbath be a day of joy, healing and celebration, finding time and making space for you.

Wednesday 23rd January   Mark 3:1–6

Again he entered the synagogue, and a man was there who had a withered hand. They watched him to see whether he would cure him on the sabbath, so that they might accuse him. And he said to the man who had the withered hand, "Come forward." Then he said to them, "Is it lawful to do good or to do harm on the sabbath, to save life or to kill?" But they were silent. He looked around at them with anger; he was grieved at their hardness of heart and said to the man, "Stretch out your hand." He stretched it out, and his hand was restored. The Pharisees went out and immediately conspired with the Herodians against him, how to destroy him.

- Lord, when you celebrated the Lord's day by healing, the Pharisees responding by plotting to kill you. You were stressing that God does not want to make our lives more difficult, and does not impose arbitrary rules on us.
- The great commandment is the law of love. Would people who know me be able to say that I follow the "law of love"?

Thursday 24th January, St. Francis de Sales   John 15:9–17

As the Father has loved me, so I have loved you; abide in my love. If you keep my commandments, you will abide in my love, just as I have kept my Father's commandments and abide in his love. I have said these things to you so that my joy may be in

you, and that your joy may be complete. 'This is my commandment, that you love one another as I have loved you. No one
has greater love than this, to lay down one's life for one's friends.
You are my friends if you do what I command you. I do not call
you servants any longer, because the servant does not know what
the master is doing; but I have called you friends, because I have
made known to you everything that I have heard from my Father.
You did not choose me but I chose you. And I appointed you to
go and bear fruit, fruit that will last, so that the Father will give
you whatever you ask him in my name. I am giving you these
commands so that you may love one another.

- Listen to Jesus saying to you, "I call you my friend . . ." He has chosen me. But it's not like a job interview, where I'm hoping they'll
  think I'm better than I really am. He knows my strengths—and
  weaknesses—and still chooses me.
- He has chosen me to be part of his mission. Can I talk to him
  about what it is he wants me to do?

Friday 25th January, Conversion of St. Paul   Acts 22:4–11
Paul said: "I persecuted this Way up to the point of death by
binding both men and women and putting them in prison,
as the high priest and the whole council of elders can testify about
me. From them I also received letters to the brothers in Damascus, and I went there in order to bind those who were there and
to bring them back to Jerusalem for punishment. While I was
on my way and approaching Damascus, about noon a great light
from heaven suddenly shone about me. I fell to the ground and
heard a voice saying to me, 'Saul, Saul, why are you persecuting
me?' I answered, 'Who are you, Lord?' Then he said to me, 'I am
Jesus of Nazareth whom you are persecuting.' Now those who
were with me saw the light but did not hear the voice of the one
who was speaking to me. I asked, 'What am I to do, Lord?' The

Lord said to me, 'Get up and go to Damascus; there you will be told everything that has been assigned to you to do.' Since I could not see because of the brightness of that light, those who were with me took my hand and led me to Damascus.

- Twice in the Acts of the Apostles, Paul describes what happened on the road to Damascus. He remembers the brilliant light, the fall (always pictured as from a horse, though no horse is mentioned), and the dialogue with heaven. It is the model of all conversion experiences.
- Today let me linger on such moments in my life, when God touched me unexpectedly.

Saturday 26th January   Mark 3:20–21

Then Jesus went home; and the crowd came together again, so that they could not even eat. When his family heard it, they went out to restrain him, for people were saying, "He has gone out of his mind."

- They said: "He has gone out of his mind." There was a melee round Jesus that embarrassed his relatives. They felt he was making a show of them, and wanted to take control of him.
- Lord, there have been times in my life when I felt I was causing my relatives embarrassment, disapproval or concern. I did not enjoy the experience; it confused or even infuriated me. You have been there before me.

Something to think and pray about each day this week:

Opening the Door

Before we end the month of January, our prayer might take a lead from the Roman god who gave January its name. Janus was the god of gates and doorways, and was pictured facing in both directions. So we might look back and reflect on our experience of the last month. Did I start the year with resolutions? How are they faring? How has God touched me in this month? And then look forward. In the Northern Hemisphere the prospect is exciting. In some reckonings, spring starts on 1st February. Already we may be seeing snowdrops and winter anemones. As Gerard Manley Hopkins wrote, the "dearest freshness deep down things" has survived the winter and is ready to break out. Maybe I would ask God for a springtime in my own heart, no matter what my age or health.

The Presence of God

As I sit here with my book, God is here.
Around me, in my sensations, in my thoughts and deep within me.
I pause for a moment, and become aware
of God's life-giving presence.

Freedom

I need to close out the noise, to rise above the noise;
The noise that interrupts, that separates,
The noise that isolates.
I need to listen to God again.

Consciousness

I remind myself that I am in the presence of the Lord.
I will take refuge in His loving heart.
He is my strength in times of weakness.
He is my comforter in times of sorrow.

The Word

God speaks to each one of us individually. I need to listen to
what he is saying to me. (Please turn to your scripture on the
following pages. Inspiration points are there should you need
them. When you are ready, return here to continue.)

Conversation

Do I notice myself reacting as I pray with the Word of God?
Do I feel challenged, comforted, angry?
Imagining Jesus sitting or standing by me,
I speak out my feelings, as one trusted friend to another.

Conclusion

Glory be to the Father, and to the Son, and to the Holy Spirit,
As it was in the beginning, is now and ever shall be,
World without end. Amen

Sunday 27th January,
Third Sunday in Ordinary Time 1 Corinthians 1:10–13, 17

Now I appeal to you, brothers and sisters, by the name of our Lord Jesus Christ, that all of you be in agreement and that there be no divisions among you, but that you be united in the same mind and the same purpose. For it has been reported to me by Chloe's people that there are quarrels among you, my brothers and sisters. What I mean is that each of you says, "I belong to Paul," or "I belong to Apollos," or "I belong to Cephas," or "I belong to Christ." Has Christ been divided? Was Paul crucified for you? Or were you baptized in the name of Paul? For Christ did not send me to baptize but to proclaim the gospel, and not with eloquent wisdom, so that the cross of Christ might not be emptied of its power.

- "I appeal that there be no dissensions among you." We live with the scandal of a divided Christendom; but we can make it better or worse. We make it worse if we focus on the differences between Christians, better if we keep our eyes on what unites us.
- We are all baptized in the name of the Father, Son and Holy Spirit. In worship, belief, morality, and in the love of Jesus, we share great areas of agreement; and we are traveling in hope towards one flock and one shepherd.
- Let me ponder this during this Octave of prayer for unity among Christians.

Monday 28th January,
St. Thomas Aquinas   Matthew 23:8–12

Jesus said to the crowds, "But you are not to be called rabbi, for you have one teacher, and you are all students. And call no one your father on earth, for you have one Father—the one in heaven. Nor are you to be called instructors, for you have one instructor, the Messiah. The greatest among you will be your servant. All who exalt themselves will be humbled, and all who humble themselves will be exalted."

- Anyone who has worked in a school knows that a teacher's authority is earned, not given by the system. The best teacher, parent, or instructor is one who does not rely on his or her position, one who does not demand respect, but earns it through humble service and devotion.

- Remember Addison's line: "'Tis not in mortals to command success, but we'll do more, Sempronius, we'll deserve it."

Tuesday 29th January   Mark 3:31–35

Then the mother and brothers of Jesus came; and standing outside, they sent to him and called him. A crowd was sitting around him; and they said to him, "Your mother and your brothers and sisters are outside, asking for you." And he replied, "Who are my mother and my brothers?" And looking at those who sat around him, he said, "Here are my mother and my brothers! Whoever does the will of God is my brother and sister and mother."

- "Here are my mother and my brothers!" This is a new family, with ties stronger even than the ties of blood.

- Mary shows us the way by saying Yes to God's will in the most profound way. Can I follow her?

Wednesday 30th January   Mark 4:1–12

Again he began to teach beside the sea. Such a very large crowd gathered around him that he got into a boat on the sea and sat there, while the whole crowd was beside the sea on the land. He began to teach them many things in parables, and in his teaching he said to them: "Listen! A sower went out to sow. And as he sowed, some seed fell on the path, and the birds came and ate it up. Other seed fell on rocky ground, where it did not have much soil, and it sprang up quickly, since it had no depth of soil. And when the sun rose, it was scorched; and since it had no root, it withered away. Other seed fell among thorns, and the thorns grew up and choked it, and it yielded no grain. Other seed fell into good soil and brought forth grain, growing up and increasing and yielding thirty and sixty and a hundredfold." And he said, "Let anyone with ears to hear listen!" When he was alone, those who were around him along with the twelve asked him about the parables. And he said to them, "To you has been given the secret of the kingdom of God, but for those outside, everything comes in parables; in order that 'they may indeed look, but not perceive, and may indeed listen, but not understand; so that they may not turn again and be forgiven.'"

- If your word is like a seed, Lord, then it is an organism, with a life of its own. My part is to receive it, give it roots and depth so that it survives hardships; and protect it from the thorns of multiple cares and desires.
- If I allow your word some space in my life, there is no limit to the fruit it may bear.

Thursday 31st January,
St. John Bosco   Matthew 18:1–5

At that time the disciples came to Jesus and asked, "Who is the greatest in the kingdom of heaven?" He called a child, whom he put among them, and said, "Truly I tell you, unless you change and become like children, you will never enter the kingdom of heaven. Whoever becomes humble like this child is the greatest in the kingdom of heaven. Whoever welcomes one such child in my name welcomes me."

- Lord, you saw something in this child that you want to see in me: the capacity to wonder at the world, its smells and taste and sounds and sights; and a readiness to depend on others rather than be full of myself; and above all, a trust in you as my Father, for whom my destiny is all-important.
- Give me that childlike confidence in your love.

Friday 1st February   Mark 4:26–34

Jesus said to the crowd, "The kingdom of God is as if someone would scatter seed on the ground, and would sleep and rise night and day, and the seed would sprout and grow, he does not know how. The earth produces of itself, first the stalk, then the head, then the full grain in the head. But when the grain is ripe, at once he goes in with his sickle, because the harvest has come." He also said, "With what can we compare the kingdom of God, or what parable will we use for it? It is like a mustard seed, which, when sown upon the ground, is the smallest of all the seeds on earth; yet when it is sown it grows up and becomes the greatest of all shrubs, and puts forth large branches, so that the birds of the air can make nests in its shade." With many such parables he spoke the word to them, as they were able to hear it; he did not speak to them except in parables, but he explained everything in private to his disciples.

- Thank you, Lord, for this most consoling of images. I was not brought into this world to help you out of a mess. You above all are the one who is working.
- Your dynamism, active in nature from the beginning of time, should humble me. You are the force of growth, and if you privilege me with the chance to add incrementally to that growth, that is your gift to me, not mine to you.

Saturday 2nd February,
The Presentation of the Lord Luke 2:22–24

When the time came for their purification according to the law of Moses, they brought him up to Jerusalem to present him to the Lord (as it is written in the law of the Lord, "Every firstborn male shall be designated as holy to the Lord"), and they offered a sacrifice according to what is stated in the law of the Lord, "a pair of turtledoves or two young pigeons."

- These verses tell us much about Jesus' family. He was born under the Jewish Law, and observed it. After eight days he was circumcised, the sign of the Covenant with God. Forty days after birth, his mother underwent purification in the Temple, and gave the offering—a lamb for richer people, two pigeons for the poor.

- Lord God, I often resent the law, and I often resent poverty. But I do not aim to be a law unto myself. I love your covenant. And poverty pinches less when it is shared with Jesus.

february 3–9

Something to think and pray about each day this week:

Healing Through Weakness

Stories of healing from sickness and disability run through the bible and through the history of the church. This week the gospel readings show Jesus in physical contact with the blind, the paralytic, the fever-ridden, and the disturbed. He feels for those whom illness has cut off from their fellows, and who cannot work or move themselves, so are often condemned to being alone. Following his example, religious orders were founded to look after the sick. It is not surprising that places like Lourdes attract Christians and non-Christians alike, not so much by the promise of cure, as by the way such places draw out love and compassion for the sick. Part of their distress is that they often find it hard to pray, and have to fall back on St Paul's promise (Romans 8:26): "The Spirit helps us in our weakness; for we do not know how to pray as we ought, but that very Spirit intercedes with sighs too deep for words."

The Presence of God

At any time of the day or night we can call on Jesus.
He is always waiting, listening for our call.
What a wonderful blessing.
No phone needed, no emails, just a whisper.

Freedom

I will ask God's help,
to be free from my own preoccupations,
to be open to God in this time of prayer,
to come to love and serve him more.

Consciousness

How am I really feeling? Light-hearted? Heavy-hearted?
I may be very much at peace, happy to be here.
Equally, I may be frustrated, worried or angry.
I acknowledge how I really am. It is the real me that the
Lord loves.

The Word

I read the Word of God slowly, a few times over, and I listen to
what God is saying to me. (Please turn to your scripture on the
following pages. Inspiration points are there should you need
them. When you are ready, return here to continue.)

Conversation

Remembering that I am still in God's presence,
I imagine Jesus himself standing or sitting beside me,
and say whatever is on my mind, whatever is in my heart,
speaking as one friend to another.

Conclusion

Glory be to the Father, and to the Son, and to the Holy Spirit,
As it was in the beginning, is now and ever shall be,
World without end. Amen

Sunday 3rd February,
Fourth Sunday in Ordinary Time   Matthew 5:1–12

When Jesus saw the crowds, he went up the mountain; and after he sat down, his disciples came to him. Then he began to speak, and taught them, saying: Blessed are the poor in spirit, for theirs is the kingdom of heaven. Blessed are those who mourn, for they will be comforted. Blessed are the meek, for they will inherit the earth. Blessed are those who hunger and thirst for righteousness, for they will be filled. Blessed are the merciful, for they will receive mercy. Blessed are the pure in heart, for they will see God. Blessed are the peacemakers, for they will be called children of God. Blessed are those who are persecuted for righteousness' sake, for theirs is the kingdom of heaven. Blessed are you when people revile you and persecute you and utter all kinds of evil against you falsely on my account. Rejoice and be glad, for your reward is great in heaven, for in the same way they persecuted the prophets who were before you.

- We have no portrait of you, Lord, but in the Beatitudes you show us your interior landscape, the source of your joy. This is not a set of regulations, but a vision of where true happiness lies.
- Let me taste it, phrase by phrase.

Monday 4th February   2 Samuel 16:5–12

When King David came to Bahurim, a man of the family of the house of Saul came out whose name was Shimei son of Gera; he came out cursing. He threw stones at David and at all the servants of King David. Shimei shouted while he cursed, "Out! Out! Murderer! Scoundrel! The LORD has avenged on all of you the blood of the house of Saul, in whose place you have reigned; and the LORD has given the kingdom into the hand of your son Absalom. See, disaster has overtaken you; for you are a man of blood." Then Abishai son of Zeruiah said to the king, "Why should this dead dog curse my lord the king? Let me go over and take off his head." David said to Abishai and to all his servants, "My own son seeks my life; how much more now may this Benjaminite! Let him alone, and let him curse; for the LORD has bidden him. It may be that the LORD will look on my distress, and the LORD will repay me with good for this cursing of me today."

- Lord, I like this story because it reminds me of what I sometimes feel: that I can welcome some punishment in my life, as David did. You have your own plans for me, and some of them feel like a parent correcting me.
- It strengthens me, and may compensate for the bad things I have done and got away with. Those who take the trouble to scold us are often closer to us than sweet-talkers.

Tuesday 5th February   Mark 5:21–43

When Jesus had crossed again in the boat to the other side, a great crowd gathered around him; and he was by the sea. Then one of the leaders of the synagogue named Jairus came and, when he saw him, fell at his feet and begged him repeatedly, "My little daughter is at the point of death. Come and lay your hands on her, so that she may be made well, and live." So he went with him. And a large crowd followed him and pressed in on him. Now there was a woman who had been suffering from hemorrhages for twelve years. She had endured much under many physicians, and had spent all that she had; and she was no better, but rather grew worse. She had heard about Jesus, and came up behind him in the crowd and touched his cloak, for she said, "If I but touch his clothes, I will be made well." Immediately her hemorrhage stopped; and she felt in her body that she was healed of her disease. Immediately aware that power had gone forth from him, Jesus turned about in the crowd and said, "Who touched my clothes?" And his disciples said to him, "You see the crowd pressing in on you; how can you say, 'Who touched me?'" He looked all around to see who had done it. But the woman, knowing what had happened to her, came in fear and trembling, fell down before him, and told him the whole truth. He said to her, "Daughter, your faith has made you well; go in peace, and be healed of your disease." While he was still speaking, some people came from the leader's house to say, "Your daughter is dead. Why trouble the teacher any further?" But overhearing what they said, Jesus said to the leader of the synagogue, "Do not fear, only believe." He allowed no one to follow him except Peter, James, and John, the brother of James. When they came to the house of the leader of the synagogue, he saw a commotion, people weeping and wailing loudly. When he had entered, he said to them, "Why do you make a commotion and weep? The child is not dead but sleeping." And they laughed at him. Then he put them all outside, and took the child's father and mother and those who were with him, and went in where the child was. He took her by the hand and said to her, "*Talitha cum*," which means, "Little girl, get up!" And immediately the girl got up and began to walk about (she was twelve years of age). At this they were overcome with amazement. He strictly ordered them that no one should know this, and told them to give her something to eat.

- Here are two healings by Jesus, of a girl dying after twelve years of life, and of a woman sick for twelve years. In both there is physical contact with Jesus. The woman reaches out through the crowd to touch him. Jesus takes the little girl by the hand.

- Lord, I cannot touch you, but I reach out to you in faith. You said of the little girl: "She is not dead but sleeping." And you woke her up. I am waiting for your hand on me, to make me more fully alive. Let me hear you say to me: "*Talitha cumi.*"

Wednesday 6th February, Ash Wednesday   Matthew 6:1–4

Jesus said to his disciples, "So whenever you give alms, do not sound a trumpet before you, as the hypocrites do in the synagogues and in the streets, so that they may be praised by others. Truly I tell you, they have received their reward. But when you give alms, do not let your left hand know what your right hand is doing, so that your alms may be done in secret; and your Father who sees in secret will reward you."

- The forty days of Lent recall the desert where the People of Israel, and then John the Baptist, and then Jesus himself, made their journey to a new life. The desert was not a destination, but a place for travelers going somewhere. In our liturgy that somewhere is Easter, the feast of the risen Lord.
- In each of our lives, Lent can be more than that; it can be the start of a second journey. It is a time to regain the freedom of my tongue, a time to tame my appetites for food, sex, drink, sleep or whatever I feel has too much of a hold on me.

Thursday 7th February   Luke 9:22–25

Jesus said to his disciples: "The Son of Man must undergo great suffering, and be rejected by the elders, chief priests, and scribes, and be killed, and on the third day be raised." Then he said to them all, "If any want to become my followers, let them deny themselves and take up their cross daily and follow me. For those who want to save their life will lose it, and those who lose their life for my sake will save it. What does it profit them if they gain the whole world, but lose or forfeit themselves?"

- Deny yourself and take up your cross daily. Lord, I used to think this meant looking for mortifications. You have taught me that my cross is myself, my ego, the pains in my body, my awkwardness, my mistakes.
- To follow you is to move beyond ego-trips. It means coping with the business of life without trampling on others or making them suffer. There is a world here to be explored this Lent.

Friday 8th February   Isaiah 58:5–9

Is such the fast that I choose, a day to humble oneself? Is it to bow down the head like a bulrush, and to lie in sackcloth and ashes? Will you call this a fast, a day acceptable to the Lord? Is not this the fast that I choose: to loose the bonds of injustice, to undo the thongs of the yoke, to let the oppressed go free, and to break every yoke? Is it not to share your bread with the hungry, and bring the homeless poor into your house; when you see the naked, to cover them, and not to hide yourself from your own kin? Then your light shall break forth like the dawn, and your healing shall spring up quickly; your vindicator shall go before you, the glory of the Lord shall be your rear guard. Then you shall call, and the Lord will answer; you shall cry for help, and he will say, Here I am.

- "Loosing the bonds of injustice, undoing the thongs of the yoke and letting the oppressed go free." All around me there are people suffering from unfairness; they may be children, old people, immigrants, each unable to raise their voice in protest.
- Lord, you are inviting me to have an eye for injustice, and take a stand against it, or at least never connive with it. Give my heart a habit of justice, restless when faced with what is unfair.

Saturday 9th February   Luke 5:27–32

After this he went out and saw a tax collector named Levi, sitting at the tax booth; and he said to him, "Follow me." And he got up, left everything, and followed him. Then Levi gave a great banquet for him in his house; and there was a large crowd of tax collectors and others sitting at the table with them. The Pharisees and their scribes were complaining to his disciples, saying, "Why do you eat and drink with tax collectors and sinners?" Jesus answered, "Those who are well have no need of a physician, but those who are sick; I have come to call not the righteous but sinners to repentance."

- Where are the Levis in my world? The drug-pushers, pedophiles, wife-batterers, rapists, those who cheat on tax or social welfare, those who are headlined for hatred in the tabloid press.

- Lord, these are the sick who need you as physician. Can I help you to reach out to them?

february 10–16

Something to think and pray about each day this week:

Growing Pains

Lent reflects the rhythm of our spiritual life, between Tabor and Gethsemani, the Transfiguration and the Agony in the Garden. There are times when God shows himself, as on Tabor: prayer is easy, our hearts are light. We feel loved and loving, on holy ground. J.D. Salinger wrote: "All we do our whole lives is go from one little piece of holy ground to the next."

Then there are times of disagreeable growth. You remember the parable of the barren fig tree (Luke 13:6), and the farmer who said: "I need a year to dig around it and manure it." We can feel God doing this to us, feel the pain when our roots are struck by the spade. We feel useless, past our best, no good to anyone, a failure in the most important things we tried, whether marriage, vocation, rearing children, our job and career. Life loses its savor. We cannot pray. We sense that some people think the world would be better off without us.

St. Ignatius called this state desolation; and he advised: "remember that it will pass . . . In consolation, think about how you will conduct yourself in time of desolation. And insist more on prayer." Then you come to see—gradually—that this same ground, however stinking, is holy, and we can find God there. He is wielding the spade, spreading the dung.

The Presence of God

For a few moments, I think of God's veiled presence in things:
in the elements, giving them existence;
in plants, giving them life; in animals, giving them sensation;
and finally, in me, giving me all this and more,
making me a temple, a dwelling-place of the Spirit.

Freedom

God is not foreign to my freedom.
Instead the Spirit breathes life into my most intimate desires,
gently nudging me towards all that is good.
I ask for the grace to let myself be enfolded by the Spirit.

Consciousness

Knowing that God loves me unconditionally,
I can afford to be honest about how I am.
How has the last day been, and how do I feel now?
I share my feelings openly with the Lord.

The Word

The word of God comes down to us through the scriptures.
May the Holy Spirit enlighten my mind and my heart to respond to the gospel teachings. (Please turn to your scripture
on the following pages. Inspiration points are there should you
need them. When you are ready, return here to continue.)

Conversation

How has God's Word moved me? Has it left me cold?
Has it consoled me or moved me to act in a new way?
I imagine Jesus standing or sitting beside me,
I turn and share my feelings with him.

Conclusion

Glory be to the Father, and to the Son, and to the Holy Spirit,
As it was in the beginning, is now and ever shall be,
World without end. Amen

Sunday 10th February,
First Sunday of Lent
Matthew 4:1–4

Then Jesus was led up by the Spirit into the wilderness to be tempted by the devil. He fasted forty days and forty nights, and afterwards he was famished. The tempter came and said to him, "If you are the Son of God, command these stones to become loaves of bread." But he answered, "It is written, 'One does not live by bread alone, but by every word that comes from the mouth of God.'"

- I too have known times of temptation when I felt on my own except for irrational forces that were messing up my life. Lord, you felt the influence of evil, and were tested. You were purified as you came through a difficult time.
- When I was in the middle of such a time, it did not feel like God's hand, but like desolation and despair. When I look back, I can see how God was shaping me.

Monday 11th February
Matthew 25:34–40

"When the Son of Man comes in his glory, and all the angels with him, then he will sit on the throne of his glory. All the nations will be gathered before him, and he will separate people one from another as a shepherd separates the sheep from the goats, and he will put the sheep at his right hand and the goats at the left. Then the king will say to those at his right hand, 'Come, you that are blessed by my Father, inherit the kingdom prepared for you from the foundation of the world; for I was hungry and you gave me food, I was thirsty and you gave me something to drink, I was a stranger and you welcomed me, I was naked and you gave me clothing, I was sick and you took care of me, I was in prison and you visited me.' Then the righteous will answer him, 'Lord, when was it that we saw you hungry and gave you food, or thirsty and gave you something to drink? And when was it that we saw you a stranger and welcomed you, or naked and gave you clothing? And when was it that we saw you sick or in prison and visited you?' And the king will answer them, 'Truly I tell you, just as you did it to one of the least of these who are members of my family, you did it to me.'

- The Last Judgment, the *Dies Irae*, stirs my heart with fear. Yet in the end, Lord, your message is simple, your command easy. You are there beside me in the needy.
- I have only to reach them to reach you.

Tuesday 12th February   Matthew 6:11

Give us this day our daily bread.

- The Greek word translated as "daily" is *epiousios*. Until recently it was unknown, occurring in this sentence in the Gospel but nowhere else in ancient literature. Then on a fragment of papyrus they found the word on a woman's shopping list, indicating that she needed to get supplies of a certain food for the coming day.
- That is the deep meaning of this workaday word: Lord, give me what I need to get through the day, to manage my business, keep the children happy, and survive myself. Give me thy love and grace just for today.

Wednesday 13th February   Jonah 3:1–5

The word of the Lord came to Jonah a second time, saying, "Get up, go to Nineveh, that great city, and proclaim to it the message that I tell you." So Jonah set out and went to Nineveh, according to the word of the Lord. Now Nineveh was an exceedingly large city, a three days' walk across. Jonah began to go into the city, going a day's walk. And he cried out, "Forty days more, and Nineveh shall be overthrown!" And the people of Nineveh believed God; they proclaimed a fast, and everyone, great and small, put on sackcloth.

- Sin is a reality in the life of every one of us, but so is God's mercy and forgiveness. Sin is not a matter of committing one of a list of forbidden acts, but of turning away from God when I make a decision.
- If I am honest with myself, I know when I am doing this. Is there some area of my life where this is going on, where I am keeping God out, because doing the right thing might be inconvenient? The Good News is this: all I have to do is turn back.

Thursday 14th February,
Sts. Cyril and Methodius   Luke 10:1–9

After this the Lord appointed seventy others and sent them on ahead of him in pairs to every town and place where he himself intended to go. He said to them, "The harvest is plentiful, but the laborers are few; therefore ask the Lord of the harvest to send out laborers into his harvest. Go on your way. See, I am sending you out like lambs into the midst of wolves. Carry no purse, no bag, no sandals; and greet no one on the road. Whatever house you enter, first say, 'Peace to this house!' And if anyone is there who shares in peace, your peace will rest on that person; but if not, it will return to you. Remain in the same house, eating and drinking whatever they provide, for the laborer deserves to be paid. Do not move about from house to house. Whenever you enter a town and its people welcome you, eat what is set before you; cure the sick who are there, and say to them, 'The kingdom of God has come near to you.'"

- Jesus, you came as one bringing peace, and told us to greet people with a word of peace, not hostility, or judgment.

- May your blessing flow through me, so that when I leave people, they may feel approved of, contented and tranquil.

Friday 15th February　　　　　　　　　Matthew 5:20–26

Jesus said to his disciples, "For I tell you, unless your righteousness exceeds that of the scribes and Pharisees, you will never enter the kingdom of heaven. You have heard that it was said to those of ancient times, 'You shall not murder'; and 'whoever murders shall be liable to judgment.' But I say to you that if you are angry with a brother or sister, you will be liable to judgment; and if you insult a brother or sister, you will be liable to the council; and if you say, 'You fool,' you will be liable to the hell of fire. So when you are offering your gift at the altar, if you remember that your brother or sister has something against you, leave your gift there before the altar and go; first be reconciled to your brother or sister, and then come and offer your gift. Come to terms quickly with your accuser while you are on the way to court with him, or your accuser may hand you over to the judge, and the judge to the guard, and you will be thrown into prison. Truly I tell you, you will never get out until you have paid the last penny."

- Must I repress and deny all anger? You might as well deny feeling hot in the Sahara. The feeling is innocent; there are times when anger sweeps over me and has to be acknowledged. The evil arises when I act out my anger by bad-mouthing or injuring my neighbor, and when I give way to hatred.
- Lord, I come before your altar. Help me to work on the seeds of hatred in my heart. You tell me that there can be no true worship of God without justice.

Saturday 16th February Matthew 5:43–48

Jesus said to the disciples, "You have heard that it was said, 'You shall love your neighbor and hate your enemy.' But I say to you, Love your enemies and pray for those who persecute you, so that you may be children of your Father in heaven; for he makes his sun rise on the evil and on the good, and sends rain on the righteous and on the unrighteous. For if you love those who love you, what reward do you have? Do not even the tax collectors do the same? And if you greet only your brothers and sisters, what more are you doing than others? Do not even the Gentiles do the same? Be perfect, therefore, as your heavenly Father is perfect."

- There is a footnote to the biblical story of the Egyptian army being drowned in the Red Sea, while the Jews escaped dry-footed. The rabbis imagined the angels starting a paean of praise to God, but the Lord interrupting them sadly: "The work of my hands are sunk in the sea, and you would sing before me!"
- When Jesus bids us be perfect like God, he means that we try to love as generously and universally as God, and to be good even to those who dislike us.

Something to think and pray about each day this week:

Learning What We Know

In prayer we are "reminded" rather than changed. Prayer helps us to realize what we already know. The Holy Spirit is not an alien invader, but the one who enables us to be ourselves. On Whit Sunday, Peter and the apostles had the same personalities as before Pentecost, but they had the courage to be themselves, to speak out from their hearts about what they had heard from Jesus. The apostles at Pentecost did not get more lectures on Christianity. Instead they had the confidence to use what they already knew. Paddy Kavanagh, the Irish poet, used to say that we only learn what we already know. We learn by reflecting on our experience.

The Presence of God

For a few moments, I think of God's veiled presence in things:
in the elements, giving them existence;
in plants, giving them life; in animals, giving them sensation;
and finally, in me, giving me all this and more,
making me a temple, a dwelling-place of the Spirit.

Freedom

God is not foreign to my freedom.
Instead the Spirit breathes life into my most intimate desires,
gently nudging me towards all that is good.
I ask for the grace to let myself be enfolded by the Spirit.

Consciousness

Knowing that God loves me unconditionally,
I can afford to be honest about how I am.
How has the last day been, and how do I feel now?
I share my feelings openly with the Lord.

The Word

I take my time to read the Word of God, slowly, a few times, allowing myself to dwell on anything that strikes me. (Please turn to your scripture on the following pages. Inspiration points are there should you need them. When you are ready, return here to continue.)

Conversation

How has God's Word moved me? Has it left me cold?
Has it consoled me or moved me to act in a new way?
I imagine Jesus standing or sitting beside me,
I turn and share my feelings with him.

Conclusion

Glory be to the Father, and to the Son, and to the Holy Spirit,
As it was in the beginning, is now and ever shall be,
World without end. Amen

Sunday 17th February,
Second Sunday of Lent   **Genesis 12:1–4**

Now the LORD said to Abram, "Go from your country and your kindred and your father's house to the land that I will show you. I will make of you a great nation, and I will bless you, and make your name great, so that you will be a blessing. I will bless those who bless you, and the one who curses you I will curse; and in you all the families of the earth shall be blessed." So Abram went, as the LORD had told him; and Lot went with him. Abram was seventy-five years old when he departed from Haran.

- God said to Abraham: "By you all the families of the earth shall bless themselves." Christians, Moslems and Jews are all children of Abraham. The future of civilization may depend on relishing what we share with Islam rather than focusing on our differences.
- Can we become a blessing to all the families of the earth, by our reverence and love for the one, true, and compassionate God? I marvel at the fidelity to daily prayer, and at the reverence for God shown by devout Moslems.
- Religion at its best can only unite people.

Monday 18th February   **Luke 6:36–38**

"Be merciful, just as your Father is merciful. Do not judge, and you will not be judged; do not condemn, and you will not be condemned. Forgive, and you will be forgiven; give, and it will be given to you. A good measure, pressed down, shaken together, running over, will be put into your lap; for the measure you give will be the measure you get back."

- Can I remember times when I heard people gossip about me, with no understanding of why I behaved as I did? Can I remember times when I leapt to judge others without knowing the whys and wherefores? Remember the Sioux prayer: May I never judge another until I have walked in his moccasins. Good newspapers offer us information without judgments. Shoddy papers try to do our thinking for us, leap to take sides, and express their judgments in banner headlines.

- Lord, keep me from jumping to judgment. You alone know all that is in my heart and in the hearts of those I am tempted to condemn.

Tuesday 19th February   Isaiah 1:16–17

Wash yourselves; make yourselves clean; remove the evil of your doings from before my eyes; cease to do evil, learn to do good; seek justice, rescue the oppressed, defend the orphan, plead for the widow.

- Lord, thank you for calling me to attention. There is no point in me following religious observances diligently if I continue to ignore suffering and injustice around me.
- Teach me to be just, so that I pray with a clean heart and give praise to your name.

Wednesday 20th February   Matthew 20:17–19

While Jesus was going up to Jerusalem, he took the twelve disciples aside by themselves, and said to them on the way, "See, we are going up to Jerusalem, and the Son of Man will be handed over to the chief priests and scribes, and they will condemn him to death; then they will hand him over to the Gentiles to be mocked and flogged and crucified; and on the third day he will be raised."

- There is a sense of doom and destiny in Jesus' words. Like Captain Oates going out into the Antarctic night: "I am just going outside and may be some time." Or like Aslan, the heroic lion in Narnia, walking alone into the hands of the Ice Queen.

- The anticipation of personal catastrophe chills the heart. When Jesus foretells the Passion, he mentions not just the handover, but the flogging and mocking. It is hard to imagine the terror that must have shadowed his heart in those last weeks.

Thursday 21st February   Jeremiah 17:5–8

Thus says the Lord: Cursed are those who trust in mere mortals and make mere flesh their strength, whose hearts turn away from the Lord. They shall be like a shrub in the desert, and shall not see when relief comes. They shall live in the parched places of the wilderness, in an uninhabited salt land. Blessed are those who trust in the Lord, whose trust is the Lord. They shall be like a tree planted by water, sending out its roots by the stream. It shall not fear when heat comes, and its leaves shall stay green; in the year of drought it is not anxious, and it does not cease to bear fruit.

- Lord, I know that wilderness feeling, when I am blown about like a paper bag in the wind, up and down, at the mercy of each day's events. I remember too the times when I felt rooted in you, trusting you, sensing the water of your nourishment even in bad times.
- Let me be that tree planted by water, sending out its roots to the stream of your goodness.

Friday 22nd February,
The See of St. Peter   Matthew 16:13–19

Now when Jesus came into the district of Caesarea Philippi, he asked his disciples, "Who do people say that the Son of Man is?" And they said, "Some say John the Baptist, but others Elijah, and still others Jeremiah or one of the prophets." He said to them, "But who do you say that I am?" Simon Peter answered,

"You are the Messiah, the Son of the living God." And Jesus answered him, "Blessed are you, Simon son of Jonah! For flesh and blood has not revealed this to you, but my Father in heaven. And I tell you, you are Peter, and on this rock I will build my church, and the gates of Hades will not prevail against it. I will give you the keys of the kingdom of heaven, and whatever you bind on earth will be bound in heaven, and whatever you loose on earth will be loosed in heaven."

• When I see the failings of the church, I wonder about its foundation on the rock. Then I think: the gates of Hell—sometimes in the shape of inner corruption—have not prevailed. The people of God are still vigorous, and growing, and holy in countless hidden ways, still sustained by the vision of God made visible in Jesus.

• I can still echo Peter: You are the Son of the living God.

Saturday 23rd February   **Luke 15:20–24**

While the son was still far off, his father saw him and was filled with compassion; he ran and put his arms around him and kissed him. Then the son said to him, 'Father, I have sinned against heaven and before you; I am no longer worthy to be called your son.' But the father said to his slaves, 'Quickly, bring out a robe—the best one—and put it on him; put a ring on his finger and sandals on his feet. And get the fatted calf and kill it, and let us eat and celebrate; for this son of mine was dead and is alive again; he was lost and is found!' And they began to celebrate.

• Jesus, this parable of the Prodigal Son was the closest you came to describing your heavenly Father: compassionate, generous, tender, watching out for me, not so much forgiving my sins as not noticing them—they are washed out of sight and mind by the Niagara of his love.

Something to think and pray about each day this week:

Sharing My Cross

You tell me to "carry my cross," Lord. You are not telling me to go out looking for the cross, in practices or penances. Rather I find it under my nose. Every encounter that costs me, that rubs off my ego, is part of your plan for me. I start with my own body and heart. The aches and limitations of my limbs, my awkwardness and shyness, are part of my cross. I often wish I was different, but this is me, and I will learn to love me as you do. When I can't think of anything to say in company, or when I think of the wrong things, I'm carrying my cross.

What consoles me is that you like my company. You can put up with my silences. You accept the grumpy mutterings that at times are the closest I come to conversation. I don't always feel good about myself. There are moments when, like Groucho Marx, I would not want to belong to any club that was ready to accept me as a member. You not merely accept me, but make me feel I belong, a first-born child in whom you delight.

The Presence of God
I pause for a moment
and think of the love and the grace that God showers on me,
creating me in his image and likeness, making me his temple.

Freedom
Everything has the potential to draw forth from me a fuller love
and life.
Yet my desires are often fixed, caught, on illusions of fulfillment.
I ask that God, through my freedom, may orchestrate
my desires in a vibrant loving melody rich in harmony.

Consciousness
In the presence of my loving Creator,
I look honestly at my feelings over the last day,
the highs, the lows and the level ground.
Can I see where the Lord has been present?

The Word
God speaks to each one of us individually. I need to listen to
what he is saying to me. (Please turn to your scripture on the
following pages. Inspiration points are there should you need
them. When you are ready, return here to continue.)

Conversation
What feelings are rising in me
as I pray and reflect on God's Word?
I imagine Jesus himself sitting or standing beside me,
and open my heart to him.

Conclusion
Glory be to the Father, and to the Son, and to the Holy Spirit,
As it was in the beginning, is now and ever shall be,
World without end. Amen

Sunday 24th February,
Third Sunday of Lent
John 4:5–12

So he came to a Samaritan city called Sychar, near the plot of ground that Jacob had given to his son Joseph. Jacob's well was there, and Jesus, tired out by his journey, was sitting by the well. It was about noon. A Samaritan woman came to draw water, and Jesus said to her, "Give me a drink." (His disciples had gone to the city to buy food.) The Samaritan woman said to him, "How is it that you, a Jew, ask a drink of me, a woman of Samaria?" (Jews do not share things in common with Samaritans.) Jesus said to the Samaritan woman, "If you knew the gift of God, and who it is that is saying to you, 'Give me a drink,' you would have asked him, and he would have given you living water." The woman said to him, "Sir, you have no bucket, and the well is deep. Where do you get that living water? Are you greater than our ancestor Jacob, who gave us the well, and with his sons and his flocks drank from it?"

- When Jesus crosses these religious and social barriers, speaking to this woman who is also a Samaritan, she does not retreat but responds—first in astonishment and then with curiosity.
- In her astonishment she is open to new possibilities; in her curiosity she is willing to explore what they might be.
- How am I responding to Jesus' message? Am I still curious? Do I want to know more, or have I "switched off"?

Monday 25th February
Luke 4:24–30

And he said, "Truly I tell you, no prophet is accepted in the prophet's hometown. But the truth is, there were many widows in Israel in the time of Elijah, when the heaven was shut up three years and six months, and there was a severe famine over all the land; yet Elijah was sent to none of them except to a widow at Zarephath in Sidon. There were also many lepers in Israel in the time of the prophet Elisha, and none of them was cleansed except Naaman the Syrian." When they heard this, all in the synagogue were filled with rage. They got up, drove him out of the town, and led him to the brow of the hill on which their town was built, so that they might hurl him off the cliff. But he passed through the midst of them and went on his way.

- "When they heard this, all in the synagogue were filled with rage." When we have fixed views, when our deepest expectations are confronted and overturned, then our reactions may lead us even to violence—such is the pain and offence we can feel.
- How do I categorize people, and on what basis: on appearance? family? race? nationality? What did Jesus do? Can I imitate him?

Tuesday 26th February   Daniel 3:38–41

We now have no leader, no prophet, no Prince, no burnt offering, no sacrifice, no oblation, no incense, no place where we can make offerings to you and win your favor. But may the contrite soul, the humbled spirit, be as acceptable to you as burnt offerings of rams and bullocks, as thousands of fat lambs: such let our sacrifice be to you today, and may it please you that we follow you wholeheartedly, since those who trust in you will not be shamed. And now we put our whole heart into following you, into fearing you and seeking your face once more.

- Azariah makes this prayer when all seems lost, when he and his companions are facing death for refusing to worship false gods.
- What is my prayer like when I hit rock bottom? When the news is sickening, and my life is in shreds, can I still put my heart into seeking God's face?
- But God, who knows me intimately, with all my strengths and weaknesses, is still more interested in me than in all the riches and lavish offerings other people might have to make.

Wednesday 27th February   **Deuteronomy 4:5–9**

See, just as the Lord my God has charged me, I now teach you statutes and ordinances for you to observe in the land that you are about to enter and occupy. You must observe them diligently, for this will show your wisdom and discernment to the peoples, who, when they hear all these statutes, will say, "Surely this great nation is a wise and discerning people!" For what other great nation has a god so near to it as the Lord our God is whenever we call? And what other great nation has statutes and ordinances as just as this entire law that I am setting before you today? But take care and watch yourselves closely, so as neither to forget the things that your eyes have seen nor to let them slip from your mind all the days of your life; make them known to your children and your children's children.

- Lord as the world around me changes fast, how can I find the language to pass on your word to the next generation? Teach me to make your wisdom the code of my heart, and then I shall be able to speak of it from my heart.

Thursday 28th February   **Jeremiah 7:23**

But this command I gave them, "Obey my voice, and I will be your God, and you shall be my people; and walk only in the way that I command you, so that it may be well with you."

- What way do I walk in, Lord? Sometimes it is the highway of immediate pleasure, sometimes the by-way of devious plotting, sometimes the shadowy lane of resentment or depression. I want to walk in the path of faithful love.
- Keep my feet from straying.

Friday 29th February   **Hosea 14:2, 4–7**

Take words with you and return to the Lord; say to him, "Take away all guilt; accept that which is good, and we will offer the fruit of our lips . . . I will heal their disloyalty; I will love them freely, for my anger has turned from them. I will be like the dew to Israel; he shall blossom like the lily, he shall strike root like the forests of Lebanon. His shoots shall spread out; his beauty shall be like the olive tree, and his fragrance like that of Lebanon. They shall again live beneath my shadow, they shall flourish as a garden; they shall blossom like the vine, their fragrance shall be like the wine of Lebanon.

- Lord, what lovely images these words of Hosea offer! Like the dew you make me blossom, spread my fragrance like the bouquet of good wine, flourish like a garden, my roots deep and firm.
- Wash away my guilt, Lord. That distorts me more than anything. Your love washes away my guilt, leaves me clean and smelling sweet.

Saturday 1st March   **Luke 18:9–14**

He also told this parable to some who trusted in themselves that they were righteous and regarded others with contempt: "Two men went up to the temple to pray, one a Pharisee and the other a tax collector. The Pharisee, standing by himself, was praying thus, 'God, I thank you that I am not like other people: thieves, rogues, adulterers, or even like this tax collector. I fast twice a week; I give a tenth of all my income.' But the tax collector, standing far off, would not even look up to heaven, but was beating his breast and saying, 'God, be merciful to me, a sinner!' I tell you, this man went down to his home justified rather than the other; for all who exalt themselves will be humbled, but all who humble themselves will be exalted."

- The contrast between Pharisee and tax collector has entered so deeply into our culture; Pharisee, a term of honor in Jesus' society, is not something we want to be called. To place it in our culture, read convicted rapist, pedophile, tyrant; any hate-figure of the popular press. We are sometimes persuaded to despise them as the Pharisee despised the humble tax collector. It is not for us to look down on anyone.

- How does the story hit me? I fear being an object of people's contempt. But Lord, if they knew me as you do, they might be right to feel contempt. I have no right to look down on those whose sins are paraded in the media. Be merciful to me.

march 2–8

Something to think and pray about each day this week:

The Joy of Freedom

This was once called *Laetare* Sunday, an invitation to gaiety in a somber season. Some churches treasured rose-colored vestments which they showed off, in place of the purple, on the fourth Sunday of Lent and the third of Advent. It made sense. The sort of self-control that we aim at in Lent can lift our hearts and give us a sense of freedom. We feel at peace because we are in charge of our appetites, not vice versa. People who visit Carmelites, or others of austere life, are astonished to find that there is more laughter in the convent than outside. Nietzsche and Thomas Aquinas agree on this. The gloomy pagan admitted: "The mother of dissipation is not joy but joylessness." The saintly Dominican put it more positively: "A joyful heart is a sign of temperance." I still have half of Lent in which to claw back some of my inner freedom and joy.

The Presence of God

I reflect for a moment on God's presence around me and in me.
Creator of the universe, the sun and the moon, the earth,
every molecule, every atom, everything that is:
God is in every beat of my heart. God is with me, now.

Freedom

A thick and shapeless tree-trunk would never believe
that it could become a statue, admired as a miracle of sculpture,
and would never submit itself to the chisel of the sculptor,
who sees by her genius what she can make of it. (St. Ignatius)
I ask for the grace to let myself be shaped by my loving Creator.

Consciousness

Knowing that God loves me unconditionally,
I look honestly over the last day, its events and my feelings.
Do I have something to be grateful for? Then I give thanks.
Is there something I am sorry for? Then I ask forgiveness.

The Word

I read the Word of God slowly, a few times over, and I listen to
what God is saying to me. (Please turn to your scripture on the
following pages. Inspiration points are there should you need
them. When you are ready, return here to continue.)

Conversation

What is stirring in me as I pray?
Am I consoled, troubled, left cold?
I imagine Jesus himself standing or sitting at my side,
and share my feelings with him.

Conclusion

Glory be to the Father, and to the Son, and to the Holy Spirit,
As it was in the beginning, is now and ever shall be,
World without end. Amen

Sunday 2nd March,
Fourth Sunday of Lent   John 9:1–3, 6–7

As Jesus walked along, he saw a man blind from birth. His disciples asked him, "Rabbi, who sinned, this man or his parents, that he was born blind?" Jesus answered, "Neither this man nor his parents sinned; he was born blind so that God's works might be revealed in him . . ." When he said this, he spat on the ground and made mud with the saliva and spread the mud on the man's eyes, saying to him, "Go, wash in the pool of Siloam" (which means Sent). Then he went and washed and came back able to see.

- In many parts of the ancient world, the spittle of good people was believed to be curative. In using his spittle Jesus was doing what the patient believed a doctor would do; like a good healer he built on the expectation of the sick person.
- Beyond that, Jesus was revealing the power of God. Sickness and misfortune can be a chance to show the glory of God working in our own lives.
- Lord, keep me open to you when tragedy really strikes. Let me feel your hand there.

Monday 3rd March   John 4:46b–54

Now there was a royal official whose son lay ill in Capernaum. When he heard that Jesus had come from Judea to Galilee, he went and begged him to come down and heal his son, for he was at the point of death. Then Jesus said to him, "Unless you see signs and wonders you will not believe." The official said to him, "Sir, come down before my little boy dies." Jesus said to him, "Go; your son will live." The man believed the word that Jesus spoke to him and started on his way. As he was going down, his slaves met him and told him that his child was alive. So he asked them the hour when he began to recover, and they said to him, "Yesterday at one in the afternoon the fever left him." The father realized that this was the hour when Jesus had said to him, "Your son will live." So he himself believed, along with his whole household. Now this was the second sign that Jesus did after coming from Judea to Galilee.

- "Your son will live," said Jesus who was coming ever closer to his own death, his "hour"; this sign points towards the new life, the new creation that is to come.
- Like the boy's father, can I believe, can I put my trust in God?

Tuesday 4th March   John 5:1–8

After this there was a festival of the Jews, and Jesus went up to Jerusalem. Now in Jerusalem by the Sheep Gate there is a pool, called in Hebrew Beth-zatha, which has five porticoes. In these lay many invalids—blind, lame, and paralyzed. One man was there who had been ill for thirty-eight years. When Jesus saw him lying there and knew that he had been there a long time, he said to him, "Do you want to be made well?" The sick man answered him, "Sir, I have no one to put me into the pool when the water is stirred up; and while I am making my way, someone else steps down ahead of me." Jesus said to him, "Stand up, take your mat and walk."

- What a strange question Jesus asked: Do you want to be made well? Yet for those who have been sick for years, a cure is a jolting change in their lives, from dependence and care to managing for themselves.
- Do I really want to be healed of all the physical and spiritual ailments I complain of? Am I ready for a change in my life?

Wednesday 5th March   **Isaiah 49:14–16**

Zion said, "The Lord has forsaken me, my Lord has forgotten me." Can a woman forget her nursing-child, or show no compassion for the child of her womb? Even these may forget, yet I will not forget you. See, I have inscribed you on the palms of my hands; your walls are continually before me.

- The Bible moves us here from the image of a heavenly Father to a heavenly Mother. No human passion is as strong as that of a mother for her child. The baby is part of her, and unforgettable.
- The grief of the mother whose baby has died is something that males can hardly imagine. That visceral passion is ascribed here to God, who is beyond gender, but the source of all love.

Thursday 6th March   **Psalm 105(106):19–23**

They made a calf at Horeb and worshiped a cast image. They exchanged the glory of God for the image of an ox that eats grass. They forgot God, their Savior, who had done great things in Egypt, wondrous works in the land of Ham, and awesome deeds by the Red Sea. Therefore he said he would destroy them—had not Moses, his chosen one, stood in the breach before him, to turn away his wrath from destroying them. Then they despised the pleasant land, having no faith in his promise.

- I'd better not judge the Chosen People too harshly. As I wander through my particular desert, what golden calves have caught my eye? No point dwelling too long on Golden Calves!
- "They forgot God their Savior." It is all about remembering, constantly.

Friday 7th March   **Wisdom 2:1, 12–15**

For the godless reasoned unsoundly, saying to themselves, "Short and sorrowful is our life, and there is no remedy when a life comes to its end, and no one has been known to return from Hades. Let us lie in wait for the righteous man, because he is inconvenient to us and opposes our actions; he reproaches us for sins against the law, and accuses us of sins against our training. He professes to have knowledge of God, and calls himself a child of the Lord. He became to us a reproof of our thoughts; the very sight of him is a burden to us, because his manner of life is unlike that of others, and his ways are strange."

- Who do I identify with, Lord? I can grasp what the godless are feeling because I have sometimes felt the same niggling resentment when my mediocrity is shown up by the integrity of some good person.
- Have I the courage to stand up for goodness, and to take the criticism and hostility that will provoke?

Saturday 8th March   John 7:40–47

When they heard these words, some in the crowd said, "This is really the prophet." Others said, "This is the Messiah." But some asked, "Surely the Messiah does not come from Galilee, does he? Has not the scripture said that the Messiah is descended from David and comes from Bethlehem, the village where David lived?" So there was a division in the crowd because of him. Some of them wanted to arrest him, but no one laid hands on him. Then the temple police went back to the chief priests and Pharisees, who asked them, "Why did you not arrest him?" The police answered, "Never has anyone spoken like this!" Then the Pharisees replied, "Surely you have not been deceived too, have you?"

- Here are two ways of approaching Jesus: some hear him, see how he lives, and love and enjoy him. Others go back to their books and argue about his pedigree.
- Lord, save me from losing you in the babble of books and arguments. May I meet and know and enjoy you.

march 9–15

Something to think and pray about each day this week:

Freedom and Forgiveness

This was once the week of Passion Sunday—that title has now moved to next Sunday—when statues and ornaments in churches were covered in purple until Easter Sunday. During Advent, we prepared for Christmas in the spirit of Mary, in a mood of expectation and happiness. These two weeks of Passiontide are spent in the shadow of Calvary. Jesus' enemies are smelling victory. The just and innocent man is to be framed by false allegations and put to death. We are struggling with the ancient problem of evil: Why do the wicked prosper? But in the passion of Jesus the wicked do not defeat goodness. They do not drive him to despair or bitterness. His heart remains free and forgiving. In my own life I have known such moments. Has my heart turned to blame and bitterness, or is it free?

The Presence of God

In the silence of my innermost being,
in the fragments of my yearned-for wholeness,
can I hear the whispers of God's presence?
Can I remember when I felt God's nearness?
When we walked together and I let myself be embraced by
God's love?

Freedom

There are very few people
who realize what God would make of them
if they abandoned themselves into his hands,
and let themselves be formed by his grace. (St. Ignatius)
I ask for the grace to trust myself totally to God's love.

Consciousness

How do I find myself today?
Where am I with God? With others?
Do I have something to be grateful for? Then I give thanks.
Is there something I am sorry for? Then I ask forgiveness.

The Word

I take my time to read the Word of God, slowly, a few times, allowing myself to dwell on anything that strikes me. (Please turn
to your scripture on the following pages. Inspiration points are
there should you need them. When you are ready, return here
to continue.)

Conversation

Do I notice myself reacting as I pray with the Word of God?
Do I feel challenged, comforted, angry?
Imagining Jesus sitting or standing by me,
I speak out my feelings, as one trusted friend to another.

Conclusion

Glory be to the Father, and to the Son, and to the Holy Spirit,
As it was in the beginning, is now and ever shall be,
World without end. Amen

116

Sunday 9th March, Fifth Sunday of Lent John 11:32–37

When Mary came where Jesus was and saw him, she knelt at his feet and said to him, "Lord, if you had been here, my brother would not have died." When Jesus saw her weeping, and the Jews who came with her also weeping, he was greatly disturbed in spirit and deeply moved. He said, "Where have you laid him?" They said to him, "Lord, come and see." Jesus began to weep. So the Jews said, "See how he loved him!" But some of them said, "Could not he who opened the eyes of the blind man have kept this man from dying?"

- "Jesus wept." Lord, you are not a cold icon. You are as vulnerable as we are to sadness, loss and grief. Remember me by name. Keep me a place in your heart as you had a place for Lazarus.

Monday 10th March Daniel 13:55–56, 60–62

Daniel said, "Indeed! Your lie recoils on you own head: the angel of God has already received from him your sentence and will cut you in half." He dismissed the man, ordered the other to be brought and said to him, "Son of Canaan, not of Judah, beauty has seduced you, lust has led your heart astray!" Then the whole assembly shouted, blessing God, the Savior of those who trust in him. And they turned on the two elders whom Daniel had convicted of false evidence out of their own mouths. As the Law of Moses prescribes, they were given the same punishment as they had schemed to inflict on their neighbor. They were put to death. And thus, that day, an innocent life was saved.

- "Beauty has deceived you and lust has perverted your heart." Plenty of others—more men than women—have followed those old men in being led by lust into personal disaster. Out-of-control hormones can trigger what looks from the outside like self-destructive madness.

- These are not happy characters. Dissipation and addiction is a form of imprisonment in which the chains are inside us, not outside; so the pain is greater.

- Thomas Aquinas put it more positively: "A joyful heart is a sure sign of temperance and self-control." Do I show that sign?

Tuesday 11th March   Numbers 21:4–9

From Mount Hor they set out by the way to the Red Sea, to go around the land of Edom; but the people became impatient on the way. The people spoke against God and against Moses, "Why have you brought us up out of Egypt to die in the wilderness? For there is no food and no water, and we detest this miserable food." Then the LORD sent poisonous serpents among the people, and they bit the people, so that many Israelites died. The people came to Moses and said, "We have sinned by speaking against the LORD and against you; pray to the LORD to take away the serpents from us." So Moses prayed for the people. And the LORD said to Moses, "Make a poisonous serpent, and set it on a pole; and everyone who is bitten shall look at it and live." So Moses made a serpent of bronze, and put it upon a pole; and whenever a serpent bit someone, that person would look at the serpent of bronze and live.

- That image of a coiled serpent still adorns clinics to symbolize the healing work of doctors. It prefigures the image of Jesus raised up on the Cross, an image that can heal bitterness and self-pity when we are in the wilderness.

- How am I affected by the challenge to be a healer?

Wednesday 12th March   John 8:31–32

Then Jesus said to the Jews who had believed in him, "If you continue in my word, you are truly my disciples; and you will know the truth, and the truth will make you free."

- That is a grand, bold phrase: "The truth will make you free." It is used in all sorts of modern rhetoric, but when it comes to the crunch, it can terrify me.
- But can I handle the truth: of my own addictions? of the unfaithfulness of somebody close to me? of the signs in my body of approaching death?
- Yet when I acknowledge such truths, they can liberate me.

Thursday 13th March   Genesis 17:3–8

Then Abram fell on his face; and God said to him, "As for me, this is my covenant with you: You shall be the ancestor of a multitude of nations. No longer shall your name be Abram, but your name shall be Abraham; for I have made you the ancestor of a multitude of nations. I will make you exceedingly fruitful; and I will make nations of you, and kings shall come from you. I will establish my covenant between me and you, and your offspring after you throughout their generations, for an everlasting covenant, to be God to you and to your offspring after you. And I will give to you, and to your offspring after you, the land where you are now an alien, all the land of Canaan, for a perpetual holding; and I will be their God."

- Father Abraham, the common spiritual ancestor for Christians, Jews and Moslems, is more important than ever today. If we children of Abraham, in these three great religions, could rediscover and cherish all that we have in common, the world would be a safer place.
- What can I do to move this process along?

Friday 14th March   Psalm 17(18):1–3

I love you, O LORD, my strength. The LORD is my rock, my fortress, and my deliverer, my God, my rock in whom I take refuge, my shield, and the horn of my salvation, my stronghold.

I call upon the LORD, who is worthy to be praised, so I shall be saved from my enemies

- Thank you, Lord, for the simple psalms. They remain with me when my head has abandoned faith, and all that is left is a sense of needing God desperately. Then I can cry out, "I love you O Lord, my strength."

Saturday 15th March   John 11:47–52

So the chief priests and the Pharisees called a meeting of the council, and said, "What are we to do? This man is performing many signs. If we let him go on like this, everyone will believe in him, and the Romans will come and destroy both our holy place and our nation." But one of them, Caiaphas, who was high priest that year, said to them, "You know nothing at all! You do not understand that it is better for you to have one man die for the people than to have the whole nation destroyed." He did not say this on his own, but being high priest that year he prophesied that Jesus was about to die for the nation, and not for the nation only, but to gather into one the dispersed children of God.

- Caiaphas was a Sadducee; ruthless, political, determined to buttress the status quo and the privileges of his class. He uses the argument of the powerful in every age: we must eliminate the awkward trouble-maker in the name of the common good—namely, the comfort of Sadducees.
- This man spoke more wisely than he knew. One man, Jesus, was to die for the people, and for me.

Something to think and pray about each day this week:

The Model of Prayer

Jesus moves towards his fate as the Jews stumbled into the gas chambers of Auschwitz, calling on God but hearing no answer. The more we know of suffering, the harder it is to live fully in this week of the Passion. Yet Jesus in Gethsemani is the model of prayer. He shows no self-pity. The chalice of rejection and torture seems humanly unbearable, and he asks God to let it pass from him. Like us, he has to interpret not just God's dialogues with us, but also God's silence. Jesus redeems us not by his miracles and preaching, but by his suffering. When he accepts the chalice, he rises strong to meet his executioners. It is our human duty to fight suffering, but there are times when like Jesus we are reduced to passivity and passion.

The Presence of God
God is with me, but more,
God is within me, giving me existence.
Let me dwell for a moment on God's life-giving presence
in my body, my mind, my heart
and in the whole of my life.

Freedom
Many countries are at this moment suffering
the agonies of war.
I bow my head in thanksgiving for my freedom.
I pray for all prisoners and captives.

Consciousness
I remind myself that I am in the presence of the Lord.
I will take refuge in His loving heart.
He is my strength in times of weakness.
He is my comforter in times of sorrow.

The Word
I read the Word of God slowly, a few times over, and I listen to
what God is saying to me. (Please turn to your scripture on the
following pages. Inspiration points are there should you need
them. When you are ready, return here to continue.)

Conversation
How has God's Word moved me? Has it left me cold?
Has it consoled me or moved me to act in a new way?
I imagine Jesus standing or sitting beside me,
I turn and share my feelings with him.

Conclusion
Glory be to the Father, and to the Son, and to the Holy Spirit,
As it was in the beginning, is now and ever shall be,
World without end. Amen

Sunday 16th March,
Palm Sunday of the Lord's Passion   Matthew 21:1–11

When they had come near Jerusalem and had reached Bethphage, at the Mount of Olives, Jesus sent two disciples, saying to them, "Go into the village ahead of you, and immediately you will find a donkey tied, and a colt with her; untie them and bring them to me. If anyone says anything to you, just say this, 'The Lord needs them.' And he will send them immediately." This took place to fulfill what had been spoken through the prophet, saying, "Tell the daughter of Zion, Look, your king is coming to you, humble, and mounted on a donkey, and on a colt, the foal of a donkey." The disciples went and did as Jesus had directed them; they brought the donkey and the colt, and put their cloaks on them, and he sat on them. A very large crowd spread their cloaks on the road, and others cut branches from the trees and spread them on the road. The crowds that went ahead of him and that followed were shouting, "Hosanna to the Son of David! Blessed is the one who comes in the name of the Lord! Hosanna in the highest heaven!" When he entered Jerusalem, the whole city was in turmoil, asking, "Who is this?" The crowds were saying, "This is the prophet Jesus from Nazareth in Galilee."

- "Who is this?" As we recall this joyous celebration of the arrival of the prophet, Jesus of Nazareth, we are also aware of what lies ahead, as Jesus was.
- At the start of this momentous week, let me sit and ponder this familiar story. Can I read it afresh, as though for the first time?

Monday 17th March   John 12:1–8

Six days before the Passover Jesus came to Bethany, the home of Lazarus, whom he had raised from the dead. There they gave a dinner for him. Martha served, and Lazarus was one of those at the table with him. Mary took a pound of costly perfume made of pure nard, anointed Jesus' feet, and wiped them with her hair. The house was filled with the fragrance of the perfume. But Judas Iscariot, one of his disciples (the one who was about to betray him), said, "Why was this perfume not sold for three hundred denarii and the money given to the poor?" (He said this not because he cared about the poor, but because he was a thief; he kept the common purse and used to steal what was put into it.) Jesus said, "Leave her alone. She bought it so that she might keep it for the day of my burial. You always have the poor with you, but you do not always have me."

- Can I sit with this scene for a while. A poignant reunion and family meal become heavy with drama, and with the portents of Jesus' death and resurrection. Meanwhile, Judas' focus is elsewhere.
- Teach me, Lord, to keep my eyes fixed on you.

Tuesday 18th March　　　　　**John 13:21–27, 31–33, 36–38**

After saying this Jesus was troubled in spirit, and declared, "Very truly, I tell you, one of you will betray me." The disciples looked at one another, uncertain of whom he was speaking. One of his disciples—the one whom Jesus loved—was reclining next to him; Simon Peter therefore motioned to him to ask Jesus of whom he was speaking. So while reclining next to Jesus, he asked him, "Lord, who is it?" Jesus answered, "It is the one to whom I give this piece of bread when I have dipped it in the dish." So when he had dipped the piece of bread, he gave it to Judas son of Simon Iscariot. After he received the piece of bread, Satan entered into him. Jesus said to him, "Do quickly what you are going to do." . . . When Judas had gone out, Jesus said, "Now the Son of Man has been glorified, and God has been glorified in him. If God has been glorified in him, God will also glorify him in himself and will glorify him at once. Little children, I am with you only a little longer. You will look for me; and as I said to the Jews so now I say to you, 'Where I am going, you cannot come.' Simon Peter said to him, "Lord, where are you going?" Jesus answered, "Where I am going, you cannot follow me now; but you will follow afterward." Peter said to him, "Lord, why can I not follow you now? I will lay down my life for you." Jesus answered, "Will you lay down your life for me? Very truly, I tell you, before the cock crows, you will have denied me three times.

- The Gospel does not spare Simon Peter. We hear him protesting undying faithfulness, and before the night is out he acts the traitor. But it is unlike the treachery of Judas, who has plotted his betrayal and haggled over the price.
- Peter's denial of Jesus comes from the weakness of human ego, being shamed by a servant in Caiaphas' house.
- St. Philip Neri used to pray: "Lord, beware of this Philip or he will betray you! Lay your hand upon my head, for without you there is not a sin I may not commit this day."

Wednesday 19th March   **Isaiah 50:4–9**

The Lord God has given me the tongue of a teacher, that I may know how to sustain the weary with a word. Morning by morning he wakens—wakens my ear to listen as those who are taught. The Lord God has opened my ear, and I was not rebellious, I did not turn backwards. I gave my back to those who struck me, and my cheeks to those who pulled out the beard; I did not hide my face from insult and spitting. The Lord God helps me; therefore I have not been disgraced; therefore I have set my face like flint, and I know that I shall not be put to shame; he who vindicates me is near. Who will contend with me? Let us stand up together. Who are my adversaries? Let them confront me. It is the Lord God who helps me; who will declare me guilty? All of them will wear out like a garment; the moth will eat them up.

- Let us take our time to contemplate these wonderful words of the prophet Isaiah.
- This Suffering Servant is a carer, a pupil, a listener, a person who asserts what is right, and one who persists to the end. Above all, this servant accepts all that comes from the Lord God.

Thursday 20th March, Holy Thursday   John 13:12–16

After Jesus had washed their feet, had put on his robe, and had returned to the table, he said to them, "Do you know what I have done to you? You call me Teacher and Lord—and you are right, for that is what I am. So if I, your Lord and Teacher, have washed your feet, you also ought to wash one another's feet. For I have set you an example, that you also should do as I have done to you. Very truly, I tell you, servants are not greater than their master, nor are messengers greater than the one who sent them."

- Where the other three gospels describe the Eucharist, John substitutes the washing of the feet. Why? From the beginning Christians have argued about the Eucharist; but works of service put us all on a level with Jesus, beyond argument.
- What used to be called menial work is no longer the job of slaves but the most secure way to God. Jesus has turned it from slave-work into an expression of love.
- Jesus kneeling with a towel round his waist is pointing to that aspect of Christianity in which there is no hierarchy, and the only rule is to meet the needs of others.

Friday 21st March, Good Friday   John 19:25–30

Meanwhile, standing near the cross of Jesus were his mother, and his mother's sister, Mary the wife of Clopas, and Mary Magdalene. When Jesus saw his mother and the disciple whom he loved standing beside her, he said to his mother, "Woman, here is your son." Then he said to the disciple, "Here is your mother." And from that hour the disciple took her into his own home. After this, when Jesus knew that all was now finished, he said (in order to fulfill the scripture), "I am thirsty." A jar full of sour wine was standing there. So they put a sponge full of the wine on a branch of hyssop and held it to his mouth. When Jesus had received the wine, he said, "It is finished." Then he bowed his head and gave up his spirit.

- Now we are at the heart of Jesus' mission: to suffer appallingly and to die without faltering in his love for us. This is where the gospel begins and ends.
- Love demands that we trust in a goodness and a life beyond our own. Lord, it is hard to contemplate. I pull away from the pain and injustice of this Cross. Your love draws me back.

Saturday 22nd March, Holy Saturday   John 19:38–42

After these things, Joseph of Arimathea, who was a disciple of Jesus, though a secret one because of his fear of the Jews, asked Pilate to let him take away the body of Jesus. Pilate gave him permission; so he came and removed his body. Nicodemus, who had at first come to Jesus by night, also came, bringing a mixture of myrrh and aloes, weighing about a hundred pounds. They took the body of Jesus and wrapped it with the spices in linen cloths, according to the burial custom of the Jews. Now there was a garden in the place where he was crucified, and in the garden there was a new tomb in which no one had ever been laid. And so, because it was the Jewish day of Preparation, and the tomb was nearby, they laid Jesus there.

- Joseph of Arimathea and Nicodemus were like many of us, secret admirers of Jesus, but afraid to raise their voice. They were members of the Sanhedrin which had framed the charge against Jesus. Out of fear they had stayed silent in that assembly, and now they were trying to make amends. A word in support of the living Jesus would have meant more than a new tomb, a load of spices and a shroud.
- Lord, may I not wait for a funeral to show my friends how I love and admire them.

march 23–29

Something to think and pray about each day this week:

At the Center of our Faith

This is a feast for our bodies, these marvelous shapely organisms that we have lived with for years, and are as central to us as our minds or memories. We shape our bodies, especially our faces, as the years pass. As the proverb has it, the face we have at forty is the face that we deserve. But we feel the body's frailty in every scratch and hiccup, in every backache and sleepless night.

The apostles and the holy women did not see a ghost of Jesus. They saw him in the flesh, but in different flesh, as the oak tree is different from the acorn from which it grew. We touch on the mystery of a body, not just Jesus' body but our own, which will express us at our best, will not blunt our spirit with weariness and rebellion, but express it with ease and joy. This is a mystery beyond our imagination, but it is the center of our faith. As we grow older, nothing in our faith makes more sense than the Passion and Resurrection, the certainty that our body, like Jesus', must suffer and die, and the certainty that we, in our bodies, have a life beyond death.

The Presence of God

To be present is to arrive as one is and open up to the other.
At this instant, as I arrive here, God is present waiting for me.
God always arrives before me, desiring to connect with me
even more than my most intimate friend.
I take a moment and greet my loving God.

Freedom

"In these days, God taught me
as a schoolteacher teaches a pupil" (St. Ignatius).
I remind myself that there are things God has to teach me yet,
and ask for the grace to hear them and let them change me.

Consciousness

How am I really feeling? Light-hearted? Heavy-hearted?
I may be very much at peace, happy to be here.
Equally, I may be frustrated, worried or angry.
I acknowledge how I really am. It is the real me that the Lord loves.

The Word

I take my time to read the Word of God, slowly, a few times, allowing myself to dwell on anything that strikes me. (Please turn
to your scripture on the following pages. Inspiration points are
there should you need them. When you are ready, return here
to continue.)

Conversation

What feelings are rising in me
as I pray and reflect on God's Word?
I imagine Jesus himself sitting or standing beside me,
and open my heart to him.

Conclusion

Glory be to the Father, and to the Son, and to the Holy Spirit,
As it was in the beginning, is now and ever shall be,
World without end. Amen

Sunday 23rd March, Easter Sunday   John 20:1–9

Early on the first day of the week, while it was still dark, Mary Magdalene came to the tomb and saw that the stone had been removed from the tomb. So she ran and went to Simon Peter and the other disciple, the one whom Jesus loved, and said to them, "They have taken the Lord out of the tomb, and we do not know where they have laid him." Then Peter and the other disciple set out and went toward the tomb. The two were running together, but the other disciple outran Peter and reached the tomb first. He bent down to look in and saw the linen wrappings lying there, but he did not go in. Then Simon Peter came, following him, and went into the tomb. He saw the linen wrappings lying there, and the cloth that had been on Jesus' head, not lying with the linen wrappings but rolled up in a place by itself. Then the other disciple, who reached the tomb first, also went in, and he saw and believed; for as yet they did not understand the scripture, that he must rise from the dead.

- During 2006, two miners in Australia spent 14 days trapped underground, facing slow death. After their rescue, their families and small community rejoiced as did their nation. People across the world followed their story.
- We are enthralled by such stories, about people who look disaster in the eye and make a new beginning. It is as though new life is granted to those who survive against such odds.
- Let me sit a while to contemplate the joy of the Easter story, of Jesus who lives, and who is present.

Monday 24th March   Matthew 28:8–10

So the women left the tomb quickly with fear and great joy, and ran to tell his disciples. Suddenly Jesus met them and said, "Greetings!" And they came to him, took hold of his feet, and worshiped him. Then Jesus said to them, "Do not be afraid; go and tell my brothers to go to Galilee; there they will see me."

- God chose women as the first witnesses of Jesus' resurrection. They had been beside him on Calvary, and been first to the tomb on Sunday morning. Here as throughout his life Jesus chooses women as the carriers of hope.
- Thank you, my sisters, for sustaining us men with hope when we have lost it, for sharing and tending our suffering as Mary shared the cross of her son. Thank you for clinging to the deep values, of patience, and love, and new life.

Tuesday 25th March   John 20:11–17

As Mary wept, she bent over to look into the tomb; and she saw two angels in white, sitting where the body of Jesus had been lying, one at the head and the other at the feet. They said to her, "Woman, why are you weeping?" She said to them, "They have taken away my Lord, and I do not know where they have laid him." When she had said this, she turned around and saw Jesus standing there, but she did not know that it was Jesus. Jesus said to her, "Woman, why are you weeping? Whom are you looking for?" Supposing him to be the gardener, she said to him, "Sir, if you have carried him away, tell me where you have laid him, and I will take him away." Jesus said to her, "Mary!" She turned and said to him in Hebrew, "Rabbouni!" (which means Teacher). Jesus said to her, "Do not hold on to me, because I have not yet ascended to the Father. But go to my brothers and say to them, 'I am ascending to my Father and your Father, to my God and your God.'"

- One word triggers this wonderful moment of recognition: Mary! Let me picture you, Lord, in the garden, in a shape which at first I do not recognize.

- Let me picture and hear you as you call me by name, and I respond: Lord and teacher!

Wednesday 26th March   Acts 3:1–8

One day Peter and John were going up to the temple at the hour of prayer, at three o'clock in the afternoon. And a man lame from birth was being carried in. People would lay him daily at the gate of the temple called the Beautiful Gate so that he could ask for alms from those entering the temple. When he saw Peter and John about to go into the temple, he asked them for alms. Peter looked intently at him, as did John, and said, "Look at us." And he fixed his attention on them, expecting to receive something from them. But Peter said, "I have no silver or gold, but what I have I give you; in the name of Jesus Christ of Nazareth, stand up and walk." And he took him by the right hand and raised him up; and immediately his feet and ankles were made strong. Jumping up, he stood and began to walk, and he entered the temple with them, walking and leaping and praising God.

- All through history people ask the church to bankroll good causes, to dispense money; and the church responds.
- But as Peter reminds us here, our real treasure in the church is the living, present Christ. The knowledge and touch of Jesus, in the gospels and sacraments, is better than silver and gold; it has power to change our lives.

Thursday 27th March   Luke 24:36–43

While they were talking about this, Jesus himself stood among them and said to them, "Peace be with you." They were startled and terrified, and thought that they were seeing a ghost. He said to them, "Why are you frightened, and why do doubts arise in your hearts? Look at my hands and my feet; see that it is I myself. Touch me and see; for a ghost does not have flesh and bones as you see that I have." And when he had said this, he showed them his hands and his feet. While in their joy they were disbelieving and still wondering, he said to them, "Have you anything here to eat?" They gave him a piece of broiled fish, and he took it and ate in their presence.

- When we are threatened by violence, or by the law, or some catastrophe, we can feel that we are on the edge of existence, and take fright easily. At such times the words of Jesus have the power we need: "Peace be with you."
- Lord, I know my worrying does not solve any problems; rather it makes them worse. Lord, teach me to place my trust in you.

Friday 28th March   John 21:2–8

Gathered there together were Simon Peter, Thomas called the Twin, Nathanael of Cana in Galilee, the sons of Zebedee, and two others of his disciples. Simon Peter said to them, "I am going fishing." They said to him, "We will go with you." They went out and got into the boat, but that night they caught nothing. Just after daybreak, Jesus stood on the beach; but the disciples did not know that it was Jesus. Jesus said to them, "Children, you have no fish, have you?" They answered him, "No." He said to them, "Cast the net to the right side of the boat, and you will find some." So they cast it, and now they were not able to haul it in because there were so many fish. That disciple whom Jesus loved said to Peter, "It is the Lord!" When Simon Peter heard that it was the Lord, he put on some clothes, for he was naked, and jumped into the sea. But the other disciples came in the boat, dragging the net full of fish, for they were not far from the land, only about a hundred yards off.

- Tradition places this daybreak encounter at Dalmanutha. The apostles were bored and dithering until Peter took the lead and went fishing. He was still, in his own eyes, as much a traitor as Judas, but his heart was in a different place. When he suspected that the stranger was Jesus, he rushed headlong toward him, not doubting for a moment that he would be forgiven.

- Lord, I want to have that same confidence in you in all my dealings.

Saturday 29th March   Acts 4:18–21

So they called Peter and John and ordered them not to speak or teach at all in the name of Jesus. But Peter and John answered them, "Whether it is right in God's sight to listen to you rather than to God, you must judge; for we cannot keep from speaking about what we have seen and heard." After threatening them again, they let them go, finding no way to punish them because of the people, for all of them praised God for what had happened.

- Lord, in a way I envy Peter and John. They could not keep from speaking about what they had seen and heard. But I have not seen or heard it, and when I speak about your love, it sometimes sounds as though I have learned it out of a book.
- Yet I have felt your presence: sometimes in moments of anguish and incompleteness when I know that I am made for something beyond this; sometimes in moments of transcending joy, when I feel the glory of being loved. Give me words to do justice to my own experience.

Something to think and pray about each day this week:

Entering Sacred Space
In these weeks after Easter, the daily readings recount the appearances of the risen Jesus. He showed himself sometimes to individuals such as Mary Magdalene, and sometimes to groups such as the twelve Apostles and larger gatherings. Sitting alone with your book or at your computer in Sacred Space, your religious world may seem to consist of God and yourself. We need reminding that our faith would not survive without the support of other Christians. We are part of a body of believers, who not only try to live their lives by Christian principles, but who turn to God together: maybe not like the dramatically serried rows of Moslems kneeling towards Mecca, but still in the consciousness of a faith shared by the largest body of believers on this planet. When you come to Sacred Space, and from there raise your mind and heart to God, you are one of thousands upon thousands, young, middle-aged, and older people, who are praying with you, in every continent, some of them far removed from any Christian community. Sacred Space, whether as a book or a cyber-community in twenty languages, is growing all the time, with a distinctive dynamism, and joined by a common bond with Our Father in heaven.

The Presence of God
What is present to me is what has a hold on my becoming.
I reflect on the presence of God always there in love,
amidst the many things that have a hold on me.
I pause and pray that I may let God
affect my becoming in this precise moment.

Freedom
If God were trying to tell me something, would I know?
If God were reassuring me or challenging me, would I notice?
I ask for the grace to be free of my own preoccupations
and open to what God may be saying to me.

Consciousness
Knowing that God loves me unconditionally,
I can afford to be honest about how I am.
How has the last day been, and how do I feel now?
I share my feelings openly with the Lord.

The Word
God speaks to each one of us individually. I need to listen to
what he is saying to me. (Please turn to your scripture on the
following pages. Inspiration points are there should you need
them. When you are ready, return here to continue.)

Conversation
What is stirring in me as I pray?
Am I consoled, troubled, left cold?
I imagine Jesus himself standing or sitting at my side,
and share my feelings with him.

Conclusion
Glory be to the Father, and to the Son, and to the Holy Spirit,
As it was in the beginning, is now and ever shall be,
World without end. Amen

march 2008

Sunday 30th March,
Second Sunday of Easter   John 20:24–29

But Thomas (who was called the Twin), one of the twelve, was not with them when Jesus came. So the other disciples told him, "We have seen the Lord." But he said to them, "Unless I see the mark of the nails in his hands, and put my finger in the mark of the nails and my hand in his side, I will not believe." A week later his disciples were again in the house, and Thomas was with them. Although the doors were shut, Jesus came and stood among them and said, "Peace be with you." Then he said to Thomas, "Put your finger here and see my hands. Reach out your hand and put it in my side. Do not doubt but believe." Thomas answered him, "My Lord and my God!" Jesus said to him, "Have you believed because you have seen me? Blessed are those who have not seen and yet have come to believe."

- Thomas' pessimism is a blessing for us. We can almost feel his resentment at having missed Jesus' first appearance, his resistance to the good news and to the enthusiasm of his friends. He retreated to the role of skeptic.
- But because of his skepticism, we enjoy this rich scene of his personal, physical encounter with the risen Jesus.
- When I feel alone in my doubts, I will remember your words, Lord: Blessed are those who have not see and yet have come to believe.

Monday 31st March,
Annunciation of the Lord   Luke 1:26–32, 34–35, 38a

In the sixth month the angel Gabriel was sent by God to a town in Galilee called Nazareth, to a virgin whose name was Mary. And he came to her and said, "Greetings, favored one! The Lord is with you." But she was much perplexed by his words and pondered what sort of greeting this might be. The angel said to her, "Do not be afraid, Mary, for you have found favor with God. And now, you will conceive in your womb and bear a son, and you will name him Jesus. He will be great, and will be called the Son of the Most High, and the Lord God will give to him the throne of his ancestor David." Mary said to the angel, "How can this be, since I am a virgin?" The angel said to her, "The Holy Spirit will come upon you, and the power of the Most High will overshadow you; therefore the child to be born will be holy; he will be called Son of God." Then Mary said, "Here am I, the servant of the Lord; let it be with me according to your word."

- As I look at this familiar scene, the question hits me: How do I react in a crisis? How does Mary? She is not flattered but perplexed, and she voices her perplexity. She hears God's messenger but wonders can this be true? How does it square with my virginity? She knows that she is free to say "Yes" or "No."
- She ponders the invitation in her heart, as she ponders later events in the life of her son. Then her response is from a full heart.
- Seat of Wisdom, teach me how to use my head and heart in a crisis.

Tuesday 1st April   John 3:7–8

Jesus said to Nicodemus, "Do not be astonished that I said to you, 'You must be born from above.' The wind blows where it chooses, and you hear the sound of it, but you do not know where it comes from or where it goes. So it is with everyone who is born of the Spirit."

- In the face of questioning from Nicodemus, Jesus does not give answers but proposes another way: "You must be born from above."

- Like Nicodemus, I am invited to become a child again, an infant new-born, listening to the Spirit of God and letting go so that the Spirit is my guide. How can I do that today?

Wednesday 2nd April   John 3:16–17

Jesus said to Nicodemus, "For God so loved the world that he gave his only Son, so that everyone who believes in him may not perish but may have eternal life. Indeed, God did not send the Son into the world to condemn the world, but in order that the world might be saved through him."

- The gospel is not about condemnation—we get enough of that in newspaper headlines—but about the promise of a good life here and hereafter.

Thursday 3rd April   Psalm 33(34):8, 18

O taste and see that the Lord is good, happy are those who take refuge in him. The Lord is near to the broken-hearted, and saves the crushed in spirit.

- There are times when I want to cut out any thoughts except of God and me. It is you, Lord, who know me, and love me as I am. You heal my broken spirit with the touch of a mother.
- I am happy to take refuge in you, to taste your sweetness.

Friday 4th April   John 6:5–11

When he looked up and saw a large crowd coming toward him, Jesus said to Philip, "Where are we to buy bread for these people to eat?" He said this to test him, for he himself knew what he was going to do. Philip answered him, "Six months' wages would not buy enough bread for each of them to get a little." One of his disciples, Andrew, Simon Peter's brother, said to him, "There is a boy here who has five barley loaves and two fish. But what are they among so many people?" Jesus said, "Make the people sit down." Now there was a great deal of grass in the place; so they sat down, about five thousand in all. Then Jesus took the loaves, and when he had given thanks, he distributed them to those who were seated; so also the fish, as much as they wanted.

- I imagine myself in the scene. Am I the little boy, ready to share my picnic with others? Am I Philip, the practical man from Bethsaida, someone with local knowledge? Am I one of the large crowd? Who am I?

- Jesus does not lose patience and send the intrusive crowd away. He does not conjure a magical banquet from the sky. Instead he says: Use what you have.

- Lord, you teach me that even the little I have to offer can help others, if I have the courage to reach out towards them.

Saturday 5th April   **John 6:16–21**

When evening came, his disciples went down to the sea, got into a boat, and started across the sea to Capernaum. It was now dark, and Jesus had not yet come to them. The sea became rough because a strong wind was blowing. When they had rowed about three or four miles, they saw Jesus walking on the sea and coming near the boat, and they were terrified. But he said to them, "It is I; do not be afraid." Then they wanted to take him into the boat, and immediately the boat reached the land toward which they were going.

- Jesus has gone up a mountain to pray while the disciples row across the lake. He does not forget them, but from his high ground keeps an eye on their plight. All the time they are struggling with the waves, Jesus has his eyes on them.

- Lord, I am written in your heart. Even when I forget you in my struggle to survive, you do not forget me.

april 6–11

Something to think and pray about each day this week:

Praying Together

This period between the Resurrection and Pentecost is marked in the Gospels by a strong sense of community. When Mary Magdalene found the stone had been moved from the tomb, she went running to tell Simon Peter and the others. When Cleopas and his companion met Jesus on the road to Emmaus, they hurried back to Jerusalem to tell the Eleven. The disciples show their need for one another, from the evening of the Last Supper to the thunderous revelation of Pentecost. Though individuals are mentioned, such as Mary Magdalene and Thomas, they feel incomplete as individuals. They are joint witnesses to the life, death and resurrection of Jesus, and they realize their companionship when they share their memories: Were not our hearts burning within us as he talked to us on the road?

This raises issues for us, who live in a culture that encourages us to operate simply as individuals. When we get sick, we quickly discover that we were not made to survive as individuals. Now in prayer I ask: Where is my community? Who shares my life? Do I ever share my faith with anyone? If I have nobody, then maybe I should look around to fill that gap. Am I more likely to share my reactions to TV programs, sport or politics than to talk to others about deeper issues? For that, I need community.

The Presence of God

At any time of the day or night we can call on Jesus.
He is always waiting, listening for our call.
What a wonderful blessing.
No phone needed, no emails, just a whisper.

Freedom

I need to close out the noise, to rise above the noise;
The noise that interrupts, that separates,
The noise that isolates.
I need to listen to God again.

Consciousness

Help me, Lord, to be more conscious of your presence.
Teach me to recognize your presence in others.
Fill my heart with gratitude for the times your love
has been shown to me through the care of others.

The Word

I read the Word of God slowly, a few times over, and I listen to
what God is saying to me. (Please turn to your scripture on the
following pages. Inspiration points are there should you need
them. When you are ready, return here to continue.)

Conversation

Do I notice myself reacting as I pray with the Word of God?
Do I feel challenged, comforted, angry?
Imagining Jesus sitting or standing by me,
I speak out my feelings, as one trusted friend to another.

Conclusion

Glory be to the Father, and to the Son, and to the Holy Spirit,
As it was in the beginning, is now and ever shall be,
World without end. Amen

Sunday 6th April, Third Sunday of Easter   Luke 24:28–32

As they came near the village to which they were going, he walked ahead as if he were going on. But they urged him strongly, saying, "Stay with us, because it is almost evening and the day is now nearly over." So he went in to stay with them. When he was at the table with them, he took bread, blessed and broke it, and gave it to them. Then their eyes were opened, and they recognized him; and he vanished from their sight. They said to each other, "Were not our hearts burning within us while he was talking to us on the road, while he was opening the scriptures to us?"

- "Stay with us, because it is almost evening." The two disciples offer hospitality; they insist he stay without realizing that it was Jesus they were inviting to eat with them.
- The guest becomes the host: he who receives hospitality from the disciples, in turn offers them the hospitality of God.
- How am I open to the hospitality of God?

Monday 7th April   John 6:26–27

Jesus answered them, "Very truly, I tell you, you are looking for me, not because you saw signs, but because you ate your fill of the loaves. Do not work for the food that perishes, but for the food that endures for eternal life, which the Son of Man will give you.

- "Do not work for food that perishes." Lord, I know about what perishes. We are the waste-makers. In the western world we make mountains of garbage which in the poor countries would supply their daily bread: not just food but clothes, toys, household goods.
- I do not want to set my heart on what will be obsolete tomorrow. You, Lord, are the beauty ever ancient, ever new. You gave us the

things of this world to use, but our hearts are made to find joy in you.

Tuesday 8th April   Acts 7:55–8:1

B ut filled with the Holy Spirit, Stephen gazed into heaven and saw the glory of God and Jesus standing at the right hand of God. "Look," he said, "I see the heavens opened and the Son of Man standing at the right hand of God!" But they covered their ears, and with a loud shout all rushed together against him. Then they dragged him out of the city and began to stone him; and the witnesses laid their coats at the feet of a young man named Saul. While they were stoning Stephen, he prayed, "Lord Jesus, receive my spirit." Then he knelt down and cried out in a loud voice, "Lord, do not hold this sin against them." When he had said this, he died. And Saul approved of their killing him. That day a severe persecution began against the church in Jerusalem, and all except the apostles were scattered throughout the countryside of Judea and Samaria.

- The notion of people legally stoning helpless fellow humans—or legally killing them by bullet, rope or lethal injection—is horrifying. That change of sensibility is surely a movement of grace. In Stephen's killing, the executioners' savagery is overcome by his prayer, echoing that of Jesus on the cross: Lord, forgive my killers.
- In the face of such violence, I must look at myself, Lord: Is there anyone I feel I cannot forgive?

Wednesday 9th April   John 6:35–40

J esus said to them, "I am the bread of life. Whoever comes to me will never be hungry, and whoever believes in me will never be thirsty. But I said to you that you have seen me and yet do not believe. Everything that the Father gives me will come to me, and anyone who comes to me I will never drive away; for I have come down from heaven, not to do my own will, but the will of him who sent me. And this is the will of him who sent me, that I should lose nothing of all that he has given me, but raise it up on the last day. This is indeed the will of my Father, that all who see the Son and believe in him may have eternal life; and I will raise them up on the last day."

- "Whoever comes to me will never be hungry." The invitation is there to each of us, alongside the promise: "And anyone who comes to me I will never drive away."
- I may stumble but the invitation remains, always. Can I respond?

Thursday 10th April   Acts 8:26–39

Then an angel of the Lord said to Philip, "Get up and go towards the south to the road that goes down from Jerusalem to Gaza." (This is a wilderness road.) So he got up and went. Now there was an Ethiopian eunuch, a court official of the Candace, queen of the Ethiopians, in charge of her entire treasury. He had come to Jerusalem to worship and was returning home; seated in his chariot, he was reading the prophet Isaiah. Then the Spirit said to Philip, "Go over to this chariot and join it." So Philip ran up to it and heard him reading the prophet Isaiah. He asked, "Do you understand what you are reading?" He replied, "How can I, unless someone guides me?" And he invited Philip to get in and sit beside him. Now the passage of the scripture that he was reading was this: 'Like a sheep he was led to the slaughter, and like a lamb silent before its shearer, so he does not open his mouth. In his humiliation justice was denied him. Who can describe his generation? For his life is taken away from the earth.' The eunuch asked Philip, "About whom, may I ask you, does the prophet say this, about himself or about someone else?" Then Philip began to speak, and starting with this scripture, he proclaimed to him the good news about Jesus. As they were going along the road, they came to some water; and the eunuch said, "Look, here is water! What is to prevent me from being baptized?" He commanded the chariot to stop, and both of them, Philip and the eunuch, went down into the water, and Philip baptized him. When they came up out of the water, the Spirit of the Lord snatched Philip away; the eunuch saw him no more, and went on his way rejoicing. But Philip found himself at Azotus, and as he was passing through the region, he proclaimed the good news to all the towns until he came to Caesarea.

- This is a sunny encounter, full of promise. As the eunuch is driven in his chariot, he is reading aloud. He symbolizes the hunger of the unbeliever for some understanding of life.
- Philip, attentive to the Holy Spirit's guidance, has the courage to speak about Jesus. The baptism that follows is a reflection of the eunuch's profession: Jesus Christ is the Son of God.
- Lord, I would wish to find the same joy as the eunuch in the discovery of you as the meaning of my life.

Friday 11th April   John 6:56–59

"Those who eat my flesh and drink my blood abide in me, and I in them. Just as the living Father sent me, and I live because of the Father, so whoever eats me will live because of me. This is the bread that came down from heaven, not like that which your ancestors ate, and they died. But the one who eats this bread will live for ever." He said these things while he was teaching in the synagogue at Capernaum.

- Lord, you speak to me here of nourishment, of the bread that sustains my life. You come to me in a form that I can take into myself, and join intimately with.

148

- You take a humble, material shape in order to give me life and vigor and answer my deepest desires.

Saturday 12th April   John 6:64–69

"But among you there are some who do not believe." For Jesus knew from the first who were the ones that did not believe, and who was the one that would betray him. And he said, "For this reason I have told you that no one can come to me unless it is granted by the Father." Because of this many of his disciples turned back and no longer went about with him. So Jesus asked the twelve, "Do you also wish to go away?" Simon Peter answered him, "Lord, to whom can we go? You have the words of eternal life. We have come to believe and know that you are the Holy One of God."

- "Do you also wish to go away?" I hear those voices every day tempting me to give up my faith, offering me any number of alternatives. I can never find a better response than Simon Peter's: "Lord, to whom can we go? You have the words of eternal life."
- We have come to believe and know that you are the Holy One of God.

april 13–19

Something to think and pray about each day this week:

The Ebb and Flow

The death and resurrection of Jesus push us back to our own experiences of death and resurrection. Perhaps it was the serious illness of a child, and her subsequent recovery. Perhaps it was a failure in some enterprise, a failure that left us disheartened and hopeless—until with a friend's help we gradually worked back confidence and enthusiasm. Perhaps it was the breakdown of a friendship, with some sense of betrayal. We felt it was all over, until a moment of mutual forgiveness, and the friendship lived again as though it had never died. When we tasted healthy living again, there was a particular joy, of having loved and lost and found again. There are countless such dips and surges in my life. Ignatius Loyola urges us to remember during the dips that this will pass, and that it is a bad time to make decisions.

The Presence of God

As I sit here, the beating of my heart,
the ebb and flow of my breathing, the movements of my mind
are all signs of God's ongoing creation of me.
I pause for a moment, and become aware
of this presence of God within me.

Freedom

I will ask God's help,
to be free from my own preoccupations,
to be open to God in this time of prayer,
to come to love and serve him more.

Consciousness

Knowing that God loves me unconditionally,
I look honestly over the last day, its events and my feelings.
Do I have something to be grateful for? Then I give thanks.
Is there something I am sorry for? Then I ask forgiveness.

The Word

I take my time to read the Word of God, slowly, a few times, allowing myself to dwell on anything that strikes me. (Please turn to your scripture on the following pages. Inspiration points are there should you need them. When you are ready, return here to continue.)

Conversation

Remembering that I am still in God's presence,
I imagine Jesus himself standing or sitting beside me,
and say whatever is on my mind, whatever is in my heart,
speaking as one friend to another.

Conclusion

Glory be to the Father, and to the Son, and to the Holy Spirit,
As it was in the beginning, is now and ever shall be,
World without end. Amen

Sunday 13th April,
Fourth Sunday of Easter   **John 10:9–10**

Jesus said to the people, "I am the gate. Whoever enters by me will be saved, and will come in and go out and find pasture. The thief comes only to steal and kill and destroy. I came that they may have life, and have it abundantly."

- This is a seminal saying: Jesus has come that we may have abundant life. The signs of his presence are love, joy, growth, change and activity, which vary at different ages. Not necessarily health—we cannot control that—but love and growth as the years pass.

- I wonder, have I more abundant life today than yesterday?

Monday 14th April   **John 10:14–16**

Jesus said to the people, "I am the good shepherd. I know my own and my own know me, just as the Father knows me and I know the Father. And I lay down my life for the sheep. I have other sheep that do not belong to this fold. I must bring them also, and they will listen to my voice. So there will be one flock, one shepherd."

- Jesus wants to give life to all, by both his life and his death, to share with us the life he shares with the Father.

- He calls me to listen, to let go, and to share my life with others.

Tuesday 15th April   **Acts 11:26**

The disciples went to Antioch. So it was that for an entire year they met with the church and taught a great many people, and it was in Antioch that the disciples were first called "Christians."

- They were called Christians, and pagans remarked how they loved one another.

- I have seen it sometimes, a group of people who enjoyed one another, shared with one another, were gentle, with an eye to others' needs.

Wednesday 16th April   John 12:46

Jesus said to the people: "I have come as light into the world, so that everyone who believes in me should not remain in the darkness."

- Lord you are a special sort of light: a kindly light who leads me; but also a light mixed with darkness. There can be obscurity in my faith, periods when, like John of the Cross, I leave the understanding behind, in order to go to God by love.
- In that sort of darkness I can always return to the memory of Jesus' humanity, and God shining through it.

Thursday 17th April   John 13:16–17

After he had washed their feet, had put on his robe, and had returned to the table, he said to them, "Very truly, I tell you, servants are not greater than their master, nor are messengers greater than the one who sent them. If you know these things, you are blessed if you do them."

- Lord, you are teaching me here: it is not what you say that stays with me, so much as the sight of you doing a slave's job and loving it. As you kneel at our feet, you put all hierarchies into perspective.
- This is the ultimate ecumenism, the unity of those who serve with love. In that unity we are guided, not by rules or rituals, but by the needs of others.

Friday 18th April   John 14:1–3

Jesus said to his disciples, "Do not let your hearts be troubled. Believe in God, believe also in me. In my Father's house there are many dwelling places. If it were not so, would I have told you that I go to prepare a place for you? And if I go and prepare a place for you, I will come again and will take you to myself, so that where I am, there you may be also."

- As we strain to imagine what lies beyond the grave, these words comfort and excite me: "In my Father's house there are many dwelling places."

- Clouds and heavenly palaces may not mean much to people who have lived in grass huts or igloos or on the side of the road. God's mercy and hospitality are wider than our imagination. I relish Belloc's wisdom: Kings live in Palaces, and Pigs in sties, and youth in Expectation. Youth is wise.

Saturday 19th April   John 14:7–9a

Jesus said to his disciples, "If you know me, you will know my Father also. From now on you do know him and have seen him." Philip said to him, "Lord, show us the Father, and we will be satisfied." Jesus said to him, "Have I been with you all this time, Philip, and you still do not know me? Whoever has seen me has seen the Father."

- Scripture never lets us forget that God is beyond our imagination, always greater than any concept we have of him. We dare not domesticate God. Even the title Father is a metaphor. God is a spirit, invisible, beyond body or gender or space or time.

- As we learn more about our universe, our sense of the Creator's transcendence grows sharper. But in Jesus we have access to God, not just as creatures who know him, but as his children, like Jesus.

april 20–26

Something to think and pray about each day this week:

Getting in Touch

If we are to encounter God truthfully in prayer, we must be real to ourselves. We need to be aware of what we are feeling. A mother will see her son come in from school, and know from his face and body language that he is depressed, or resentful, or anxious, or whatever. If she asks him how he is, he is likely to say, "Fine." Most mothers will have the intuition and wit to lead him gently to put words on what he is feeling, and then to trace the happenings that led him to this state, such as a failure in school, a quarrel with a friend or worry about an exam. I remember a girl in school startling me—when I was a teacher—by asking, "Why are you angry today?" She was right, but up to that point I had not realized that I was angry.

It is only when we are in touch with what is going on inside us that we can come before the Lord. Then I can experience the real me connecting with the real God. It is not a case of apologizing for my emotions. They are as pre-moral and innocent as feeling cold or shivery. When I bring those feelings to consciousness, as the Psalmist does with his anger and despair, then prayer become authentic.

The Presence of God

I pause for a moment
and reflect on God's life-giving presence
in every part of my body, in everything around me,
in the whole of my life.

Freedom

God is not foreign to my freedom.
Instead the Spirit breathes life into my most intimate desires,
gently nudging me towards all that is good.
I ask for the grace to let myself be enfolded by the Spirit.

Consciousness

How do I find myself today?
Where am I with God? With others?
Do I have something to be grateful for? Then I give thanks.
Is there something I am sorry for? Then I ask forgiveness.

The Word

God speaks to each one of us individually. I need to listen to
what he is saying to me. (Please turn to your scripture on the
following pages. Inspiration points are there should you need
them. When you are ready, return here to continue.)

Conversation

How has God's Word moved me? Has it left me cold?
Has it consoled me or moved me to act in a new way?
I imagine Jesus standing or sitting beside me,
I turn and share my feelings with him.

Conclusion

Glory be to the Father, and to the Son, and to the Holy Spirit,
As it was in the beginning, is now and ever shall be,
World without end. Amen

Sunday 20th April, Fifth Sunday of Easter   1 Peter 2:9

You are a chosen race, a royal priesthood, a holy nation, God's own people, in order that you may proclaim the mighty acts of him who called you out of darkness into his marvelous light.

- Lord, I do not always feel chosen, royal or holy. I often feel ordinary and irrelevant.
- But you have called me into your marvelous light, and when I am praying, you are more active in me than I am.

Monday 21st April   John 14:25–26

Jesus said to his disciples: "I have said these things to you while I am still with you. The Advocate, the Holy Spirit, whom the Father will send in my name, will teach you everything, and remind you of all that I have said to you."

- Here is a new image of God. The vine-grower has a sharp knife, and a keen eye to the vine's health. If he cuts out, it is to make the plant more vigorous and fruitful.
- Lord, when I feel your sharp touch, I may resent it; but I trust your love for me.

Tuesday 22nd April   John 14:27–29

Jesus said to his disciples, "Peace I leave with you; my peace I give to you. I do not give to you as the world gives. Do not let your hearts be troubled, and do not let them be afraid. You heard me say to you, 'I am going away, and I am coming to you.' If you loved me, you would rejoice that I am going to the Father, because the Father is greater than I. And now I have told you this before it occurs, so that when it does occur, you may believe."

- Peace, shalom, does not mean escape from trouble, or its avoidance. It means being grounded in God: *In la sua volontà é nostra pace*, said Dante. Then no experience, even prison or pain or loss, can shake our peace.

- How do I experience God's peace?

Wednesday 23rd April   John 15:5–8

Jesus said to his disciples, "I am the vine, you are the branches. Those who abide in me and I in them bear much fruit, because apart from me you can do nothing. Whoever does not abide in me is thrown away like a branch and withers; such branches are gathered, thrown into the fire, and burned. If you abide in me, and my words abide in you, ask for whatever you wish, and it will be done for you. My Father is glorified by this, that you bear much fruit and become my disciples."

- To abide in Jesus means more than carrying the name of Christian, or rendering lip service to the Lord. It means bearing fruit, showing our faith in our life and work, living in such a way that our life would make no sense if God did not exist.
- Do I accept this challenge today?

Thursday 24th April   John 15:9–11

Jesus said to his disciples, "As the Father has loved me, so I have loved you; abide in my love. If you keep my commandments, you will abide in my love, just as I have kept my Father's commandments and abide in his love. I have said these things to you so that my joy may be in you, and that your joy may be complete."

- There are times when I seem to understand what this love means. Paul spoke of the love of God which is poured out in our hearts through the Holy Spirit who is given to us. Sometimes we can experience that love going through us, giving us joy in loving others. There is an energy in us which is not of our making.

- I think of one or two friends who radiate contentment; I think they are abiding in God's love, and feeling joy from it. Lord, maybe you will one day surprise me with this joy.

Friday 25th April, St. Mark the Evangelist   1 Peter 5:5–11

And all of you must clothe yourselves with humility in your dealings with one another, for "God opposes the proud, but gives grace to the humble." Humble yourselves therefore under the mighty hand of God, so that he may exalt you in due time. Cast all your anxiety on him, because he cares for you. Discipline yourselves; keep alert. Like a roaring lion your adversary the devil prowls around, looking for someone to devour. Resist him, steadfast in your faith, for you know that your brothers and sisters throughout the world are undergoing the same kinds of suffering. And after you have suffered for a little while, the God of all grace, who has called you to his eternal glory in Christ, will himself restore, support, strengthen, and establish you. To him be the power for ever and ever. Amen.

- Here we have a *Quick Guide to Christian Living*, a series of bullet points for daily living.
- Self-discipline, steadfast faith, and suffering are part of the journey. But we do not journey alone: "For you know that your brothers and sisters throughout the world are undergoing the same kinds of suffering."
- *Sacred Space* is part of that community, sharing that journey.

Saturday 26th April   John 15:18–21

Jesus said to his disciples: "If the world hates you, be aware that it hated me before it hated you. If you belonged to the world, the world would love you as its own. Because you do not belong to the world, but I have chosen you out of the world—therefore the world hates you. Remember the word that I said to you,

'Servants are not greater than their master.' If they persecuted me, they will persecute you; if they kept my word, they will keep yours also. But they will do all these things to you on account of my name, because they do not know him who sent me."

- This talk about hatred is distasteful stuff, Lord. But I have to admit that it rings true. It happens that good Christians are slandered and hated, for whatever reason.
- It is then I need to remember how you were hated and kept your peace, and did not let your heart flame up in resentment.

april 27–may 3

Something to think and pray about each day this week:

The Invitation

Have you ever prepared to meet somebody who mattered a lot to you? You reach the door of the room where your friend is waiting, and pause before opening the door. Saint Ignatius suggests this picture as a preparation for prayer. Gather yourself, with your hand on the door-knob, and think: Something important is about to happen to me. Somebody important is waiting for me. I am walking onto holy ground, stepping into sacred space, going to meet the Lord of my life, the one whose name is I AM. I am preparing to invite God to deal with me, to speak to my heart. I will be receptive. I do not know what words to say, what thoughts to think, so I trust in the Holy Spirit, who will teach me from the inside. In that mood of confidence I open the door, to find God looking at me . . .

The Presence of God

The world is charged with the grandeur of God (Gerard Manley Hopkins).
I dwell for a moment on the presence of God
around me, in every part of my body,
and deep within my being.

Freedom

Everything has the potential to draw forth from me a fuller love and life.
Yet my desires are often fixed, caught, on illusions of fulfillment.
I ask that God, through my freedom, may orchestrate
my desires in a vibrant loving melody rich in harmony.

Consciousness

In God's loving presence I unwind the past day,
starting from now and looking back, moment by moment.
I gather in all the goodness and light, in gratitude.
I attend to the shadows and what they say to me,
seeking healing, courage, forgiveness.

The Word

I read the Word of God slowly, a few times over, and I listen to
what God is saying to me. (Please turn to your scripture on the
following pages. Inspiration points are there should you need
them. When you are ready, return here to continue.)

Conversation

What feelings are rising in me
as I pray and reflect on God's Word?
I imagine Jesus himself sitting or standing beside me,
and open my heart to him.

Conclusion

Glory be to the Father, and to the Son, and to the Holy Spirit,
As it was in the beginning, is now and ever shall be,
World without end. Amen

Sunday 27th April, Sixth Sunday of Easter   John 14:15–21

Jesus said to his disciples, "If you love me, you will keep my commandments. And I will ask the Father, and he will give you another Advocate, to be with you forever. This is the Spirit of truth, whom the world cannot receive, because it neither sees him nor knows him. You know him, because he abides with you, and he will be in you. I will not leave you orphaned; I am coming to you. In a little while the world will no longer see me, but you will see me; because I live, you also will live. On that day you will know that I am in my Father, and you in me, and I in you."

- The Father will give you another Counsellor, "the Spirit of truth . . . you know him, for he dwells with you and will be in you." I know, Lord, that the same Holy Spirit joins me to you as joined Jesus to his Father.
- That Spirit dwells in me, an abiding presence whose voice can easily be drowned by my everyday plans and concerns.
- To be open to the Spirit, I must quieten first my body, then my heart.

Monday 28th April   John 15:26–27

Jesus said to his disciples, "When the Advocate comes, whom I will send to you from the Father, the Spirit of truth who comes from the Father, he will testify on my behalf. You also are to testify because you have been with me from the beginning.

- To testify and bear witness to something, I must have personal experience, so that I can say: This is true, and I know it.
- Lord, I have not been with you from the beginning. I am one of those who did not see and yet believed. Show me yourself, strengthen your spirit in me, so that my life and my words may testify to you.

Tuesday 29th April   John 16:5–7

Jesus said to his disciples, "But now I am going to him who sent me; yet none of you asks me, 'Where are you going?' But because I have said these things to you, sorrow has filled your hearts. Nevertheless I tell you the truth: it is to your advantage that I go away, for if I do not go away, the Advocate will not come to you; but if I go, I will send him to you."

- These words of Jesus at the Last Supper reflect some of the heavy sorrow of that meal, darkened by the disciples' awareness that they were losing Jesus.
- What he says to them applies to us also: Jesus remains with us through his spirit, the Paraclete dwelling in us and linking us to the Father as he linked Jesus to the Father.

Wednesday 30th April   Acts 17:22–28

Then Paul stood in front of the Areopagus and said, "Athenians, I see how extremely religious you are in every way. For as I went through the city and looked carefully at the objects of your worship, I found among them an altar with the inscription, 'To an unknown god.' What therefore you worship as unknown, this I proclaim to you. The God who made the world and everything in it, he who is Lord of heaven and earth, does not live in shrines made by human hands, nor is he served by human hands, as though he needed anything, since he himself gives to all mortals life and breath and all things. From one ancestor he made all nations to inhabit the whole earth, and he allotted the times of their existence and the boundaries of the places where they would live, so that they would search for God and perhaps grope for him and find him—though indeed he is not far from each one of us. For 'In him we live and move and have our being'; as even some of your own poets have said, 'For we too are his offspring.'"

- Lord, I thank you for this mind-blowing meeting of the Christian Paul with the splendid culture of Athens. He spoke under the shadow of the Acropolis, in the city which has left such a mark on Western literature, philosophy, art, history and politics.
- Paul did not rail against paganism; instead he paid tribute to the searching of the Greeks and the glimmerings of God in their poets.
- Teach me to be like Paul and to find your traces in unexpected places.

Thursday 1st May   John 16:16–20

Jesus said to his disciples, "A little while, and you will no longer see me, and again a little while, and you will see me." Then some of his disciples said to one another, "What does he mean by saying to us, 'A little while, and you will no longer see me, and again a little while, and you will see me'; and 'Because I am going to the Father'?" They said, "What does he mean by this 'a little while'? We do not know what he is talking about." Jesus knew that they wanted to ask him, so he said to them, "Are you discussing among yourselves what I meant when I said, 'A little while, and you will no longer see me, and again a little while, and you will see me'? Very truly, I tell you, you will weep and mourn, but the world will rejoice; you will have pain, but your pain will turn into joy."

- Lord, you see the way we are with one another: we find it hard to say Goodbye. Our last words always carry the promise of further meeting: See you; au revoir, auf wiedersehen; arrivederci.
- In these goodbyes to your friends, you were holding out a scarcely believable promise, of a meeting on the far side of the grave.

Friday 2nd May John 16:20–23

Jesus said to his disciples, "Very truly, I tell you, you will weep and mourn, but the world will rejoice; you will have pain, but your pain will turn into joy. When a woman is in labor, she has pain, because her hour has come. But when her child is born, she no longer remembers the anguish because of the joy of having brought a human being into the world. So you have pain now; but I will see you again, and your hearts will rejoice, and no one will take your joy from you. On that day you will ask nothing of me. Very truly, I tell you, if you ask anything of the Father in my name, he will give it to you."

- Lord, there are times when this metaphor of yours hits me hard. Life feels like the labor of a pregnant woman. It weighs me down with its difficulties.
- Nourish in me the conviction that this is not a labor unto death, but a labor unto birth, unto a joy with you that will last.

Saturday 3rd May, Sts. Philip and James John 14:8–10a

Philip said to Jesus, "Lord, show us the Father, and we will be satisfied." Jesus said to him, "Have I been with you all this time, Philip, and you still do not know me? Whoever has seen me has seen the Father. How can you say, 'Show us the Father'? Do you not believe that I am in the Father and the Father is in me?"

- On this feast of Saints Philip and James, the gospel quotes a curious remark of Philip to Jesus: "Show us the Father and we will be satisfied." It reminds me of what I have often heard on the lips of exasperated mothers to their children: You're never satisfied.
- Am I ever? Augustine said our hearts are restless till they rest in God. When I see Jesus I see a human vision of the Infinite God who is beyond imagination.

Something to think and pray about each day this week:

Time to Pray

Jesus gave an instruction on prayer: When you pray, go into your room and shut the door. You want to be present to God alone, fully in the Now. Shut the door on the past, and shut it on the future. To be fully alert to the Now is a rare grace and gift, but very occasionally we see glimpses of it, people for whom in prayer, time stands still.

There is a story about St. Francis Xavier when he was living in Goa. One day as he retired to his room, he asked his friend Andrew to call him at two o'clock, as he had to visit the Viceroy of Portugal, the highest official in the city. So at two Andrew came to his room, and found Francis sitting in a chair, with his eyes raised to heaven, and his face inflamed: he was in a trance. Andrew tried shuffling his feet noisily, rattled the door, coughed aloud—no use. Xavier was lost to the world, so Andrew left him there. He came back later and got Francis' attention by tugging at his clothes. "What time is it?" asked Xavier. "It's gone four," said Andrew. "Come on," said Francis, "let's go." But he was still deep in prayer, and as they walked through the city he lost his way, and they wandered round till evening, never reaching the viceroy. "Son," said Xavier, "we shall have time for that some other day. God wished this day for himself."

The Presence of God

As I sit here, God is present,
breathing life into me and into everything around me.
For a few moments, I sit silently,
and become aware of God's loving presence.

Freedom

There are very few people
who realize what God would make of them
if they abandoned themselves into his hands,
and let themselves be formed by his grace. (St. Ignatius)
I ask for the grace to trust myself totally to God's love.

Consciousness

I exist in a web of relationships—links to nature, people, God.
I trace out these links, giving thanks for the life that flows
through them.
Some links are twisted or broken: I may feel regret, anger,
disappointment.
I pray for the gift of acceptance and forgiveness.

The Word

I take my time to read the Word of God, slowly, a few times, allowing myself to dwell on anything that strikes me. (Please turn to your scripture on the following pages. Inspiration points are there should you need them. When you are ready, return here to continue.)

Conversation

What is stirring in me as I pray?
Am I consoled, troubled, left cold?
I imagine Jesus himself standing or sitting at my side,
and share my feelings with him.

Conclusion

Glory be to the Father, and to the Son, and to the Holy Spirit,
As it was in the beginning, is now and ever shall be,
World without end. Amen

Sunday 4th May,
Ascension of the Lord   Matthew 28:16–20

Now the eleven disciples went to Galilee, to the mountain to which Jesus had directed them. When they saw him, they worshipped him; but some doubted. And Jesus came and said to them, "All authority in heaven and on earth has been given to me. Go therefore and make disciples of all nations, baptizing them in the name of the Father and of the Son and of the Holy Spirit, and teaching them to obey everything that I have commanded you. And remember, I am with you always, to the end of the age."

- "When they saw Jesus, they worshipped him; but some doubted." These are the eleven disciples—Judas has not yet been replaced—who have walked with Jesus for three years.
- Yet here on the mountain of revelation, their faith and worship is mixed with questioning and doubt. We know how it feels. It is to these shaky, ambivalent men that Jesus gives the mandate to preach to all nations. To them, and to us, he says: I am with you. I need you to be with me, Lord.

Monday 5th May   John 16:32b–33

Jesus said to his disciples, "I am not alone because the Father is with me. I have said this to you, so that in me you may have peace. In the world you face persecution. But take courage; I have conquered the world!"

- Before this Maundy Thursday is over, the disciples are going to see Jesus at his weakest, sweating blood in Gethsemini, mocked and scourged and crucified. They will see the world doing its worst to Jesus, and yet failing to defeat him.
- Life can do its worst to me, but in the power of the Cross I will not be defeated.

- To each of us he says, I am with you.

Tuesday 6th May — John 17:1–3

After Jesus had spoken these words, he looked up to heaven and said, "Father, the hour has come; glorify your Son so that the Son may glorify you, since you have given him authority over all people, to give eternal life to all whom you have given him. And this is eternal life, that they may know you, the only true God, and Jesus Christ whom you have sent."

- What we are seeking in *Sacred Space* is just this, to know the one true God and Jesus Christ whom God has sent. The prophet Habbakuk dreamt of a Golden Age in which "the earth shall be filled with the knowledge of God."
- We are all invited to be mystics, not just having thoughts, but knowing in the biblical sense, seeking intimacy with God through prayer.

Wednesday 7th May — Acts 20:32–35

Paul said to the elders of the church of Ephesus: "Now I commend you to God and to the message of his grace, a message that is able to build you up and to give you the inheritance among all who are sanctified. I coveted no one's silver or gold or clothing. You know for yourselves that I worked with my own hands to support myself and my companions. In all this I have given you an example that by such work we must support the weak, remembering the words of the Lord Jesus, for he himself said, 'It is more blessed to give than to receive.'"

- With these words Paul farewells the people of Ephesus whom he lived among for three years. There are tears and great sadness. But they will recall his preaching and how he worked hard while he was with them.

- Do I work hard, in whatever I do? Do I only work for myself or do I work for others too?
- What can I learn from Paul's example?

Thursday 8th May   John 17:20–21

Jesus looked up to heaven and said, "Father, I ask not only on behalf of these, but also on behalf of those who will believe in me through their word, that they may all be one. As you, Father, are in me and I am in you, may they also be in us, so that the world may believe that you have sent me."

- Lord, I treasure all the chances of true fellowship with others who do not believe in you. When I work or talk with them, or love them, or serve or pray with them, your grace is at work in us.
- These occasions may not be labeled "ecumenical events," but they reveal your presence among us.

Friday 9th May   John 21:15–19

When they had finished breakfast, Jesus said to Simon Peter, "Simon son of John, do you love me more than these?" He said to him, "Yes, Lord; you know that I love you." Jesus said to him, "Feed my lambs." A second time he said to him, "Simon son of John, do you love me?" He said to him, "Yes, Lord; you know that I love you." Jesus said to him, "Tend my sheep." He said to him the third time, "Simon son of John, do you love me?" Peter felt hurt because he said to him the third time, "Do you love me?" And he said to him, "Lord, you know everything; you know that I love you." Jesus said to him, "Feed my sheep. Very truly, I tell you, when you were younger, you used to fasten your own belt and to go wherever you wished. But when you grow old, you will stretch out your hands, and someone else will fasten a belt around you and take you where you do not wish to go."

(He said this to indicate the kind of death by which he would glorify God.) After this he said to him, "Follow me."

- This is a scene to savor slowly. John's gospel summarizes what was probably a long morning's conversation between Jesus and Peter.
- Jesus with his triple questioning is reminding Peter of his triple betrayal—the most painful memory imaginable—but he does it with delicacy. Peter loved Jesus before his cowardly betrayal of him; he loved him more deeply afterwards.
- Am I disturbed by such weakness in others—and myself—or does it remind me of God's constant saving love?

Saturday 10th May   John 21:20–24

Peter turned and saw the disciple whom Jesus loved following them; he was the one who had reclined next to Jesus at the supper and had said, "Lord, who is it that is going to betray you?" When Peter saw him, he said to Jesus, "Lord, what about him?" Jesus said to him, "If it is my will that he remain until I come, what is that to you? Follow me!" So the rumor spread in the community that this disciple would not die. Yet Jesus did not say to him that he would not die, but, "If it is my will that he remain until I come, what is that to you?" This is the disciple who is testifying to these things and has written them, and we know that his testimony is true.

- Is there is an undercurrent of sibling rivalry here? Jesus has just given Peter the leadership, but also warned of a premature death. When Peter asks about John's future, Jesus answers: "What is that to you? Follow me!"
- Lord I am not above sibling rivalry, that foolish waste of emotion. Teach me, as you taught Peter, that the following of you places all of us on the same level.

Something to think and pray about each day this week:

One in the Spirit

It is no accident that the Holy Spirit came down on a group, not an individual. The story of Pentecost is of a community. John Donne's wonderful sermon echoes here: "No man is an island. The church is Catholic, universal, so are all her actions; all that she does belongs to all." From the beginning, huddled in fear in the Upper Room, the first Christians prayed together, talked together, learned together. The tongues of fire appeared on all of them. We are called into communion with one another. When Paul and Peter and James disagreed about the need to circumcise Christian converts, they did not make separate calls on the Holy Spirit. Instead, at the First Council of Jerusalem, they talked and listened to one another, and shared their experience; after all that they were able to say: "It has seemed good to the Holy Spirit and to us . . ." For many people the gathering for worship on a Sunday is the only occasion on which they rub shoulders with a crowd. We strengthen our faith and love by contact with one another, and through one another, with the Holy Spirit.

The Presence of God
As I sit here with my book, God is here.
Around me, in my sensations, in my thoughts and deep within me.
I pause for a moment, and become aware
of God's life-giving presence.

Freedom
A thick and shapeless tree-trunk would never believe
that it could become a statue, admired as a miracle of sculpture,
and would never submit itself to the chisel of the sculptor,
who sees by her genius what she can make of it. (St. Ignatius)
I ask for the grace to let myself be shaped by my loving Creator.

Consciousness
How am I really feeling? Light-hearted? Heavy-hearted?
I may be very much at peace, happy to be here.
Equally, I may be frustrated, worried or angry.
I acknowledge how I really am. It is the real me that the Lord loves.

The Word
God speaks to each one of us individually. I need to listen to
what he is saying to me. (Please turn to your scripture on the
following pages. Inspiration points are there should you need
them. When you are ready, return here to continue.)

Conversation
Do I notice myself reacting as I pray with the Word of God?
Do I feel challenged, comforted, angry?
Imagining Jesus sitting or standing by me,
I speak out my feelings, as one trusted friend to another.

Conclusion
Glory be to the Father, and to the Son, and to the Holy Spirit,
As it was in the beginning, is now and ever shall be,
World without end. Amen

Sunday 11th May, Pentecost   1 Corinthians 12:4–7, 12–13

Now there are varieties of gifts, but the same Spirit; and there are varieties of services, but the same Lord; and there are varieties of activities, but it is the same God who activates all of them in everyone. To each is given the manifestation of the Spirit for the common good. For just as the body is one and has many members, and all the members of the body, though many, are one body, so it is with Christ. For in the one Spirit we were all baptized into one body—Jews or Greeks, slaves or free—and we were all made to drink of one Spirit.

- "Varieties of gifts, but the same spirit." Lord, I do not see myself as having gifts in any variety. I am just me. But I can look at my sisters and brothers and admire their gifts with a touch of green in my gaze.

- How do I accept my gifts, and the gifts of those around me? What sense is there in being proud of my gifts? If I am good-looking, attractive, intelligent, good company, I can be happy in my skin, but not proud. It is a gift, not of my making.

- Thanks be to you, Lord. "I thank you for the wonder of my being."

Monday 12th May   Mark 8:11–13

The Pharisees came and began to argue with Jesus, asking him for a sign from heaven, to test him. And he sighed deeply in his spirit and said, "Why does this generation ask for a sign? Truly I tell you, no sign will be given to this generation." And he left them, and getting into the boat again, he went across to the other side.

- There are times, Lord, when I too look for something abnormal to proclaim your presence. In fact it is all around me. There are signs enough of you in my every day.

- Do I ignore what is under my nose? Can I think for a moment about some obvious signs I see each day?

Tuesday 13th May   James 1:12–18

Blessed is anyone who endures temptation. Such a one has stood the test and will receive the crown of life that the Lord has promised to those who love him. No one, when tempted, should say, "I am being tempted by God"; for God cannot be tempted by evil and he himself tempts no one. But one is tempted by one's own desire, being lured and enticed by it; then, when that desire has conceived, it gives birth to sin, and that sin, when it is fully grown, gives birth to death. Do not be deceived, my beloved. Every generous act of giving, with every perfect gift, is from above, coming down from the Father of lights, with whom there is no variation or shadow due to change. In fulfillment of his own purpose he gave us birth by the word of truth, so that we would become a kind of first fruits of his creatures.

- As always, James speaks to us directly, pulling no punches, exhorting us to demonstrate faith by the way we live and act towards others.

- Do I demonstrate my faith in the ways I act? Can I do a little better today?

Wednesday 14th May   James 1:19–25

You must understand this, my beloved: let everyone be quick to listen, slow to speak, slow to anger; for your anger does not produce God's righteousness. Therefore rid yourselves of all sordidness and rank growth of wickedness, and welcome with meekness the implanted word that has the power to save your souls. But be doers of the word, and not merely hearers who deceive themselves. For if any are hearers of the word and not doers, they are like those who look at themselves in a mirror; for they look at themselves and, on going away, immediately forget what they were like. But those who look into the perfect law, the law of liberty, and persevere, being not hearers who forget but doers who act—they will be blessed in their doing.

- "Welcome with meekness the implanted word." This starting point is important for James; we must start first as ready pupils of the Word, with a truly teachable spirit. It is only then that we can be doers of the word and not merely hearers.
- Do I acknowledge the shortcomings I have; look honestly at what I see in the mirror? And try to change?

Thursday 15th May   Mark 8:27–33

Jesus went on with his disciples to the villages of Caesarea Philippi; and on the way he asked his disciples, "Who do people say that I am?" And they answered him, "John the Baptist; and others, Elijah; and still others, one of the prophets." He asked them, "But who do you say that I am?" Peter answered him, "You are the Messiah." And he sternly ordered them not to tell anyone about him. Then he began to teach them that the Son of Man must undergo great suffering, and be rejected by the elders, the chief priests, and the scribes, and be killed, and after three days rise again. He said all this quite openly. And Peter took him aside and began to rebuke him. But turning and looking at his disciples, he rebuked Peter and said, "Get behind me, Satan! For you are setting your mind not on divine things but on human things."

- How hard it is to listen to forecasts of misfortune, no matter how realistic! When Jesus says openly that he must suffer and be rejected, Peter cannot stomach it. He thinks the Messiah must be mighty, glorious, all-conquering, not a "loser."

- In Peter's memory this day would stand out for its huge joy, when he recognized Jesus as the Messiah; and also for the pain of a sharp word from Jesus, correcting Peter as to the sort of Messiah Jesus would be, a model of self-sacrificing love.

Friday 16th May   Mark 8:34–9:1

Jesus called the crowd with his disciples, and said to them, "If any want to become my followers, let them deny themselves and take up their cross and follow me. For those who want to save their life will lose it, and those who lose their life for my sake, and for the sake of the gospel, will save it. For what will it profit them to gain the whole world and forfeit their life? Indeed, what can they give in return for their life? Those who are ashamed of me and of my words in this adulterous and sinful generation, of them the Son of Man will also be ashamed when he comes in the glory of his Father with the holy angels." And he said to them, "Truly I tell you, there are some standing here who will not taste death until they see that the kingdom of God has come with power."

- Jesus is offering me a choice here, and telling me the plain truth about what that choice will mean. I can live for myself, concentrate on my life, my ambitions, my pleasures, and stay closed up in my own little world. I can choose that if I want to, and nobody will stop me.
- Or I can choose to be a "person for others." This does not mean making myself a doormat or neglecting my real needs, but giving of myself for others, wanting other people's lives to have been better because I have lived.

Saturday 17th May   Mark 9:2–8

Six days later, Jesus took with him Peter and James and John, and led them up a high mountain apart, by themselves. And he was transfigured before them, and his clothes became dazzling white, such as no one on earth could bleach them. And there appeared to them Elijah with Moses, who were talking with Jesus. Then Peter said to Jesus, "Rabbi, it is good for us to be here; let us make three dwellings, one for you, one for Moses, and one for Elijah." He did not know what to say, for they were terrified. Then a cloud overshadowed them, and from the cloud there came a voice, "This is my Son, the Beloved; listen to him!" Suddenly when they looked around, they saw no one with them any more, but only Jesus.

- Mount Tabor is Holy Ground, a peak experience. Peter wants it to go on for ever, but Jesus brings him back to earth.
- We live on the memory of such moments, and draw heart from the hope that they will happen again.

Something to think and pray about each day this week:

Living in the Spirit

If we celebrate this Sunday as the feast of the Blessed Trinity, it is not an invitation to theological speculation about three persons in one God. Rather it recalls the experience of Jesus, our brother. He spoke of himself as a beloved son, as one who does not send himself but is sent on a mission, and as being joined by the Holy Spirit to the Father (this was the metaphor he liked to use for the sublime majesty of God). We too, sisters and brothers of Jesus, are sent into this world with a purpose, we are God's beloved children, and we are joined to God by the Holy Spirit—we are temples of the Spirit. Already we are living in the life of the Trinity.

The Presence of God
Jesus waits silent and unseen to come into my heart.
I will respond to His call.
He comes with His infinite power and love
May I be filled with joy in His presence.

Freedom
I ask for the grace
to let go of my own concerns
and be open to what God is asking of me,
to let myself be guided and formed by my loving Creator.

Consciousness
Knowing that God loves me unconditionally,
I can afford to be honest about how I am.
How has the last day been, and how do I feel now?
I share my feelings openly with the Lord.

The Word
I read the Word of God slowly, a few times over, and I listen to
what God is saying to me. (Please turn to your scripture on the
following pages. Inspiration points are there should you need
them. When you are ready, return here to continue.)

Conversation
Remembering that I am still in God's presence,
I imagine Jesus himself standing or sitting beside me,
and say whatever is on my mind, whatever is in my heart,
speaking as one friend to another.

Conclusion
Glory be to the Father, and to the Son, and to the Holy Spirit,
As it was in the beginning, is now and ever shall be,
World without end. Amen

Sunday 18th May, Trinity Sunday   2 Corinthians 13:11–13

Finally, brothers and sisters, farewell. Put things in order, listen to my appeal, agree with one another, live in peace; and the God of love and peace will be with you. Greet one another with a holy kiss. All the saints greet you. The grace of the Lord Jesus Christ, the love of God, and the communion of the Holy Spirit be with all of you.

- What is the Blessed Trinity?
- I do not understand it, Lord; but I try to live it. Patrick Kavanagh hoped, "That through the hole in reason's ceiling We can fly to knowledge Without ever going to college."
- Let me sit within this mystery for a while.

Monday 19th May   Mark 9:20–24

And the crowd brought the speechless boy to Jesus. When the spirit saw him, immediately it convulsed the boy, and he fell on the ground and rolled about, foaming at the mouth. Jesus asked the father, "How long has this been happening to him?" And he said, "From childhood. It has often cast him into the fire and into the water, to destroy him; but if you are able to do anything, have pity on us and help us." Jesus said to him, "If you are able! All things can be done for the one who believes." Immediately the father of the child cried out, "I believe; help my unbelief!" Jesus took the boy by the hand and lifted him up, and he was able to stand. When he had entered the house, his disciples asked him privately, "Why could we not cast out the spirit?" He said to them, "This kind can come out only through prayer."

- Help my unbelief, Lord. At this distance of two millennia and repeated culture-shocks, I cling to my faith; there is darkness there as well as light. It might be easier if I was standing in front of you, feeling your compassion and power. Perhaps.

- You were saying to your disciples: You don't live close enough to God. You might well say that to me. At least let me give time to you, minutes stolen from my work, so that I may sense your compassion and power, and you may help my unbelief.

Tuesday 20th May   Mark 9:30–37

They went on from there and passed through Galilee. He did not want anyone to know it; for he was teaching his disciples, saying to them, "The Son of Man is to be betrayed into human hands, and they will kill him, and three days after being killed, he will rise again." But they did not understand what he was saying and were afraid to ask him. Then they came to Capernaum; and when he was in the house he asked them, "What were you arguing about on the way?" But they were silent, for on the way they had argued with one another who was the greatest. He sat down, called the twelve, and said to them, "Whoever wants to be first must be last of all and servant of all." Then he took a little child and put it among them; and taking it in his arms, he said to them, "Whoever welcomes one such child in my name welcomes me, and whoever welcomes me welcomes not me but the one who sent me."

- Lord, you were trying to prepare your friends for bad news (the Passion) and good news (the Resurrection), but they did not want to hear you.
- They were caught up, as I am often caught up, in private competitions and jealousies. It takes a lifetime to realize the silliness of my ego-trips. Do not despair of my silliness, Lord. Go on teaching me.

Wednesday 21st May   James 4:13–15

Come now, you who say, "Today or tomorrow we will go to such and such a town and spend a year there, doing business and making money." Yet you do not even know what tomorrow will bring. What is your life? For you are a mist that appears for a little while and then vanishes. Instead you ought to say, "If the Lord wishes, we will live and do this or that."

- "What is your life?" Again, James challenges us to see things as they really are, not as we would rather they were.
- Do I live as though life is a journey, on a path towards God? Am I thankful for the day, my gifts, each grace? How will I live today?

Thursday 22nd May   Mark 9:50

Jesus said: "Salt is good; but if salt has lost its saltiness, how can you season it? Have salt in yourselves, and be at peace with one another."

- "Salt is good." Have I still any saltiness in me, Lord, or am I bland, flavorless, anxious simply to please and merge with my surroundings?
- When I am tempted to go along with worldliness, have I the courage to be different? I want to be the salt of the earth, Lord. Help me!

Friday 23rd May   Mark 10:1–9

Jesus left that place and went to the region of Judea and beyond the Jordan. And crowds again gathered around him; and, as was his custom, he again taught them. Some Pharisees came, and to test him they asked, "Is it lawful for a man to divorce his wife?" He answered them, "What did Moses command you?" They said, "Moses allowed a man to write a certificate of dismissal and to divorce her." But Jesus said to them, "Because of your hardness of heart he wrote this commandment for you. But from the beginning of creation, 'God made them male and female.' 'For this reason a man shall leave his father and mother and be joined to his wife, and the two shall become one flesh.' So they are no longer two, but one flesh. Therefore what God has joined together, let no one separate."

- Lord, I cannot read this without sorrow, remembering my many friends whose marriages have broken. The scholars have argued over these verses, because so much happiness hangs on them.
- One thing I know: that you were speaking up for women, who at the time were on an uneven playing-field. A woman might be divorced with or without her will, but a man only with his will. You were calling us back to an ideal, a loving and faithful union of mutual respect.

Saturday 24th May   Mark 10:13–16

People were bringing little children to him in order that he might touch them; and the disciples spoke sternly to them. But when Jesus saw this, he was indignant and said to them, "Let the little children come to me; do not stop them; for it is to such as these that the kingdom of God belongs. Truly I tell you, whoever does not receive the kingdom of God as a little child will never enter it." And he took them up in his arms, laid his hands on them, and blessed them.

- "He took children up in his arms, laid his hands on them, and blessed them." Lord, you uttered dire warnings against those who lead little ones astray. That did not mean that you were afraid to touch children, bless them and love them.
- Children need our attention, and they need to be stroked, in ways that meet their needs, not ours. Save me from the fearfulness that would turn child protection into child rejection.

Something to think and pray about each day this week:

Being Together
In this coming week many in their local communities are re-membering and giving thanks for the great gift of Eucharist, our word which comes from the Greek for "thanksgiving."

There is another important word to consider here: "sacrament," which means a sign pointing to something bigger than itself. Eu-charist is such a sign, and that is why it is a measure of the quality of our fellowship and community. Where there is no real com-munity there can be no real Eucharist, even though the church building is beautiful, the vestments are splendid and the choir sings the most heavenly music.

Some people ask why they have to come on Sundays and why they cannot pray at home. Of course, they can pray at home and sometimes that is a better place to pray. But the weekly Eu-charist is not just a time for praying; it is a time for celebrating community. That cannot be done at home; we can only do that together.

The Presence of God

I pause for a moment
and think of the love and the grace that God showers on me,
creating me in his image and likeness, making me his temple.

Freedom

Lord, grant me the grace to be free from the excesses of this life.
Let me not get caught up with the desire for wealth.
Keep my heart and mind free to love and serve you.

Consciousness

In the presence of my loving Creator,
I look honestly at my feelings over the last day,
the highs, the lows and the level ground.
Can I see where the Lord has been present?

The Word

God speaks to each one of us individually. I need to listen to
what he is saying to me. (Please turn to your scripture on the
following pages. Inspiration points are there should you need
them. When you are ready, return here to continue.)

Conversation

Sometimes I wonder what I might say
if I were to meet You in person, Lord.
I might say "Thank You, Lord" for always being there for me.
I know with certainty there were times when you carried me.
When through your strength I got through the dark times in
my life.

Conclusion

Glory be to the Father, and to the Son, and to the Holy Spirit,
As it was in the beginning, is now and ever shall be,
World without end. Amen

Sunday 25th May,
The Body and Blood of Christ   1 Corinthians 10:16–17

The cup of blessing that we bless, is it not a sharing in the blood of Christ? The bread that we break, is it not a sharing in the body of Christ? Because there is one bread, we who are many are one body, for we all partake of the one bread.

- Sharing in Christ's body and blood leads us also, despite our great diversity, to share with each other: "For we all partake of the one bread."
- Let me sit with Paul's words, and think about the unifying power of Christ's presence.

Monday 26th May   Mark 10:17–22

As he was setting out on a journey, a man ran up and knelt before him, and asked him, "Good Teacher, what must I do to inherit eternal life?" Jesus said to him, "Why do you call me good? No one is good but God alone. You know the commandments: 'You shall not murder; You shall not commit adultery; You shall not steal; You shall not bear false witness; You shall not defraud; Honor your father and mother.'" He said to him, "Teacher, I have kept all these since my youth." Jesus, looking at him, loved him and said, "You lack one thing; go, sell what you own, and give the money to the poor, and you will have treasure in heaven; then come, follow me." When he heard this, he was shocked and went away grieving, for he had many possessions.

- Mark can arrest us with a phrase: "Jesus looking at him, loved him." People were held by your gaze, Lord, and remembered it.
- It stayed in the memory of that man, even though he walked away grieving. He would not rise to the invitation, for his possessions held him in thrall. You let him go, Lord: no coercion.

Tuesday 27th May 　　　　　　　　　　　　　**Mark 10:28–31**

Peter began to say to Jesus, "Look, we have left everything and followed you." Jesus said, "Truly I tell you, there is no one who has left house or brothers or sisters or mother or father or children or fields, for my sake and for the sake of the good news, who will not receive a hundredfold now in this age—houses, brothers and sisters, mothers and children, and fields with persecutions—and in the age to come eternal life. But many who are first will be last, and the last will be first."

- I reflect on this exchange as St. Peter might have done at the end of his life. What has it meant to me to follow Jesus? What have I given up?
- What was my hundredfold, in the way of joy, contentment, peace of soul?

Wednesday 28th May 　　　　　　　　　　　　**Mark 10:32–34**

They were on the road, going up to Jerusalem, and Jesus was walking ahead of them; they were amazed, and those who followed were afraid. He took the twelve aside again and began to tell them what was to happen to him, saying, "See, we are going up to Jerusalem, and the Son of Man will be handed over to the chief priests and the scribes, and they will condemn him to death; then they will hand him over to the Gentiles; they will mock him, and spit upon him, and flog him, and kill him; and after three days he will rise again."

- Moving ever closer to Jerusalem, Jesus' followers are still unsettled so again Jesus lays out the future in blunt terms. He tries to prepare them but his message is not what they want to hear. Again, they do not understand.

- Is there something here for me to think about? How do I block out Jesus' message? Do I really want to understand? Am I afraid of how I may change if I follow more closely, and hear more clearly?

Thursday 29th May   1 Peter 2:2–5

Like newborn infants, long for the pure, spiritual milk, so that by it you may grow into salvation—if indeed you have tasted that the Lord is good. Come to him, a living stone, though rejected by mortals yet chosen and precious in God's sight, and like living stones, let yourselves be built into a spiritual house, to be a holy priesthood, to offer spiritual sacrifices acceptable to God through Jesus Christ.

- "Like living stones, let yourselves be built into a spiritual house"; each of us is a living stone, firm but vibrant, strong but malleable.
- There are rich images here that we can dwell on.

Friday 30th May, Feast of the Sacred Heart   1 John 4:7–10

Beloved, let us love one another, because love is from God; everyone who loves is born of God and knows God. Whoever does not love does not know God, for God is love. God's love was revealed among us in this way: God sent his only Son into the world so that we might live through him. In this is love, not that we loved God but that he loved us and sent his Son to be the atoning sacrifice for our sins.

- Religious practice and doctrine may be a help in sustaining a community of believers, but the measure of my Christian commitment is not my adherence to these. The measure is: Do I love?
- Love can be expressed in many ways. Saying "I love you" is the easiest. But it is in what we do and how we treat other people that love is made real, just as God's love for us was expressed most clearly by what Jesus did.

- If I think of the people I have encountered in the last few days, and am likely to encounter today and tomorrow, how might this self-giving love be expressed in the way I deal with them?

Saturday 31st May,
Visitation of the Virgin Mary to Elizabeth   Luke 1:39–47

In those days Mary set out and went with haste to a Judean town in the hill country, where she entered the house of Zechariah and greeted Elizabeth. When Elizabeth heard Mary's greeting, the child leaped in her womb. And Elizabeth was filled with the Holy Spirit and exclaimed with a loud cry, "Blessed are you among women, and blessed is the fruit of your womb. And why has this happened to me, that the mother of my Lord comes to me? For as soon as I heard the sound of your greeting, the child in my womb leaped for joy. And blessed is she who believed that there would be a fulfillment of what was spoken to her by the Lord." And Mary said, "My soul magnifies the Lord, and my spirit rejoices in God my Savior."

- Let me stay with this joyful scene. Both of these pregnant women are aware that something awesome is at work in them. In their meeting there is the ordinariness of friends meeting, the love of affectionate cousins, and also a profound sense of destiny.
- In her later years Mary would have looked back on this joyful mystery as a time when the world was young and full of promise. Let me savor the memory with her.

june 1–7

Something to think and pray about each day this week:

Community Prayer

Why have churches? We need to find God, and find him in community; and the church offers what we call the Real Presence. We are not praying in empty vaults, but before our Lord in the tabernacle. The Curè of Ars used to see an old countryman sitting for hours in the parish church, and one day he asked him what he was doing. "I look at the good God and the good God looks at me." In every parish there are mystics who do not know they are mystics, people whose prayer has reached a simplicity and intimacy beyond words. You feel the aura of their prayers when you come into their church. It witnessed their baptism, sheltered them in sorrow, confirmed the young and celebrated committed love. It expresses the dream, the vision, the reaching out towards God, of the local people and their visitors over the generations.

The Presence of God

As I sit here with my book, God is here.
Around me, in my sensations, in my thoughts and deep within me.
I pause for a moment, and become aware
of God's life-giving presence.

Freedom

A thick and shapeless tree-trunk would never believe
that it could become a statue, admired as a miracle of sculpture,
and would never submit itself to the chisel of the sculptor,
who sees by her genius what she can make of it. (St. Ignatius)
I ask for the grace to let myself be shaped by my loving Creator.

Consciousness

How am I really feeling? Light-hearted? Heavy-hearted?
I may be very much at peace, happy to be here.
Equally, I may be frustrated, worried or angry.
I acknowledge how I really am. It is the real me that the Lord loves.

The Word

The word of God comes down to us through the scriptures.
May the Holy Spirit enlighten my mind and my heart to respond to the gospel teachings. (Please turn to your scripture
on the following pages. Inspiration points are there should you
need them. When you are ready, return here to continue.)

Conversation

Do I notice myself reacting as I pray with the Word of God?
Do I feel challenged, comforted, angry?
Imagining Jesus sitting or standing by me,
I speak out my feelings, as one trusted friend to another.

Conclusion

Glory be to the Father, and to the Son, and to the Holy Spirit,
As it was in the beginning, is now and ever shall be,
World without end. Amen

Sunday 1st June,
Ninth Sunday in Ordinary Time Deuteronomy 11:18, 26–28

You shall put these words of mine in your heart and soul, and you shall bind them as a sign on your hand, and fix them as an emblem on your forehead. See, I am setting before you today a blessing and a curse: the blessing, if you obey the commandments of the Lord your God that I am commanding you today; and the curse, if you do not obey the commandments of the Lord your God, but turn from the way that I am commanding you today, to follow other gods that you have not known.

- "Put these words of mine in your heart and your soul." Scripture repeats this message in so many ways, in so many places, yet I am often more comfortable understanding with my head than with my heart. Perhaps my head helps me to "keep my distance."
- It is not enough to say the right words; I must act on them. Lord, teach me again.

Monday 2nd June   2 Peter 1:2–7

May grace and peace be yours in abundance in the knowledge of God and of Jesus our Lord. His divine power has given us everything needed for life and godliness, through the knowledge of him who called us by his own glory and goodness. Thus he has given us, through these things, his precious and very great promises, so that through them you may escape from the corruption that is in the world because of lust, and may become participants of the divine nature. For this very reason, you must make every effort to support your faith with goodness, and goodness with knowledge, and knowledge with self-control, and self-control with endurance, and endurance with godliness, and godliness with mutual affection, and mutual affection with love.

- "Support your faith with goodness." Lord, you will not examine me on my creed, my thoughts or my words, but on how I have lived, and especially how I have related to those in need.
- My faith challenges the way I behave. Lord, let me live a life in which faith, action and love are united.

Tuesday 3rd June
Mark 12:13–17

Then they sent to Jesus some Pharisees and some Herodians to trap him in what he said. And they came and said to him, "Teacher, we know that you are sincere, and show deference to no one; for you do not regard people with partiality, but teach the way of God in accordance with truth. Is it lawful to pay taxes to the emperor, or not? Should we pay them, or should we not?" But knowing their hypocrisy, he said to them, "Why are you putting me to the test? Bring me a denarius and let me see it." And they brought one. Then he said to them, "Whose head is this, and whose title?" They answered, "The emperor's." Jesus said to them, "Give to the emperor the things that are the emperor's, and to God the things that are God's." And they were utterly amazed at him.

- Many have enlisted this response from Jesus, to support revolution against an oppression or to affirm their conservatism. How should it challenge me, Lord?
- Do I hunger and thirst for justice, and hear the cry of the poor? In all your preaching you championed the cause of the destitute. How do my actions measure up today?

Wednesday 4th June
Mark 12:18–27

Some Sadducees, who say there is no resurrection, came to Jesus and asked him a question, saying, "Teacher, Moses wrote for us that 'if a man's brother dies, leaving a wife but no child, the man shall marry the widow and raise up children for his brother.'

There were seven brothers; the first married and, when he died, left no children; and the second married her and died, leaving no children; and the third likewise; none of the seven left children. Last of all the woman herself died. In the resurrection whose wife will she be? For the seven had married her." Jesus said to them, "Is not this the reason you are wrong, that you know neither the scriptures nor the power of God? For when they rise from the dead, they neither marry nor are given in marriage, but are like angels in heaven. And as for the dead being raised, have you not read in the book of Moses, in the story about the bush, how God said to him, 'I am the God of Abraham, the God of Isaac, and the God of Jacob'? He is God not of the dead, but of the living; you are quite wrong."

- The Sadducees ask a question that matters to me too: "What is heaven like?" In our imagination we shape it to our heart's desire. For American Indians it is a happy hunting ground, rich with game. I would like to imagine a green and pleasant land with rivers and lakes.

- But God goes beyond the limitations of our imagination: "What no eye has seen, nor ear heard, nor the human heart conceived, God has prepared for those who love him."

Thursday 5th June   Mark 12:28–34

One of the scribes came near and heard them disputing with one another, and seeing that Jesus answered them well, he asked him, "Which commandment is the first of all?" Jesus answered, "The first is, 'Hear, O Israel: the Lord our God, the Lord is one; you shall love the Lord your God with all your heart, and with all your soul, and with all your mind, and with all your strength.' The second is this, 'You shall love your neighbor as yourself.' There is no other commandment greater than these."

Then the scribe said to him, "You are right, Teacher; you have truly said that 'he is one, and besides him there is no other'; and 'to love him with all the heart, and with all the understanding, and with all the strength,' and 'to love one's neighbor as oneself,'—this is much more important than all whole burnt offerings and sacrifices." When Jesus saw that he answered wisely, he said to him, "You are not far from the kingdom of God." After that no one dared to ask him any question.

- Lord, with what affection and regard you answered this scribe. Unlike others scribes, he was seeking wisdom, not an argument. He relished Jesus' answer, and placed it in the context of the Scriptures.
- Jesus rewarded him with that grave compliment: "You are not far from the kingdom of God." Could you say it to me, Lord? Is my search as serious as that scribe's?

Friday 6th June   **Psalm 15(16):1–2, 5, 7–8, 11**

Protect me, O God, for in you I take refuge. I say to the LORD, "You are my Lord; I have no good apart from you." The LORD is my chosen portion and my cup; you hold my lot. I bless the LORD who gives me counsel; in the night also my heart instructs me. I keep the LORD always before me; because he is at my right hand, I shall not be moved. You show me the path of life. In your presence there is fullness of joy; in your right hand are pleasures forevermore.

- "I have no good apart from you, Lord." Of course there are countless other goods, the pleasures of the body, the love of friends, the pastimes that fill idle hours.
- I thank you for all these pleasures, but the fullness of joy is found only in you, Lord. That is what I look for. In your right hand are pleasures for evermore.

Saturday 7th June　　　　　　　　　　**Mark 12:38–44**

As Jesus taught, he said, "Beware of the scribes, who like to walk around in long robes, and to be greeted with respect in the marketplaces, and to have the best seats in the synagogues and places of honor at banquets! They devour widows' houses and for the sake of appearance say long prayers. They will receive the greater condemnation." He sat down opposite the treasury, and watched the crowd putting money into the treasury. Many rich people put in large sums. A poor widow came and put in two small copper coins, which are worth a penny. Then he called his disciples and said to them, "Truly I tell you, this poor widow has put in more than all those who are contributing to the treasury. For all of them have contributed out of their abundance; but she out of her poverty has put in everything she had, all she had to live on."

- Everything you say, Lord, touches my conscience. You warn me against coveting a flash car—the equivalent of long robes—or front page publicity, or a high public profile.
- You remind me how women have always been imposed upon by religious charlatans. You tell me that self-advertisement is not a sacred duty but a weakness.
- You who lived a hidden life for nine tenths of your years on earth, are a model of how to walk humbly before our God. How am I to follow you in this?

june 8–14

Something to think and pray about each day this week:

Staying Focused

Those who entered religious life as novices (in the days when there were lots of novices and novitiates) were introduced to a notion that nowadays may seem quaint: custody of the eyes. We were advised that in preparation for prayer it is useful to limit our exposure to distracting sights and sounds; in fact for the most part it would be useful to keep our eyes on the ground. In other words, we were warned against rubber-necking. This was at a time when there were fewer visual distractions than today: there was no TV or internet, radios were limited to the living room at home, and newspapers carried few illustrations. With this in mind, look at your own day-by-day experience. Are you hungry for visual stimulation, or can you control what enters your mind via your eyes? Do you feel besieged by advertisements and seductive screens? Do you resist the siege, or, on the contrary, feel a hunger for distractions?

The Presence of God

For a few moments, I think of God's veiled presence in things:
in the elements, giving them existence;
in plants, giving them life; in animals, giving them sensation;
and finally, in me, giving me all this and more,
making me a temple, a dwelling-place of the Spirit.

Freedom

I ask for the grace to believe
in what I could be and do
if I only allowed God, my loving Creator,
to continue to create me, guide me and shape me.

Consciousness

In the presence of my loving Creator,
I look honestly at my feelings over the last day,
the highs, the lows and the level ground.
Can I see where the Lord has been present?

The Word

I take my time to read the Word of God, slowly, a few times, allowing myself to dwell on anything that strikes me. (Please turn
to your scripture on the following pages. Inspiration points are
there should you need them. When you are ready, return here
to continue.)

Conversation

How has God's Word moved me? Has it left me cold?
Has it consoled me or moved me to act in a new way?
I imagine Jesus standing or sitting beside me,
I turn and share my feelings with him.

Conclusion

Glory be to the Father, and to the Son, and to the Holy Spirit,
As it was in the beginning, is now and ever shall be,
World without end. Amen

Sunday 8th June,
Tenth Sunday in Ordinary Time   Matthew 9:9–13

As Jesus was walking along, he saw a man called Matthew sitting at the tax booth; and he said to him, "Follow me." And he got up and followed him. And as he sat at dinner in the house, many tax collectors and sinners came and were sitting with him and his disciples. When the Pharisees saw this, they said to his disciples, "Why does your teacher eat with tax collectors and sinners?" But when he heard this, he said, "Those who are well have no need of a physician, but those who are sick. Go and learn what this means, 'I desire mercy, not sacrifice.' For I have come to call not the righteous but sinners."

- Lord, I used to think religion was a matter of keeping the rules. But when you walked this earth, you preferred to mix with those who had broken the rules—not because they broke the rules, but because their hearts were open and humble.
- Dare I say that I can be grateful for my sins? They are carriers of grace.

Monday 9th June   Matthew 5:1–6

When Jesus saw the crowds, he went up the mountain; and after he sat down, his disciples came to him. Then he began to speak, and taught them, saying: "Blessed are the poor in spirit, for theirs is the kingdom of heaven. "Blessed are those who mourn, for they will be comforted. "Blessed are the meek, for they will inherit the earth. "Blessed are those who hunger and thirst for righteousness, for they will be filled."

- On this occasion Jesus sat down to teach. This was the posture of a master, instructing the disciples in a solemn way. The Greek text is significant here: "He taught them" is in the imperfect tense, meaning these words sum up the teaching which Jesus habitually gave to his inner circle.

- The Beatitudes are the concentrated memory of many hours of heart-to-heart communion between Jesus and his disciples. Let me savor them.

Tuesday 10th June   Matthew 5:13

Jesus said to the disciples, "You are the salt of the earth; but if salt has lost its taste, how can its saltiness be restored? It is no longer good for anything, but is thrown out and trampled under foot."

- Let me remember why salt has always been prized. It gives flavor to what is bland, and lifts the everyday to something interesting.
- In the same way a new baby brings a family together; a visit from an old friend banishes my boredom and restores my zest for living; a leader gives a sense of purpose to a whole community.
- Yet I can lose my saltiness, by self-indulgence or sin or by focusing totally on myself. Lord, may I always have other people with whom I can engage.

Wednesday 11th June   Matthew 5:17–19

Jesus said to the crowds, "Do not think that I have come to abolish the law or the prophets; I have come not to abolish but to fulfill. For truly I tell you, until heaven and earth pass away, not one letter, not one stroke of a letter, will pass from the law until all is accomplished. Therefore, whoever breaks one of the least of these commandments, and teaches others to do the same, will be called least in the kingdom of heaven; but whoever does them and teaches them will be called great in the kingdom of heaven."

- When I read these words I am troubled, Lord. Some scholars deny the authenticity of these verses. After all, Jesus nowhere insists on observance of all 613 precepts of Old Testament law, much of it ceremonial.
- What sense have these words for me? If the meaning of the law is love of God and of my neighbor, how does that affect me today?

Thursday 12th June   Matthew 5:21–24

Jesus said to the crowds, "You have heard that it was said to those of ancient times, 'You shall not murder'; and 'whoever murders shall be liable to judgment.' But I say to you that if you are angry with a brother or sister, you will be liable to judgment; and if you insult a brother or sister, you will be liable to the council; and if you say, 'You fool,' you will be liable to the hell of fire. So when you are offering your gift at the altar, if you remember that your brother or sister has something against you, leave your gift there before the altar and go; first be reconciled to your brother or sister, and then come and offer your gift."

- Lord, you are pushing my conscience inwards. I will be judged not just by what I have done in the external forum, but by the voluntary movements of my heart. God sees the heart, and sees how far I go along with feelings of hatred, lust or pride.
- In other words, I should be of one piece, the same on the inside as I am on the outside, responding more to God's gaze than to other people's.

Friday 13th June, St. Anthony of Padua   Isaiah 61:1–3a

The spirit of the Lord GOD is upon me, because the LORD has anointed me; he has sent me to bring good news to the oppressed, to bind up the brokenhearted, to proclaim liberty to the captives, and release to the prisoners; to proclaim the year of the Lord's favor, and the day of vengeance of our God; to comfort all who mourn; to provide for those who mourn in Zion—to give them a garland instead of ashes, the oil of gladness instead of mourning, the mantle of praise instead of a faint spirit.

- We need saints, the heroes and heroines who express the ideals we aspire to.
- The saints are just like us; they are forgiven sinners. They rejoiced in forgiveness and refused to be overwhelmed by their sin. That gives me hope.

Saturday 14th June   Matthew 5:33–37

Jesus said to the crowds, "Again, you have heard that it was said to those of ancient times, 'You shall not swear falsely, but carry out the vows you have made to the Lord.' But I say to you, Do not swear at all, either by heaven, for it is the throne of God, or by the earth, for it is his footstool, or by Jerusalem, for it is the city of the great King. And do not swear by your head, for you cannot make one hair white or black. Let your word be 'Yes, Yes' or 'No, No'; anything more than this comes from the evil one."

- Lord, when will I meet someone like that, whose Yes means Yes, without expletives or curses? What a refreshment to hear plain speech, free of the boring swearwords and the mindless use of profanity. The person who speaks the simple truth is a rarer creature than the most eloquent wordsmith.
- How do I speak?

Something to think and pray about each day this week:

Beyond Words
There is a stage in prayer where we go beyond words and thoughts: the hard bit is to stop thinking. A mystic is quoted as hearing from God: "I will not have thy thoughts instead of thee." So to prepare for prayer, it helps to focus on something other than the mind. "Be still and know that I am God." I stop the body moving. I focus on something physical: the breath flowing into me, or the sounds that invade my stillness, or the awareness of my enveloping skin. Then I give space to the Lord who created me, who is more central to my being than my own mind is, yet who is beyond my imagination.

The Presence of God

I remind myself that, as I sit here now,
God is gazing on me with love and holding me in being.
I pause for a moment and think of this.

Freedom

I need to close out the noise, to rise above the noise;
The noise that interrupts, that separates,
The noise that isolates.
I need to listen to God again.

Consciousness

In God's loving presence I unwind the past day,
starting from now and looking back, moment by moment.
I gather in all the goodness and light, in gratitude.
I attend to the shadows and what they say to me,
seeking healing, courage, forgiveness.

The Word

I take my time to read the Word of God, slowly, a few times, allowing myself to dwell on anything that strikes me. (Please turn
to your scripture on the following pages. Inspiration points are
there should you need them. When you are ready, return here
to continue.)

Conversation

Do I notice myself reacting as I pray with the Word of God?
Do I feel challenged, comforted, angry?
Imagining Jesus sitting or standing by me,
I speak out my feelings, as one trusted friend to another.

Conclusion

Glory be to the Father, and to the Son, and to the Holy Spirit,
As it was in the beginning, is now and ever shall be,
World without end. Amen

Sunday 15th June,
Eleventh Sunday in Ordinary Time   Matthew 9:36–38

When he saw the crowds, he had compassion for them, because they were harassed and helpless, like sheep without a shepherd. Then he said to his disciples, "The harvest is plentiful, but the laborers are few; therefore ask the Lord of the harvest to send out laborers into his harvest."

- In many countries ordained priests are few, many parishes are priestless, and seminarians are few. Is there is message here from God?
- But even where fewer priests are being ordained, the church is thriving in some places where the Christian community is reduced to basics.
- Lord, I ask you for the courage and the opportunity to be active in my community, and to make it a growth-point of Christian living.

Monday 16th June   Matthew 5:38–42

Jesus said to the crowds, "You have heard that it was said, 'An eye for an eye and a tooth for a tooth.' But I say to you, Do not resist an evildoer. But if anyone strikes you on the right cheek, turn the other also; and if anyone wants to sue you and take your coat, give your cloak as well; and if anyone forces you to go one mile, go also the second mile. Give to everyone who begs from you, and do not refuse anyone who wants to borrow from you."

- The desire for revenge can burn fiercely after an injury. The ancient *Lex Talionis* (an eye for an eye. . .) was designed to limit vengeance to a level equal to that of the injury revenged.
- Lord, you call me to higher virtue: to resent no insult, and to seek retaliation for no slight. The only way I can manage this is by keeping my eyes on you in your Passion.

Tuesday 17th June   Matthew 5:43–47

J esus said to the crowds, "You have heard that it was said, 'You shall love your neighbor and hate your enemy.' But I say to you, Love your enemies and pray for those who persecute you, so that you may be children of your Father in heaven; for he makes his sun rise on the evil and on the good, and sends rain on the righteous and on the unrighteous. For if you love those who love you, what reward do you have? Do not even the tax collectors do the same? And if you greet only your brothers and sisters, what more are you doing than others? Do not even the Gentiles do the same?"

- Where do I stand, Lord, in the face of your invitation to become godlike in my kindliness? When I am struggling to survive in a hostile world, trying to care for a family, and earn my living, how do I keep my heart free of annoyance, resentment, even hatred?
- Only by keeping my eyes on you, and being patient with myself and my falls from grace.

Wednesday 18th June   Matthew 6:1–6, 16–18

J esus said to the disciples, "Beware of practicing your piety before others in order to be seen by them; for then you have no reward from your Father in heaven. "So whenever you give alms, do not sound a trumpet before you, as the hypocrites do in the synagogues and in the streets, so that they may be praised by others. Truly I tell you, they have received their reward. But when you give alms, do not let your left hand know what your right hand is doing, so that your alms may be done in secret; and your Father who sees in secret will reward you. "And whenever you pray, do not be like the hypocrites; for they love to stand and pray in the synagogues and at the street corners, so that they may be seen by others. Truly I tell you, they have received their reward. But whenever you pray, go into your room and shut the door and pray to your Father who is in secret; and your Father who sees in secret will reward you. "And whenever you fast, do not look dismal, like the hypocrites, for they disfigure their faces so as to show others that they are fasting. Truly I tell you, they have received their reward. But when you fast, put oil on your head and wash your face, so that your fasting may be seen not by others but by your Father who is in secret; and your Father who sees in secret will reward you."

- Prayer, almsgiving, fasting: these are each central to our religious practice, each vital in our relationship with God. But do them all in secret Jesus teaches us.
- How does this work? How will others have an example to follow?
- Whatever I do, Lord, teach me to do it in your name, to the Father's glory, and not to draw attention to myself.

Thursday 19th June   Matthew 6:9–13

Jesus said to the crowds, "Pray then in this way: Our Father in heaven, hallowed be your name. Your kingdom come. Your will be done, on earth as it is in heaven. Give us this day our daily bread. And forgive us our debts, as we also have forgiven our debtors. And do not bring us to the time of trial, but rescue us from the evil one."

- "Pray then in this way." This is still good advice for us. There is no word or phrase in the Lord's Prayer which does not repay you if you mine it for meaning, and savor it. Take the prayer slowly, breathing slowly as you relish it and are led into its depths.
- Take for instance, "Your kingdom come." The word "kingdom" sounds obsolete but the idea still holds: May I leave this world better than I found it, shape it closer to the Creator's dream.

Friday 20th June   Matthew 6:19–23

Jesus said to his disciples, "Do not store up for yourselves treasures on earth, where moth and rust consume and where thieves break in and steal; but store up for yourselves treasures in heaven, where neither moth nor rust consumes and where thieves do not break in and steal. For where your treasure is, there your heart will be also. "The eye is the lamp of the body. So, if your eye is healthy, your whole body will be full of light; but if your eye is unhealthy, your whole body will be full of darkness. If then the light in you is darkness, how great is the darkness!"

- Many of us spend our days working to acquire what we believe we need, and then protect our acquisitions with locks and insurance. It is what our parents did, and what our neighbors do also. This is how we live.

- "Store up for yourselves treasures in heaven." This is a mighty challenge Lord. Teach me to focus on what is really important, to see clearly where I should be going, to be single minded.

Saturday 21st June, St. Aloysius Gonzaga   Mark 10:23–27

Then Jesus looked around and said to his disciples, "How hard it will be for those who have wealth to enter the kingdom of God!" And the disciples were perplexed at these words. But Jesus said to them again, "Children, how hard it is to enter the kingdom of God! It is easier for a camel to go through the eye of a needle than for someone who is rich to enter the kingdom of God." They were greatly astounded and said to one another, "Then who can be saved?" Jesus looked at them and said, "For mortals it is impossible, but not for God; for God all things are possible."

- Lord, you were not talking about possessing millions, but about coveting millions, about setting my heart on making money.
- It is possible to own riches and sit lightly with them, to lose them without heartache. It is possible, but rare. More often, achieving the first million kindles the desire for more.

june 22–28

Something to think and pray about each day this week:

Meeting the Competition

If prayer is a lifting of the mind and heart to God, then you, who do the lifting, need to be in charge of your mind and heart. You face competitors. It is difficult, for example, to reach the *Sacred Space* website without battling your way through a barrage of pictures and advertisements offering you holidays, medications, cheap watches, endless things to covet. You face the philosophy of the market-place: Buy, Buy, Buy. Sales people are competing for my mind, my heart and my credit card.

How do I stay in charge? By guarding my eyes and ears which are the gateways to my heart and mind. Build a personal spam filter into your eyes and ears, a half-automatic delete key to use on whatever distracts me from the Lord. It may have been easier for St. Augustine, but his words still help: "You have made us for yourself, Lord, and our hearts are restless till they rest in you."

The Presence of God

At any time of the day or night we can call on Jesus.
He is always waiting, listening for our call.
What a wonderful blessing.
No phone needed, no emails, just a whisper.

Freedom

Lord, grant me the grace to be free from the excesses of this life.
Let me not get caught up with the desire for wealth.
Keep my heart and mind free to love and serve you.

Consciousness

I exist in a web of relationships—links to nature, people, God.
I trace out these links, giving thanks for the life that flows
through them.
Some links are twisted or broken: I may feel regret, anger,
disappointment.
I pray for the gift of acceptance and forgiveness.

The Word

God speaks to each one of us individually. I need to listen to
what he is saying to me. (Please turn to your scripture on the
following pages. Inspiration points are there should you need
them. When you are ready, return here to continue.)

Conversation

Remembering that I am still in God's presence,
I imagine Jesus himself standing or sitting beside me,
and say whatever is on my mind, whatever is in my heart,
speaking as one friend to another.

Conclusion

Glory be to the Father, and to the Son, and to the Holy Spirit,
As it was in the beginning, is now and ever shall be,
World without end. Amen

Sunday 22nd June,
Twelfth Sunday in Ordinary Time   Matthew 10:26–33

Jesus said to the disciples, "So have no fear of them; for nothing is covered up that will not be uncovered, and nothing secret that will not become known. What I say to you in the dark, tell in the light; and what you hear whispered, proclaim from the housetops. Do not fear those who kill the body but cannot kill the soul; rather fear him who can destroy both soul and body in hell. Are not two sparrows sold for a penny? Yet not one of them will fall to the ground apart from your Father. And even the hairs of your head are all counted. So do not be afraid; you are of more value than many sparrows. Everyone therefore who acknowledges me before others, I also will acknowledge before my Father in heaven; but whoever denies me before others, I also will deny before my Father in heaven."

- Did you smile, Lord, when you assured your friends that they were worth more than sparrows? You were promising something much more, something quite momentous: that even the very hairs of my head are numbered.

- We mortals are born and die in our millions, many of us unregarded or forgotten. Yet you say your Father cherishes each of us personally. Without that faith I may despair.

Monday 23rd June   Matthew 7:1–5

Jesus said to the crowds, "Do not judge, so that you may not be judged. For with the judgment you make you will be judged, and the measure you give will be the measure you get. Why do you see the speck in your neighbor's eye, but do not notice the log in your own eye? Or how can you say to your neighbor, 'Let me take the speck out of your eye,' while the log is in your own eye?

You hypocrite, first take the log out of your own eye, and then you will see clearly to take the speck out of your neighbor's eye."

- Lord, it is not easy always to think the best of other people. Newspaper headlines are pointing the finger of blame every day; they see the speck in every neighbor's eye, and urge me to judge, denounce, and sue for damages.

- In truth, I never know enough of the story to form a proper judgment on anyone. Can I leave judgment to God, and try to be godlike in thinking well of others.

Tuesday 24th June,
Birth of St. John the Baptist   Luke 1:57–66

Now the time came for Elizabeth to give birth, and she bore a son. Her neighbors and relatives heard that the Lord had shown his great mercy to her, and they rejoiced with her. On the eighth day they came to circumcise the child, and they were going to name him Zechariah after his father. But his mother said, "No; he is to be called John." They said to her, "None of your relatives has this name." Then they began motioning to his father to find out what name he wanted to give him. He asked for a writing tablet and wrote, "His name is John." And all of them were amazed. Immediately his mouth was opened and his tongue freed, and he began to speak, praising God.

- Lord, my name is written in the palm of your hand, just like John's. I imagine you calling me by my name, your message is personal; not a general precept but directed to me in particular.

- I ponder my name, what went into the choosing of it, what patrons or ancestors are echoed in it. Thank you for my name.

Wednesday 25th June   Matthew 7:15–20

Jesus told the crowds, "Beware of false prophets, who come to you in sheep's clothing but inwardly are ravenous wolves. You will know them by their fruits. Are grapes gathered from thorns, or figs from thistles? In the same way, every good tree bears good fruit, but the bad tree bears bad fruit. A good tree cannot bear bad fruit, nor can a bad tree bear good fruit. Every tree that does not bear good fruit is cut down and thrown into the fire. Thus you will know them by their fruits."

- How practical your words are, Lord. The world is awash with words—such as what I am writing now—and we need some way of knowing how to discern the true and good.
- Whether the speaker is a broadcaster or a bishop, a politician or a policeman, the only safe criterion is the one you give us: "You will know them by their fruits," by the way they live.

Thursday 26th June   Matthew 7:21–29

Jesus said to his disciples, "Not everyone who says to me, 'Lord, Lord,' will enter the kingdom of heaven, but only the one who does the will of my Father in heaven. On that day many will say to me, 'Lord, Lord, did we not prophesy in your name, and cast out demons in your name, and do many deeds of power in your name?' Then I will declare to them, 'I never knew you; go away from me, you evildoers.' "Everyone then who hears these words of mine and acts on them will be like a wise man who built his house on rock. The rain fell, the floods came, and the winds blew and beat on that house, but it did not fall, because it had been founded on rock. And everyone who hears these words of mine and does not act on them will be like a foolish man who built his house on sand. The rain fell, and the floods came, and the winds blew and beat against that house, and it fell—and great was its fall!" Now when Jesus had finished saying these things, the crowds were astounded at his teaching, for he taught them as one having authority, and not as their scribes.

- "And great was its fall!" Jesus shows what a common touch his preaching has when he links house construction with the way we respond to his words. His image confronts us immediately—am I solid house or sandcastle?
- Have I really taken in your message Lord, or is lip service my way? Can I allow your words to change my day, today?

Friday 27th June   Matthew 8:1–4

When Jesus had come down from the mountain, great crowds followed him; and there was a leper who came to him and knelt before him, saying, "Lord, if you choose, you can make me clean." He stretched out his hand and touched him, saying, "I do choose. Be made clean!" Immediately his leprosy was cleansed. Then Jesus said to him, "See that you say nothing to anyone; but go, show yourself to the priest, and offer the gift that Moses commanded, as a testimony to them."

- This eager leper was breaking the law by coming closer than fifty feet to a non-leper and exchanging greetings with another. When this man's faith broke through legal limitations, Jesus not merely spoke with him but touched him. Jesus cannot bear to see us isolated from him.
- When the Irish President Mary McAleese shook the hands of lepers in Uganda or Princess Diana touched AIDS sufferers, their gestures brought great joy: moments of grace.

Saturday 28th June   Matthew 8:5–13

When he entered Capernaum, a centurion came to him, appealing to him and saying, "Lord, my servant is lying at home paralyzed, in terrible distress." And he said to him, "I will come and cure him." The centurion answered, "Lord, I am not worthy to have you come under my roof; but only speak the word, and my servant will be healed. For I also am a man under authority, with soldiers under me; and I say to one, 'Go,' and he goes, and to another, 'Come,' and he comes, and to my slave, 'Do this,' and the slave does it." When Jesus heard him, he was amazed and said to those who followed him, "Truly I tell you, in no one in Israel have I found such faith. I tell you, many will come from east and west and will eat with Abraham and Isaac and Jacob in the kingdom of heaven, while the heirs of the kingdom will be thrown into the outer darkness, where there will be weeping and gnashing of teeth." And to the centurion Jesus said, "Go; let it be done for you according to your faith." And the servant was healed in that hour.

- Along with the calm authority of the centurion there is an extraordinary feeling for his sick servant which leads him to forget his standing as an officer of the occupying power, and respectfully beg a favor. More than that, he respects the possible reluctance of a Jew to enter a Gentile's house, and bows to the greater authority he senses in Jesus.

- Are there any in my life, Lord, for whom I would go to such lengths? Yet I am one of those you welcome, who come from east and west to eat with Abraham, Isaac and Jacob. May I be worthy of that calling.

Something to think and pray about each day this week:

Pain and Healing

You could see Jesus' life as a struggle against sickness and death. He was a healer, and reached out to cure the pains that disabled people, so that they could forget their sickness and enjoy, as he said, more abundant life, like Simon Peter's mother-in-law. When Jesus cured her of a fever, she got up and prepared food. Pious people with a headache sometimes offer up the pain and continue talking about it. Better to take an aspirin and get on with the job.

Pain and sickness are obviously bad, something to be fought and resisted. Yet the Lord touches us through them, and a time comes when we can no longer feel God's touch in prayer, but we sense how he is shaping us through our suffering. It is remarkable how many people find the grace to seek whatever help medicine can offer, and then to accept the remaining pain as the background of a peaceful existence—and without talking about it. Remember the prayer of the old nun: "Lord, keep my mind free from the recital of endless details—give me wings to get to the point. Seal my lips on my aches and pains—they are interesting, and my love of rehearsing them becomes sweeter as the years go by. I dare not ask for grace enough to listen to the tales of others' pains, but help me to endure them with patience."

The Presence of God

God is with me, but more,
God is within me, giving me existence.
Let me dwell for a moment on God's life-giving presence
in my body, my mind, my heart
and in the whole of my life.

Freedom

God is not foreign to my freedom.
Instead the Spirit breathes life into my most intimate desires,
gently nudging me towards all that is good.
I ask for the grace to let myself be enfolded by the Spirit.

Consciousness

How am I really feeling? Light-hearted? Heavy-hearted?
I may be very much at peace, happy to be here.
Equally, I may be frustrated, worried or angry.
I acknowledge how I really am. It is the real me that the Lord loves.

The Word

I read the Word of God slowly, a few times over, and I listen to
what God is saying to me. (Please turn to your scripture on the
following pages. Inspiration points are there should you need
them. When you are ready, return here to continue.)

Conversation

How has God's Word moved me? Has it left me cold?
Has it consoled me or moved me to act in a new way?
I imagine Jesus standing or sitting beside me,
I turn and share my feelings with him.

Conclusion

Glory be to the Father, and to the Son, and to the Holy Spirit,
As it was in the beginning, is now and ever shall be,
World without end. Amen

Sunday 29th June, Sts. Peter and Paul   Matthew 16:13–19

Now when Jesus came into the district of Caesarea Philippi, he asked his disciples, "Who do people say that the Son of Man is?" And they said, "Some say John the Baptist, but others Elijah, and still others Jeremiah or one of the prophets." He said to them, "But who do you say that I am?" Simon Peter answered, "You are the Messiah, the Son of the living God." And Jesus answered him, "Blessed are you, Simon son of Jonah! For flesh and blood has not revealed this to you, but my Father in heaven. And I tell you, you are Peter, and on this rock I will build my church, and the gates of Hades will not prevail against it. I will give you the keys of the kingdom of heaven, and whatever you bind on earth will be bound in heaven, and whatever you loose on earth will be loosed in heaven."

- You put that question to me, Lord: "Who do you say that I am?"
- As I pray about your question, your own words echo in me: "I am the Way, the Truth and the Life."

Monday 30th June   Matthew 8:18–22

Now when Jesus saw great crowds around him, he gave orders to go over to the other side. A scribe then approached and said, "Teacher, I will follow you wherever you go." And Jesus said to him, "Foxes have holes, and birds of the air have nests; but the Son of Man has nowhere to lay his head." Another of his disciples said to him, "Lord, first let me go and bury my father." But Jesus said to him, "Follow me, and let the dead bury their own dead."

- This highly educated scribe offers himself as Jesus' disciple. What is it that makes Jesus slow to jump at the offer? Perhaps it was a suspicion that the scribe was exchanging the stability of a scholar for the stability of a disciple, still a student of God's word, a spectator.

- The authentic following of Jesus means taking risks, or being unsettled; not the role of spectator. Lord you constantly challenge me. I will try to hear your voice in what unsettles me.

Tuesday 1st July   Matthew 8:23–27

And when Jesus got into the boat, his disciples followed him. A windstorm arose on the sea, so great that the boat was being swamped by the waves; but he was asleep. And they went and woke him up, saying, "Lord, save us! We are perishing!" And he said to them, "Why are you afraid, you of little faith?" Then he got up and rebuked the winds and the sea; and there was a dead calm. They were amazed, saying, "What sort of man is this, that even the winds and the sea obey him?"

- In a storm, whether of the sea or of my own emotions, the urgent often pushes out the important. Overwhelmed by feelings of panic, I can say and do things that destroy relationships or make my plight worse. It need not be like that.
- Mother Teresa and Nelson Mandela suffered worse crises than any I have suffered; I marvel at the calm with which they could respond. Jesus' greeting is one of peace. Teach me that, Lord.

Wednesday 2nd July   Amos 5:21–24

I hate, I despise your festivals, and I take no delight in your solemn assemblies. Even though you offer me your burnt offerings and grain offerings, I will not accept them; and the offerings of well-being of your fatted animals I will not look upon. Take away from me the noise of your songs; I will not listen to the melody of your harps. But let justice roll down like waters, and righteousness like an ever-flowing stream.

- Is it as simple as this, Lord? I often feel distaste for religious festivals and solemn assemblies, and I love the image of justice rolling in waves across the land. Yet when it comes to identifying what is just and what is unjust, I am caught between conflicting voices.

- Do I support the local unemployed, or the demands and needs of immigrants; the striking workers, or the travelers stranded by blocked services? I am puzzled: where is the overflowing stream of righteousness? Teach me, Lord.

Thursday 3rd July, St. Thomas   John 20:24–29

But Thomas (who was called the Twin), one of the twelve, was not with them when Jesus came. So the other disciples told him, "We have seen the Lord." But he said to them, "Unless I see the mark of the nails in his hands, and put my finger in the mark of the nails and my hand in his side, I will not believe." A week later his disciples were again in the house, and Thomas was with them. Although the doors were shut, Jesus came and stood among them and said, "Peace be with you." Then he said to Thomas, "Put your finger here and see my hands. Reach out your hand and put it in my side. Do not doubt but believe." Thomas answered him, "My Lord and my God!" Jesus said to him, "Have you believed because you have seen me? Blessed are those who have not seen and yet have come to believe."

- "Peace be with you." In the midst of pain, loss, fear, and infidelity Jesus offers "peace." What is this peace Jesus brings?
- It is something even deeper than all that is wounded and fearful in us. This is not the peace the world gives; it is the peace of love and forgiveness; this peace goes hand-in-hand with the Cross.
- Is this the peace I pray for?

Friday 4th July   Matthew 9:9–13

As Jesus was walking along, he saw a man called Matthew sitting at the tax booth; and he said to him, "Follow me." And he got up and followed him. And as he sat at dinner in the house, many tax collectors and sinners came and were sitting with him and his disciples. When the Pharisees saw this, they said to his disciples, "Why does your teacher eat with tax collectors and sinners?" But when he heard this, he said, "Those who are well have no need of a physician, but those who are sick. Go and learn what this means, 'I desire mercy, not sacrifice.' For I have come to call not the righteous but sinners."

- Would you eat with me, Lord? Where do I stand? Do I recognize my sickness?
- I thank you for the moments when you surprise me, as you surprised Matthew, with a gesture that reveals me to myself and shows me my need of mercy.

Saturday 5th July   Matthew 9:14–17

Then the disciples of John came to him, saying, "Why do we and the Pharisees fast often, but your disciples do not fast?" And Jesus said to them, "The wedding guests cannot mourn as long as the bridegroom is with them, can they? The days will come when the bridegroom is taken away from them, and then they will fast. No one sews a piece of unshrunk cloth on an old cloak, for the patch pulls away from the cloak, and a worse tear is made. Neither is new wine put into old wineskins; otherwise, the skins burst, and the wine is spilled, and the skins are destroyed; but new wine is put into fresh wineskins, and so both are preserved."

- John's disciples, like the older brother of the Prodigal Son, have a grievance, and Jesus' answer sparkles in an unexpected way: I am the bridegroom, and the party will not last for ever. He picks up a hint of self-righteousness in their question, but he does not linger on it, just uses a metaphor.

- Perhaps they went off wondering, as I wonder sometimes: Am I an old wineskin? Lord, renew me, fill me with your new wine.

july 6–12

Something to think and pray about each day this week:

Beyond Imagining

Because we call God our "Father," we easily ascribe to him the limitations of a human father or mother. As children we always wanted to know that we had a place in our parent's mind and heart. Sibling rivalry centers on the question of how much father or mother has time for me—and how I compare in their minds with my siblings. But with my heavenly Father I have uncountable billions of siblings, stretching backwards and forwards in time. How can he have a place and thought for all of us? One thing we know: God is beyond our imagination. Every comparison, even with father or mother, limps. St. Augustine said: "God is not what you imagine or think you understand. If you understand him, you have failed." The God we believe in is outside space and time, and surpasses all that we can conceive. Yet Jesus has brought his tenderness within the compass of our imagination in the story of the Prodigal Son (Luke 15).

The Presence of God

To be present is to arrive as one is and open up to the other.
At this instant, as I arrive here, God is present waiting for me.
God always arrives before me, desiring to connect with me
even more than my most intimate friend.
I take a moment and greet my loving God.

Freedom

Everything has the potential to draw forth from me a fuller love
and life.
Yet my desires are often fixed, caught, on illusions of fulfillment.
I ask that God, through my freedom, may orchestrate
my desires in a vibrant loving melody rich in harmony.

Consciousness

Knowing that God loves me unconditionally,
I can afford to be honest about how I am.
How has the last day been, and how do I feel now?
I share my feelings openly with the Lord.

The Word

I take my time to read the Word of God, slowly, a few times, allowing myself to dwell on anything that strikes me. (Please turn
to your scripture on the following pages. Inspiration points are
there should you need them. When you are ready, return here
to continue.)

Conversation

What feelings are rising in me
as I pray and reflect on God's Word?
I imagine Jesus himself sitting or standing beside me,
and open my heart to him.

Conclusion

Glory be to the Father, and to the Son, and to the Holy Spirit,
As it was in the beginning, is now and ever shall be,
World without end. Amen

Sunday 6th July,
Fourteenth Sunday in Ordinary Time   Matthew 11:28–30

Jesus said, "Come to me, all you that are weary and are carrying heavy burdens, and I will give you rest. Take my yoke upon you, and learn from me; for I am gentle and humble in heart, and you will find rest for your souls. For my yoke is easy, and my burden is light."

- The phrase "comfort zone" describes the state where we feel life is under control and satisfactory. Jesus is inviting those who are not in that zone, who feel oppressed by anxiety and uncertainty.
- Lord, I do not ask that you bring my life completely under control. To be mortal is to face uncomfortable realities. I beg you to be my uncomfortable comfort zone.

Monday 7th July   Matthew 9:18–19, 23–26

While he was saying these things to them, suddenly a leader of the synagogue came in and knelt before him, saying, "My daughter has just died; but come and lay your hand on her, and she will live." And Jesus got up and followed him, with his disciples. When Jesus came to the leader's house and saw the flute players and the crowd making a commotion, he said, "Go away; for the girl is not dead but sleeping." And they laughed at him. But when the crowd had been put outside, he went in and took her by the hand, and the girl got up. And the report of this spread throughout that district.

- Jesus can be such an icon of perfection and reverence for us that we forget what he faced from his own people: "They laughed at him." He did not waste energy taking issue with their mockery. He focused simply on the sick girl and took her by the hand.
- Lord, take me by the hand, lift my sickness and weariness, give me hope and new life.

Tuesday 8th July   **Matthew 9:35–38**

Then Jesus went about all the cities and villages, teaching in their synagogues, and proclaiming the good news of the kingdom, and curing every disease and every sickness. When he saw the crowds, he had compassion for them, because they were harassed and helpless, like sheep without a shepherd. Then he said to his disciples, "The harvest is plentiful, but the laborers are few; therefore ask the Lord of the harvest to send out laborers into his harvest."

- In face of the helplessness and harassment that many suffer, Jesus reminds us to turn to God. It is his world, not ours. We do what we can, glad to be of service, but God did not create us to help him out of a jam. The work of the world's redemption is never complete.
- When we have done our best, we turn to our Father in heaven and say: "Thank you for giving me a share in this work. Now over to you, Lord."

Wednesday 9th July   **Matthew 10:1–7**

Then Jesus summoned his twelve disciples and gave them authority over unclean spirits, to cast them out, and to cure every disease and every sickness. These are the names of the twelve apostles: first, Simon, also known as Peter, and his brother Andrew; James son of Zebedee, and his brother John; Philip and Bartholomew; Thomas and Matthew the tax collector; James son of Alphaeus, and Thaddaeus; Simon the Cananaean, and Judas Iscariot, the one who betrayed him. These twelve Jesus sent out with the following instructions: "Go nowhere among the Gentiles, and enter no town of the Samaritans, but go rather to the lost sheep of the house of Israel. As you go, proclaim the good news, 'The kingdom of heaven has come near.'"

- Jesus commissioned the Twelve to preach to Israel; only at the end of his life did he extend their mission to the Gentiles. The message is the same: Good News, Gospel.
- Do I leave people feeling more upbeat, more hopeful, with a vision that God's kingdom is within reach?

Thursday 10th July   Hosea 11:1–4

When Israel was a child, I loved him, and out of Egypt I called my son. The more I called them, the more they went from me; they kept sacrificing to the Baals, and offering incense to idols. Yet it was I who taught Ephraim to walk, I took them up in my arms; but they did not know that I healed them. I led them with cords of human kindness, with bands of love. I was to them like those who lift infants to their cheeks. I bent down to them and fed them.

- These images of God as mother remind me to seek from God all the passionate affection we hope for from mothers. In my life I look for those cords of kindness, those bands of love.
- Even as I age, I treasure the moments when God bends down to feed me.

Friday 11th July, St. Benedict   Matthew 19:27–29

Then Peter said in reply, "Look, we have left everything and followed you. What then will we have?" Jesus said to them, "Truly I tell you, at the renewal of all things, when the Son of Man is seated on the throne of his glory, you who have followed me will also sit on twelve thrones, judging the twelve tribes of Israel. And everyone who has left houses or brothers or sisters or father or mother or children or fields, for my name's sake, will receive a hundredfold, and will inherit eternal life."

- This promise has had profound effects on the world's history, in the hundreds of thousands of good people who for Jesus' sake have left everything they held precious, in order to give themselves to serving others. Today we honor Benedict, who guided a vast community of such people, and had immense impact on the culture of Europe.
- We also remember the many men and women he has inspired over centuries.

Saturday 12th July   Matthew 10:28–31

Jesus said to his disciples, "Do not fear those who kill the body but cannot kill the soul; rather fear him who can destroy both soul and body in hell. Are not two sparrows sold for a penny? Yet not one of them will fall to the ground apart from your Father. And even the hairs of your head are all counted. So do not be afraid; you are of more value than many sparrows."

- With other teachers we may reach a point where we have learned all that they have to offer us. We may even go beyond them. Not so with Jesus.
- What sort of pupil do I make—alert? inattentive? diligent? easily distracted?

july 13–19

Something to think and pray about each day this week:

Changing Pace

In the Northern hemisphere many people are now planning holidays, for a couple of summer weeks or even longer. What do
we seek in our holidays? When we are young and feel immor-
tal, vacation can be a frantic search for new experience, which
may leave us needing further time to recover. As we grow older
and feel the pressure of modern living more acutely, the joy of
holidays is to escape from the tyranny of the clock, to savor the
full length of these lazy, crazy days, and to find leisure for the
people and things we love. We can rediscover our inner harmony
in God, who exists in an eternal Now. We change our tempo.

The Presence of God

What is present to me is what has a hold on my becoming.
I reflect on the presence of God always there in love,
amidst the many things that have a hold on me.
I pause and pray that I may let God
affect my becoming in this precise moment.

Freedom

There are very few people
who realize what God would make of them
if they abandoned themselves into his hands,
and let themselves be formed by his grace. (St. Ignatius)
I ask for the grace to trust myself totally to God's love.

Consciousness

In the presence of my loving Creator,
I look honestly at my feelings over the last day,
the highs, the lows and the level ground.
Can I see where the Lord has been present?

The Word

God speaks to each one of us individually. I need to listen to
what he is saying to me. (Please turn to your scripture on the
following pages. Inspiration points are there should you need
them. When you are ready, return here to continue.)

Conversation

What is stirring in me as I pray?
Am I consoled, troubled, left cold?
I imagine Jesus himself standing or sitting at my side,
and share my feelings with him.

Conclusion

Glory be to the Father, and to the Son, and to the Holy Spirit,
As it was in the beginning, is now and ever shall be,
World without end. Amen

Sunday 13th July,
Fifteenth Sunday in Ordinary Time   Romans 8:18–23

I consider that the sufferings of this present time are not worth comparing with the glory about to be revealed to us. For the creation waits with eager longing for the revealing of the children of God; for the creation was subjected to futility, not of its own will but by the will of the one who subjected it, in hope that the creation itself will be set free from its bondage to decay and will obtain the freedom of the glory of the children of God. We know that the whole creation has been groaning in labor pains until now; and not only the creation, but we ourselves, who have the first fruits of the Spirit, groan inwardly while we wait for adoption, the redemption of our bodies.

* Paul affirms a solidarity of the human and non-human world in the redemption of Christ. We are born onto an earth of rivers, mountains, plains, forests, animals, birds, fish and plants in their millions. This is the habitat in which God placed us, where we have evolved, and which we have made our own.

* I pray, Lord, that the heaven you prepare for me will echo in some way the earth which I have loved.

Monday 14th July   Matthew 10:37–39

Jesus said to his disciples, "Whoever loves father or mother more than me is not worthy of me; and whoever loves son or daughter more than me is not worthy of me; and whoever does not take up the cross and follow me is not worthy of me. Those who find their life will lose it, and those who lose their life for my sake will find it."

* Jesus is stating his message at its starkest: should I have to choose between the claims of God and those of my household, then God comes first.

- We do not go looking for this sort of confrontation, and pray it may never come to this. But you, Lord, have first claim on my life.

Tuesday 15th July   Matthew 11:20–24

Then Jesus began to reproach the cities in which most of his deeds of power had been done, because they did not repent. "Woe to you, Chorazin! Woe to you, Bethsaida! For if the deeds of power done in you had been done in Tyre and Sidon, they would have repented long ago in sackcloth and ashes. But I tell you, on the day of judgment it will be more tolerable for Tyre and Sidon than for you. And you, Capernaum, will you be exalted to heaven? No, you will be brought down to Hades. For if the deeds of power done in you had been done in Sodom, it would have remained until this day. But I tell you that on the day of judgment it will be more tolerable for the land of Sodom than for you."

- These verses hint at the mass of unrecorded history that the Gospels omit: the deeds of power performed by Jesus in the towns at the northern end of the Sea of Tiberias. Here were communities that listened to Jesus, and saw his miracles, but shrugged their shoulders and sent him on his way.
- Lord, open my eyes and heart to the signs of your grace around me. Help me to hear your message, even if it upsets my habits.

Wednesday 16th July   Matthew 11:25–27

At that time Jesus said, "I thank you, Father, Lord of heaven and earth, because you have hidden these things from the wise and the intelligent and have revealed them to infants; yes, Father, for such was your gracious will. All things have been handed over to me by my Father; and no one knows the Son except the Father, and no one knows the Father except the Son and anyone to whom the Son chooses to reveal him."

- When we ask about Jesus' knowledge of himself, this is a crucial passage. He calls on his Father with the intimate "Abba, Daddy." He claims to be the unique channel of the love and knowledge of God.

- Theologians have used complex words, like hypostatic union, to describe the joining of divine and human natures in Jesus. He insists that access to the Father is granted not so much to the intelligent, as to those who come to Him as his trusting children.

Thursday 17th July   Matthew 11:28–30

Jesus said, "Come to me, all you that are weary and are carrying heavy burdens, and I will give you rest. Take my yoke upon you, and learn from me; for I am gentle and humble in heart, and you will find rest for your souls. For my yoke is easy, and my burden is light."

- Jesus, you offer me rest and comfort in an invitation that is maternal in its tenderness. You speak these words to me as if for the first time.

- In that promise of rest there is a hint of the sabbath, and I remember St. Augustine's prayer: Lord give us the peace of quiet, the peace of the sabbath, a sabbath with no evening.

Friday 18th July   Matthew 12:1–8

At that time Jesus went through the grainfields on the sabbath; his disciples were hungry, and they began to pluck heads of grain and to eat. When the Pharisees saw it, they said to him, "Look, your disciples are doing what is not lawful to do on the sabbath." He said to them, "Have you not read what David did when he and his companions were hungry? He entered the house of God and ate the bread of the Presence, which it was not lawful for him or his companions to eat, but only for the priests. Or have you not read in the law that on the sabbath the priests in the temple break the sabbath and yet are guiltless? I tell you, something greater than the temple is here. But if you had known what this means, 'I desire mercy and not sacrifice,' you would not have condemned the guiltless. For the Son of Man is lord of the sabbath."

- The corn was planted in long, narrow strips, and the ground between them was always a right of way. Jewish law allowed hungry travelers to pluck and eat ears of corn when walking through a field.

- This sunny, carefree scene is suddenly overshadowed by the Pharisees quoting a rigid interpretation of the law of the sabbath. Jesus does not retreat, but takes them a step further. The sabbath is made for man, who is lord of the sabbath. The sun shines again.

Saturday 19th July   Matthew 12:14–21

But the Pharisees went out and conspired against him, how to destroy him. When Jesus became aware of this, he departed. Many crowds followed him, and he cured all of them, and he ordered them not to make him known. This was to fulfill what had been spoken through the prophet Isaiah: "Here is my servant, whom I have chosen, my beloved, with whom my soul is well pleased. I will put my Spirit upon him, and he will proclaim justice to the Gentiles. He will not wrangle or cry aloud, nor will anyone hear his voice in the streets. He will not break a bruised reed or quench a smoldering wick until he brings justice to victory. And in his name the Gentiles will hope."

- In the face of plots and conspiracies, Jesus walks on, to continue his ministry. Again, he does not retreat.

- "I will put my Spirit upon him, and he will proclaim justice to the Gentiles." Like the Suffering Servant of Isaiah, Jesus encourages us to move forward, despite our failures and limitations, to persist and not retreat.

- How do I respond?

Something to think and pray about each day this week:

The Loving Bond

The Gospels portray Jesus as a man of quite unusual physical and psychological strength. When he was with the crowds, he was always alert, dynamic, a figure you could not ignore. He would spend a long day teaching, explaining, arguing, healing, blessing, and then withdraw from the crowds and from his own disciples. But it was not a withdrawal into sleep. He went apart, often into the hills, to pray. Can we begin to imagine what happened in that dialogue with the Father? The only notion I can form is of the Trinity: Father and Son in a loving bond with one another, and that bond is the Holy Spirit. As sisters and brothers of Jesus we too enjoy that bond with the Father. "Likewise the Spirit helps us in our weakness; for we do not know how to pray as we ought, but that very Spirit intercedes with sighs too deep for words." (Romans 8:26)

The Presence of God

Jesus waits silent and unseen to come into my heart.
I will respond to His call.
He comes with His infinite power and love
May I be filled with joy in His presence.

Freedom

A thick and shapeless tree-trunk would never believe
that it could become a statue, admired as a miracle of sculpture,
and would never submit itself to the chisel of the sculptor,
who sees by her genius what she can make of it. (St. Ignatius)
I ask for the grace to let myself be shaped by my loving Creator.

Consciousness

Knowing that God loves me unconditionally,
I look honestly over the last day, its events and my feelings.
Do I have something to be grateful for? Then I give thanks.
Is there something I am sorry for? Then I ask forgiveness.

The Word

I read the Word of God slowly, a few times over, and I listen to
what God is saying to me. (Please turn to your scripture on the
following pages. Inspiration points are there should you need
them. When you are ready, return here to continue.)

Conversation

Do I notice myself reacting as I pray with the Word of God?
Do I feel challenged, comforted, angry?
Imagining Jesus sitting or standing by me,
I speak out my feelings, as one trusted friend to another.

Conclusion

Glory be to the Father, and to the Son, and to the Holy Spirit,
As it was in the beginning, is now and ever shall be,
World without end. Amen

Sunday 20th July,
Sixteenth Sunday in Ordinary Time   Matthew 13:24–30

Jesus put before them another parable: "The kingdom of heaven may be compared to someone who sowed good seed in his field; but while everybody was asleep, an enemy came and sowed weeds among the wheat, and then went away. So when the plants came up and bore grain, then the weeds appeared as well. And the slaves of the householder came and said to him, 'Master, did you not sow good seed in your field? Where, then, did these weeds come from?' He answered, 'An enemy has done this.' The slaves said to him, 'Then do you want us to go and gather them?' But he replied, 'No; for in gathering the weeds you would uproot the wheat along with them. Let both of them grow together until the harvest; and at harvest time I will tell the reapers, Collect the weeds first and bind them in bundles to be burned, but gather the wheat into my barn.'"

- Lord, you are telling me how to live with the evil in the world. Part of me is impatient to root it out, like the servants offering to weed out the darnel.
- You tell me to wait on God's judgment and trust that the goodness of his seed will prevail over the weeds. You do not ask us to coerce people into what we think is the right path—that was the illusion of the Inquisition.
- May I learn patience. When faced with violent people, I will not let their way of treating me determine my way of treating them.

Monday 21st July   Matthew 12:38–42

Then some of the scribes and Pharisees said to him, "Teacher, we wish to see a sign from you." But he answered them, "An evil and adulterous generation asks for a sign, but no sign will be given to it except the sign of the prophet Jonah. For just as Jonah was three days and three nights in the belly of the sea monster, so for three days and three nights the Son of Man will be in the heart of the earth. The people of Nineveh will rise up at the judgment with this generation and condemn it, because they repented at the proclamation of Jonah, and see, something greater than Jonah is here! The queen of the South will rise up at the judgment with this generation and condemn it, because she came from the ends of the earth to listen to the wisdom of Solomon, and see, something greater than Solomon is here!

- Jesus resisted the Jews' repeated demand for a sign that would show he was from God. They wanted to see something abnormal. Jesus brings them back to the normal, to the man Jesus whom they saw and knew.
- From the beginning of his public life, those who did not believe in Jesus' preaching or his miracles discerned nothing of the divine in his features. What do I see in Jesus?

Tuesday 22nd July, St. Mary Magdalene John 20:11–18

But Mary stood weeping outside the tomb. As she wept, she bent over to look into the tomb; and she saw two angels in white, sitting where the body of Jesus had been lying, one at the head and the other at the feet. They said to her, "Woman, why are you weeping?" She said to them, "They have taken away my Lord, and I do not know where they have laid him." When she had said this, she turned around and saw Jesus standing there, but she did not know that it was Jesus. Jesus said to her, "Woman, why are you weeping? Whom are you looking for?" Supposing him to be the gardener, she said to him, "Sir, if you have carried him away, tell me where you have laid him, and I will take him away." Jesus said to her, "Mary!" She turned and said to him in Hebrew, "Rabbouni!" (which means Teacher). Jesus said to her,

"Do not hold on to me, because I have not yet ascended to the Father. But go to my brothers and say to them, 'I am ascending to my Father and your Father, to my God and your God.'" Mary Magdalene went and announced to the disciples, "I have seen the Lord"; and she told them that he had said these things to her.

- This tear-laden, poignant recognition scene deserves to be contemplated slowly. Mary is distraught, thinking only of the Jesus whose death she has witnessed; she cannot see who stands before her. Suddenly she hears a familiar voice call her name. Her world is transformed: "I have seen the Lord." She looks across the boundary between life and death, which has met its master.

- When he points to the group of disciples, can I imagine that I am standing among them? How do I respond?

Wednesday 23rd July, St. Bridget — Galatians 2:19–20

I have been crucified with Christ; and it is no longer I who live, but it is Christ who lives in me. And the life I now live in the flesh I live by faith in the Son of God, who loved me and gave himself for me.

- Teach me, Lord Jesus, what it is to live in you, and for you to live in me. It means being in love with you, being at ease with you, finding my strength in you, and being ready, when questioned, to explain to others what you are in my life.

Thursday 24th July — Matthew 13:10–12

Jesus said to his disciples: "To those who have, more will be given, and they will have an abundance; but from those who have nothing, even what they have will be taken away."

- This apparently paradoxical statement is really an observation of life. Those who have money easily make more—if they invest, it grows. Those who practice a sport grow better at it. Those who are good to others develop habits of generosity. It is a re-statement of the parable of the talents.

- What are you telling me, Lord? That by praying I come to know about prayer; that I should use everything I have, and not let what I have lie fallow.

Friday 25th July, St. James, Apostle　　Matthew 20:20–28

Then the mother of the sons of Zebedee came to him with her sons, and kneeling before him, she asked a favor of him. And he said to her, "What do you want?" She said to him, "Declare that these two sons of mine will sit, one at your right hand and one at your left, in your kingdom." But Jesus answered, "You do not know what you are asking. Are you able to drink the cup that I am about to drink?" They said to him, "We are able." He said to them, "You will indeed drink my cup, but to sit at my right hand and at my left, this is not mine to grant, but it is for those for whom it has been prepared by my Father." When the ten heard it, they were angry with the two brothers. But Jesus called them to him and said, "You know that the rulers of the Gentiles lord it over them, and their great ones are tyrants over them. It will not be so among you; but whoever wishes to be great among you must be your servant, and whoever wishes to be first among you must be your slave; just as the Son of Man came not to be served but to serve, and to give his life a ransom for many."

- Lord, you taught James and John a gentle lesson. While the rest of the twelve were angry with the brothers, you asked them the deep question: "Can you share my chalice?"
- Rather than scold the ambitious mother and her sons, you invited them to put on the true uniform of Christians, to learn to be a servant, and share your passion. You invite me too.

Saturday 26th July, Sts. Joachim and Ann   Jeremiah 1:4–8

Now the word of the LORD came to me saying, "Before I formed you in the womb I knew you, and before you were born I consecrated you; I appointed you a prophet to the nations." Then I said, "Ah, Lord GOD! Truly I do not know how to speak, for I am only a boy." But the LORD said to me, 'Do not say, 'I am only a boy'; for you shall go to all to whom I send you, and you shall speak whatever I command you. Do not be afraid of them, for I am with you to deliver you, says the LORD."

- Lord, you did not call me to prophesy like Jeremiah, but you did call me, and your words hold for me too. I see needs around me, above all people who need me as a friend.
- I hold back through fear, and you tell me to be an adult, not to fear, but to go where I am needed.

july 27–august 2

Something to think and pray about each day this week:

God of Surprises

The end of July is a significant jubilee for many Jesuits, with the feast of Saint Ignatius Loyola. The commitment of religious vows, like that of marriage, is a solemn and free act that touches us as deeply as any act can. This gift, of all that we are and may become, suggests the image of a silver chalice, filled with all that is precious. Alas, it does not work out that way.

All of us who live by vows, whether in marriage or religious life, know that a goblet of precious wine is an inadequate image for a personal commitment. Our lives and relationships are inevitably a mixed drink, bitter-sweet. As we look back, over ten, or thirty, or sixty years, we can see what a mixture it was, at once richer and more painful than when we took our vows. Only a jubilee reveals what a complicated and unexpected mixture is there. The God we serve is a God of surprises; retrospect shows that it is his plans, not ours, that counted. He does not call us to help him out of a jam. He calls us because he loves us.

The Presence of God

As I sit here, the beating of my heart,
the ebb and flow of my breathing, the movements of my mind
are all signs of God's ongoing creation of me.
I pause for a moment, and become aware
of this presence of God within me.

Freedom

I ask for the grace
to let go of my own concerns
and be open to what God is asking of me,
to let myself be guided and formed by my loving Creator.

Consciousness

How do I find myself today?
Where am I with God? With others?
Do I have something to be grateful for? Then I give thanks.
Is there something I am sorry for? Then I ask forgiveness.

The Word

I take my time to read the Word of God, slowly, a few times, allowing myself to dwell on anything that strikes me. (Please turn to your scripture on the following pages. Inspiration points are there should you need them. When you are ready, return here to continue.)

Conversation

Remembering that I am still in God's presence,
I imagine Jesus himself standing or sitting beside me,
and say whatever is on my mind, whatever is in my heart,
speaking as one friend to another.

Conclusion

Glory be to the Father, and to the Son, and to the Holy Spirit,
As it was in the beginning, is now and ever shall be,
World without end. Amen

Sunday 27th July,
Seventeenth Sunday in Ordinary Time   1 Kings 3:5, 7–12

The LORD appeared to Solomon in a dream by night; and God said, "Ask what I should give you." And Solomon said, "You have shown great and steadfast love to your servant my father David, because he walked before you in faithfulness, in righteousness, and in uprightness of heart toward you; and you have kept for him this great and steadfast love, and have given him a son to sit on his throne today. And now, O LORD my God, you have made your servant king in place of my father David, although I am only a little child; I do not know how to go out or come in. And your servant is in the midst of the people whom you have chosen, a great people, so numerous they cannot be numbered or counted. Give your servant therefore an understanding mind to govern your people, able to discern between good and evil; for who can govern this your great people?" It pleased the Lord that Solomon had asked this. God said to him, "Because you have asked this, and have not asked for yourself long life or riches, or for the life of your enemies, but have asked for yourself understanding to discern what is right, I now do according to your word. Indeed I give you a wise and discerning mind; no one like you has been before you and no one like you shall arise after you."

- What would I seek as a prize above all other prizes? Solomon asks for a wise and discerning mind, to become a true listener. Wise people, young or old, are not so much those who know all the answers, as those who go on listening and learning.

- Boethius defined the wise person: one who savors things the way they really are.

- Lord, I wish for that mental humility. Make me a good listener.

Monday 28th July   Matthew 13:31–32

Jesus put before them another parable: "The kingdom of heaven is like a mustard seed that someone took and sowed in his field; it is the smallest of all the seeds, but when it has grown it is the greatest of shrubs and becomes a tree, so that the birds of the air come and make nests in its branches."

- Jesus gives us this wonderfully brief but graphic image of the kingdom; the seed which starts tiny, and grows so impressively.
- What is my response? How do I see my role in "growing" this kingdom?

Tuesday 29th July, St. Martha   John 11:19–27

Many of the Jews had come to Martha and Mary to console them about their brother. When Martha heard that Jesus was coming, she went and met him, while Mary stayed at home. Martha said to Jesus, "Lord, if you had been here, my brother would not have died. But even now I know that God will give you whatever you ask of him." Jesus said to her, "Your brother will rise again." Martha said to him, "I know that he will rise again in the resurrection on the last day." Jesus said to her, "I am the resurrection and the life. Those who believe in me, even though they die, will live, and everyone who lives and believes in me will never die. Do you believe this?" She said to him, "Yes, Lord, I believe that you are the Messiah, the Son of God, the one coming into the world."

- We call our world the land of the living. We might well call it the land of the dying; it is through the door of death that we pass into the land of the living. Remember John Donne's poetic words:
    Death be not proud, though some have called thee
    Mighty and dreadful, for thou art not so,
    For those whom thou think'st thou dost overthrow,

Die not, poor Death, nor yet canst thou kill me …
One short sleep past, we wake eternally,
And death shall be no more; Death, thou shalt die.

Wednesday 30th July   Matthew 13:44–46

Jesus said to the disciples, "The kingdom of heaven is like treasure hidden in a field, which someone found and hid; then in
his joy he goes and sells all that he has and buys that field. Again,
the kingdom of heaven is like a merchant in search of fine pearls;
on finding one pearl of great value, he went and sold all that he
had and bought it."

- What Jesus describes could easily happen in a troubled land like
  Palestine. Ordinary people used the ground as the safest place to
  keep their most treasured possessions. There were caches of coins
  buried all over the country, forgotten when the owner died.
- Lord, you talk of the joy of discovery. That is the sign that I have
  found your treasure, a deep happiness that nothing can separate
  me from you.

Thursday 31st July, St. Ignatius Loyola   Luke 9:23–26

Then Jesus said to the disciples, "If any want to become my
followers, let them deny themselves and take up their cross
daily and follow me. For those who want to save their life will
lose it, and those who lose their life for my sake will save it. What
does it profit them if they gain the whole world, but lose or forfeit themselves? Those who are ashamed of me and of my words,
of them the Son of Man will be ashamed when he comes in his
glory and the glory of the Father and of the holy angels."

- When we start a spiritual journey with Ignatius Loyola, as when
  we pray in *Sacred Space*, we start from where we are, not from
  where we would like to be.

- He started his journey as an almost illiterate ex-soldier, and went back to primary school, learning to read and write. "In prayer," he used to say, "God taught me like a schoolboy." He watched the movements in his own heart, and by constant reflection on that experience, he became a spiritual master.
- Lord, as you taught Ignatius, make me your pupil too.

Friday 1st August   Matthew 13:54–58

Jesus came to his home town and began to teach the people in their synagogue, so that they were astounded and said, "Where did this man get this wisdom and these deeds of power? Is not this the carpenter's son? Is not his mother called Mary? And are not his brothers James and Joseph and Simon and Judas? And are not all his sisters with us? Where then did this man get all this?" And they took offense at him. But Jesus said to them, "Prophets are not without honor except in their own country and in their own house." And he did not do many deeds of power there, because of their unbelief.

- I enter this scene as one of the townspeople. Am I blown over by Jesus' deeds of power? Fascinated to see how this young neighbor has grown? Or am I skeptical, begrudging, loath to be impressed, looking for a way to put him down?
- I am grateful for the details we might never otherwise have known, about his trade and his relations. But Lord, give me a more generous heart, to respond readily to love and the signs of your presence.

Saturday 2nd August   Psalm 68(69):15–16, 29–30

Do not let the flood sweep over me, or the deep swallow me up, or the Pit close its mouth over me. Answer me, O LORD, for your steadfast love is good; according to your abundant mercy, turn to me. But I am lowly and in pain; let your salvation, O God, protect me. I will praise the name of God with a song; I will magnify him with thanksgiving.

- There have been times when I needed psalms like this, when the imagination and mind went dumb, and all I could feel was a desperate need for God's help, when I was "lowly and in pain."
- Thank you, Lord, for these heart-wrenching psalms.

august 3–9

Something to think and pray about each day this week:

Sensing God's Presence

To prepare for prayer, clean the heart and the senses. If the weather permits, go outside and look at the sky; and stay looking. Gaze at its colors, its changes, the forms and movement of clouds, the effects of the wind, the particular pattern of the horizons all round you. There is so much to watch, not with the eye of a meteorologist or physicist who seeks to analyze, but with the eye of a beholder, seeing and marveling rather than thinking. With your energy focused on watching, your mind calms down and your heart settles. On other occasions ring the changes with the other senses: focus for a while on what you hear, or what you feel, or what you taste, or on breathing in and breathing out. This is not strictly prayer, but a preparation for prayer; it can have unexpected effects.

The Presence of God
I pause for a moment
and reflect on God's life-giving presence
in every part of my body, in everything around me,
in the whole of my life.

Freedom
I ask for the grace to believe
in what I could be and do
if I only allowed God, my loving Creator,
to continue to create me, guide me and shape me.

Consciousness
In God's loving presence I unwind the past day,
starting from now and looking back, moment by moment.
I gather in all the goodness and light, in gratitude.
I attend to the shadows and what they say to me,
seeking healing, courage, forgiveness.

The Word
God speaks to each one of us individually. I need to listen to
what he is saying to me. (Please turn to your scripture on the
following pages. Inspiration points are there should you need
them. When you are ready, return here to continue.)

Conversation
How has God's Word moved me? Has it left me cold?
Has it consoled me or moved me to act in a new way?
I imagine Jesus standing or sitting beside me,
I turn and share my feelings with him.

Conclusion
Glory be to the Father, and to the Son, and to the Holy Spirit,
As it was in the beginning, is now and ever shall be,
World without end. Amen

Sunday 3rd August,
Eighteenth Sunday in Ordinary Time   Romans 8:35, 37–39

Who will separate us from the love of Christ? Will hardship, or distress, or persecution, or famine, or nakedness, or peril, or sword? No, in all these things we are more than conquerors through him who loved us. For I am convinced that neither death, nor life, nor angels, nor rulers, nor things present, nor things to come, nor powers, nor height, nor depth, nor anything else in all creation, will be able to separate us from the love of God in Christ Jesus our Lord.

- How have I dealt with the hardships in my life? Has resentment or bitterness featured in my responses? Have I felt alone?
- "For I am convinced . . ." Where does this powerful conviction come from? Do I share Paul's belief that nothing can separate me from the love of God?

Monday 4th August   Matthew 14:15–21

When it was evening, the disciples came to him and said, "This is a deserted place, and the hour is now late; send the crowds away so that they may go into the villages and buy food for themselves." Jesus said to them, "They need not go away; you give them something to eat." They replied, "We have nothing here but five loaves and two fish." And he said, "Bring them here to me." Then he ordered the crowds to sit down on the grass. Taking the five loaves and the two fish, he looked up to heaven, and blessed and broke the loaves, and gave them to the disciples, and the disciples gave them to the crowds. And all ate and were filled; and they took up what was left over of the broken pieces, twelve baskets full. And those who ate were about five thousand men, besides women and children.

- When you help me, Lord, it is not by magic, or rabbits-out-of-a-hat. It is by showing me what riches I already possess, and telling me to share them.
- "Give them something to eat yourselves," you said. Teach me to trust my own resources, and use them for others.

Tuesday 5th August   Matthew 12:22–33

Jesus made the disciples get into the boat and go on ahead to the other side, while he dismissed the crowds. And after he had dismissed the crowds, he went up the mountain by himself to pray. When evening came, he was there alone, but by this time the boat, battered by the waves, was far from the land, for the wind was against them. And early in the morning he came walking toward them on the sea. But when the disciples saw him walking on the sea, they were terrified, saying, "It is a ghost!" And they cried out in fear. But immediately Jesus spoke to them and said, "Take heart, it is I; do not be afraid." Peter answered him, "Lord, if it is you, command me to come to you on the water." He said, "Come." So Peter got out of the boat, started walking on the water, and came toward Jesus. But when he noticed the strong wind, he became frightened, and beginning to sink, he cried out, "Lord, save me!" Jesus immediately reached out his hand and caught him, saying to him, "You of little faith, why did you doubt?" When they got into the boat, the wind ceased. And those in the boat worshiped him, saying, "Truly you are the Son of God."

- I'm fascinated by that first step of Peter as he climbed over the side of the boat. He was looking at Jesus, not at the water. His mind was charged with Jesus' invitation: "Come."
- So often the way out of depression, fear or anxiety is not a thought or a consideration, but a physical step. I take a risk, and find myself strong enough to walk forward, keeping my eyes on the Lord.

Wednesday 6th August,
Transfiguration of the Lord   Matthew 17:1–9

Six days later, Jesus took with him Peter and James and his brother John and led them up a high mountain, by themselves. And he was transfigured before them, and his face shone like the sun, and his clothes became dazzling white. Suddenly there appeared to them Moses and Elijah, talking with him. Then Peter said to Jesus, 'Lord, it is good for us to be here; if you wish, I will make three dwellings here, one for you, one for Moses, and one for Elijah.' While he was still speaking, suddenly a bright cloud overshadowed them, and from the cloud a voice said, 'This is my Son, the Beloved; with him I am well pleased; listen to him!' When the disciples heard this, they fell to the ground and were overcome by fear. But Jesus came and touched them, saying, 'Get up and do not be afraid.' And when they looked up, they saw no one except Jesus himself alone. As they were coming down the mountain, Jesus ordered them, 'Tell no one about the vision until after the Son of Man has been raised from the dead.'

- Mount Tabor remains a holy place today. This is a theophany, God showing himself.
- Let me linger in memory on moments like this, when I was lifted into intimacy with God, and felt the rapture that goes with intimacy.

Thursday 7th August   Matthew 16:13–20

Now when Jesus came into the district of Caesarea Philippi, he asked his disciples, "Who do people say that the Son of Man is?" And they said, "Some say John the Baptist, but others Elijah, and still others Jeremiah or one of the prophets." He said to them, "But who do you say that I am?" Simon Peter answered, "You are the Messiah, the Son of the living God." And Jesus answered him, "Blessed are you, Simon son of Jonah! For flesh and blood has not revealed this to you, but my Father in heaven. And I tell you, you are Peter, and on this rock I will build my church, and the gates of Hades will not prevail against it. I will give you the keys of the kingdom of heaven, and whatever you bind on earth will be bound in heaven, and whatever you loose on earth will be loosed in heaven." Then he sternly ordered the disciples not to tell anyone that he was the Messiah.

- "But who do you say that I am?" There may have been a long pause after this second question. Imagine what was going through their minds as the apostles heard the words Peter then blurted out.
- Suddenly they began to realize that Jesus was preparing them for a time when he was no longer walking with them.
- Do I believe that Jesus has a special role for me too, as he did for Peter?

Friday 8th August   Matthew 16:24–28

Then Jesus told his disciples, "If any want to become my followers, let them deny themselves and take up their cross and follow me. For those who want to save their life will lose it, and those who lose their life for my sake will find it. For what will it profit them if they gain the whole world but forfeit their life? Or what will they give in return for their life? "For the Son of Man is to come with his angels in the glory of his Father, and then he will repay everyone for what has been done. Truly I tell you, there are some standing here who will not taste death before they see the Son of Man coming in his kingdom."

- Yes, I need this reminder, Lord. You are not leading us out to a picnic in the country, or to a concert of uplifting Gregorian chant, or to a life of guaranteed prosperity.

- I want to find my life, to make something of it beyond getting and spending. For that I need a smidgeon of your fortitude.

Saturday 9th August   Matthew 17:14–20

When they came to the crowd, a man came to Jesus, knelt before him, and said, "Lord, have mercy on my son, for he is an epileptic and he suffers terribly; he often falls into the fire and often into the water. And I brought him to your disciples, but they could not cure him." Jesus answered, "You faithless and perverse generation, how much longer must I be with you? How much longer must I put up with you? Bring him here to me." And Jesus rebuked the demon, and it came out of him, and the boy was cured instantly. Then the disciples came to Jesus privately and said, "Why could we not cast it out?" He said to them, "Because of your little faith. For truly I tell you, if you have faith the size of a mustard seed, you will say to this mountain, 'Move from here to there,' and it will move; and nothing will be impossible for you."

- I take my place in this drama, wondering how it will end. Am I the distraught, despairing, beseeching father? Or the suffering epileptic son? Or the helpless disciples? Or one of the crowd, hoping against hope to see suffering relieved?
- I watch you, Lord, and ask that I may one day have the sort of mountain-moving faith you speak of.

august 10–16

Something to think and pray about each day this week:

Receiving the Gift of Prayer

Children learn prayers at their mother's knee, and for a long time they think of praying as saying prayers that someone else has invented. It is something they do, often with a sense of duty. What has my own experience been in this regard? How did I progress in prayer? Gradually I turned to prayer that did not depend on a formula. I would kneel in the church like the old French peasant quoted by the Curè of Ars: "I look at the good God and the good God looks at me." I came to realize that prayer is something we receive more than something we do. We cannot understand or imagine God. But we can open ourselves to God in silence and wait for his gift.

The Presence of God

The world is charged with the grandeur of God (Gerard Manley Hopkins).

I dwell for a moment on the presence of God
around me, in every part of my body,
and deep within my being.

Freedom

"In these days, God taught me
as a schoolteacher teaches a pupil" (St. Ignatius).

I remind myself that there are things God has to teach me yet,
and ask for the grace to hear them and let them change me.

Consciousness

Help me, Lord, to be more conscious of your presence.
Teach me to recognize your presence in others.
Fill my heart with gratitude for the times your love
has been shown to me through the care of others.

The Word

I read the Word of God slowly, a few times over, and I listen to
what God is saying to me. (Please turn to your scripture on the
following pages. Inspirations points are there should you need
them. When you are ready, return here to continue.)

Conversation

What feelings are rising in me
as I pray and reflect on God's Word?
I imagine Jesus himself sitting or standing beside me,
and open my heart to him.

Conclusion

Glory be to the Father, and to the Son, and to the Holy Spirit,
As it was in the beginning, is now and ever shall be,
World without end. Amen

Sunday 10th August,
Nineteenth Sunday in Ordinary Time   **1 Kings 19:9–13**

Elijah came to a cave, and spent the night there. Then the word of the LORD came to him, saying, "What are you doing here, Elijah?" He answered, "I have been very zealous for the LORD, the God of hosts; for the Israelites have forsaken your covenant, thrown down your altars, and killed your prophets with the sword. I alone am left, and they are seeking my life, to take it away." He said, "Go out and stand on the mountain before the LORD, for the LORD is about to pass by." Now there was a great wind, so strong that it was splitting mountains and breaking rocks in pieces before the LORD, but the LORD was not in the wind; and after the wind an earthquake, but the LORD was not in the earthquake; and after the earthquake a fire, but the LORD was not in the fire; and after the fire a sound of sheer silence. When Elijah heard it, he wrapped his face in his mantle and went out and stood at the entrance of the cave. Then there came a voice to him that said, "What are you doing here, Elijah?"

- "After the fire, a sound of sheer silence." God was not in the great wind, the earthquake or the fire, which were the traditional manifestations of his presence, but in the silence. So he is with us when we pray.
- We must be alert to God's stillness, the absence of language, and the startling question: "What are you doing here?"

Monday 11th August   **Matthew 17:22–27**

As they were gathering in Galilee, Jesus said to them, "The Son of Man is going to be betrayed into human hands, and they will kill him, and on the third day he will be raised." And they were greatly distressed. When they reached Capernaum, the collectors of the temple tax came to Peter and said, "Does your teacher not pay the temple tax?" He said, "Yes, he does." And when he came home, Jesus spoke of it first, asking, "What do you think, Simon? From whom do kings of the earth take toll or tribute? From their children or from others?" When Peter said, "From others." Jesus said to him, "Then the children are free. However, so that we do not give offence to them, go to the lake and cast a hook; take the first fish that comes up; and when you open its mouth, you will find a coin; take that and give it to them for you and me."

- Jesus shows us that he wanted to fulfill his duty as a citizen, as others do. He submits himself to local authority.
- Christian life always has a social and political dimension; a good Christian cannot be a bad citizen. It is faith that affects the way we live out those commitments. That is often a great challenge.
- Do I pursue the common good in my social and political dealings? Or do I avoid involvement in my community? Lord, guide me as I find the way forward.

Tuesday 12th August   **Matthew 18:1–5, 10**

At that time the disciples came to Jesus and asked, "Who is the greatest in the kingdom of heaven?" He called a child, whom he put among them, and said, "Truly I tell you, unless you change and become like children, you will never enter the kingdom of heaven. Whoever becomes humble like this child is the greatest in the kingdom of heaven. Whoever welcomes one such child in my name welcomes me. Take care that you do not despise one of these little ones; for, I tell you, in heaven their angels continually see the face of my Father in heaven.

- "Unless you change and become like children, you will never enter the kingdom of heaven." What is it that Jesus sees in children that adults lack? Is it the implicit trust children show others, their simple acceptance?

- Jesus asks for change, for conversion, for humility, for simplicity. Can I begin today?

Wednesday 13th August   Matthew 18:18–20

Jesus said to the disciples, "Truly I tell you, whatever you bind on earth will be bound in heaven, and whatever you loose on earth will be loosed in heaven. Again, truly I tell you, if two of you agree on earth about anything you ask, it will be done for you by my Father in heaven. For where two or three are gathered in my name, I am there among them."

- Thank you, Lord, for the freedom to gather with others in your name. It is not so in every land. I join in spirit with those isolated Christians in countries where their rights of worship are denied.
- Prayer together with others, even silent prayer, strengthens and lifts me because you are among us in a special way.

Thursday 14th August,
St. Maximilian Kolbe   John 15:16–17

Jesus said to the disciples, "You did not choose me but I chose you. And I appointed you to go and bear fruit, fruit that will last, so that the Father will give you whatever you ask him in my name. I am giving you these commands so that you may love one another."

- When a prisoner escaped from Auschwitz, the Nazis reacted by choosing at random ten others to die as punishment. One of the ten, a married man, was weeping that he would never see his wife and children again. The Franciscan Maximilian Kolbe offered to stand in for him, and then died by lethal injection.

- Lord, you chose Maximilian for heroism, and he inspires me. I feel I am in a different league, but you have some vocation for me, too.

Friday 15th August,
The Assumption of the Blessed Virgin Mary   Luke 1:39–47

In those days Mary set out and went with haste to a Judean town in the hill country, where she entered the house of Zechariah and greeted Elizabeth. When Elizabeth heard Mary's greeting, the child leaped in her womb. And Elizabeth was filled with the Holy Spirit and exclaimed with a loud cry, "Blessed are you among women, and blessed is the fruit of your womb. And why has this happened to me, that the mother of my Lord comes to me? For as soon as I heard the sound of your greeting, the child in my womb leaped for joy. And blessed is she who believed that there would be a fulfillment of what was spoken to her by the Lord." And Mary said, "My soul magnifies the Lord, and my spirit rejoices in God my Savior."

- Few Gospel encounters are as full of joy and promise as this one. Let me savor it as I see the scene: young Mary arriving to help her older cousin through pregnancy; and Elizabeth saluting her with unexpected insight, as in the Irish greeting of a pregnant woman: "God bless both of you"; and with a happiness so total that she feels the child in her womb dancing with her.

Saturday 16th August   Matthew 19:13–15

Then little children were being brought to Jesus in order that he might lay his hands on them and pray. The disciples spoke sternly to those who brought them; but Jesus said, "Let the little children come to me, and do not stop them; for it is to such as these that the kingdom of heaven belongs." And he laid his hands on them and went on his way.

- Recent surprising research has shown that women are attracted to men who are fond of children, and can tell who is and who is not fond of children just by looking at their faces. However they did it, mothers saw this quality in Jesus.
- In return Jesus gave children what they needed: attention and stroking. He is unique among ancient religious and philosophical teachers in recognizing children as significant. Can I discover why?

Something to think and pray about each day this week:

The Gaze of Love

In prayer I am brought into the dynamic life of the Trinity through the Holy Spirit, the spirit of Jesus, who cries out from within my soul: "Abba, Father." The spirit of Jesus links me into the Blessed Trinity. When God looks at me, he desires me and is saying: "You are desirable. I made you good. I want you." God sees me as his daughter or son, whom he loves. He says: "You are mine." His gaze says: "I delight in you." Can I accept this gaze of love? Or do I run back into disapproval of myself? His gaze is like sunshine: can I rest in it, bask in it, enabled by the Holy Spirit?

The Presence of God

As I sit here, God is present,
breathing life into me and into everything around me.
For a few moments, I sit silently,
and become aware of God's loving presence.

Freedom

If God were trying to tell me something, would I know?
If God were reassuring me or challenging me, would I notice?
I ask for the grace to be free of my own preoccupations
and open to what God may be saying to me.

Consciousness

How am I really feeling? Light-hearted? Heavy-hearted?
I may be very much at peace, happy to be here.
Equally, I may be frustrated, worried or angry.
I acknowledge how I really am. It is the real me that the Lord loves.

The Word

I take my time to read the Word of God, slowly, a few times, allowing myself to dwell on anything that strikes me. (Please turn to your scripture on the following pages. Inspiration points are there should you need them. When you are ready, return here to continue.)

Conversation

What is stirring in me as I pray?
Am I consoled, troubled, left cold?
I imagine Jesus himself standing or sitting at my side,
and share my feelings with him.

Conclusion

Glory be to the Father, and to the Son, and to the Holy Spirit,
As it was in the beginning, is now and ever shall be,
World without end. Amen

Sunday 17th August,
Twentieth Sunday in Ordinary Time   Matthew 15:21–28

Jesus left that place and went away to the district of Tyre and Sidon. Just then a Canaanite woman from that region came out and started shouting, "Have mercy on me, Lord, Son of David; my daughter is tormented by a demon." But he did not answer her at all. And his disciples came and urged him, saying, "Send her away, for she keeps shouting after us." He answered, "I was sent only to the lost sheep of the house of Israel." But she came and knelt before him, saying, "Lord, help me." He answered, "It is not fair to take the children's food and throw it to the dogs." She said, "Yes, Lord, yet even the dogs eat the crumbs that fall from their masters' table." Then Jesus answered her, "Woman, great is your faith! Let it be done for you as you wish." And her daughter was healed instantly.

- "He did not answer her at all." It would have been easy for this woman to give up in bitterness. She carried a triple handicap: a woman alone in a man's world; a gentile and therefore unclean; and with an afflicted daughter. But in spite of Jesus' silence she trusts him, keeps at him, and bests him in debate.
- Lord, may I never be discouraged by your silence.

Monday 18th August   Matthew 19:16–22

Then someone came to Jesus and said, "Teacher, what good deed must I do to have eternal life?" And he said to him, "Why do you ask me about what is good? There is only one who is good. If you wish to enter into life, keep the commandments." He said to him, "Which ones?" And Jesus said, "You shall not murder; You shall not commit adultery; You shall not steal; You shall not bear false witness; Honor your father and mother; also, You shall love your neighbor as yourself." The young man said to him, "I have kept all these; what do I still lack?" Jesus said to him, "If you wish to be perfect, go, sell your possessions, and give the money to the poor, and you will have treasure in heaven; then come, follow me." When the young man heard this word, he went away grieving, for he had many possessions.

- Jesus, you pick up two false notes in the approach of this good young man. There seems to be a fawning, flattering note in his use of "good"; and his question focuses on "doing good deeds."
- You bring him back to the central issue, Lord: not so much to pile up good deeds, as to be a loving person, ready to express that love in any sacrifices God may ask of us.

Tuesday 19th August   Matthew 19:23–26

Then Jesus said to his disciples, "Truly I tell you, it will be hard for a rich person to enter the kingdom of heaven. Again I tell you, it is easier for a camel to go through the eye of a needle than for someone who is rich to enter the kingdom of God." When the disciples heard this, they were greatly astounded and said, "Then who can be saved?" But Jesus looked at them and said, "For mortals it is impossible, but for God all things are possible."

- It is not so much the size of my bank balance that you are warning me against, Lord; it is my attachment to riches. I remember Dr Johnson's comment as he was shown over a luxuriously appointed castle: "These are the things that make it difficult to die."
- What would I find hard to leave? People or things?

Wednesday 20th August   Psalm 22(23):1–4

The LORD is my shepherd, I shall not want. He makes me lie down in green pastures, he leads me beside still waters, he restores my soul. He leads me in right paths for his name's sake.

Even though I walk through the darkest valley, I fear no evil; for you are with me; your rod and your staff—they comfort me.

- These holy words have been made even more holy by their constant repetition over thousands of years. Can I sit with them, mull over them, and allow their freshness to touch me?

Thursday 21st August   **Matthew 22:1–10**

Once more Jesus spoke to them in parables, saying: "The kingdom of heaven may be compared to a king who gave a wedding banquet for his son. He sent his slaves to call those who had been invited to the wedding banquet, but they would not come. Again he sent other slaves, saying, 'Tell those who have been invited: Look, I have prepared my dinner, my oxen and my fat calves have been slaughtered, and everything is ready; come to the wedding banquet.' But they made light of it and went away, one to his farm, another to his business, while the rest seized his slaves, maltreated them, and killed them. The king was enraged. He sent his troops, destroyed those murderers, and burned their city. Then he said to his slaves, 'The wedding is ready. Go therefore into the main streets, and invite everyone you find to the wedding banquet.' Those slaves went out into the streets and gathered all whom they found, both good and bad; so the wedding hall was filled with guests.

- The image of the wondrous banquet was familiar to Jesus' listeners, a sign of the coming of the Messiah, and of salvation.
- "Invite everyone you find to the wedding banquet." While the Israelites were the first invitees, Jesus' message is that all are invited, including those on the margins of society.
- Do I treasure the grace of my invitation? How am I answering?

Friday 22nd August **Matthew 22:34–40**

When the Pharisees heard that Jesus had silenced the Sadducees, they gathered together, and one of them, a lawyer, asked him a question to test him. "Teacher, which commandment in the law is the greatest?" He said to him, "'You shall love the Lord your God with all your heart, and with all your soul, and with all your mind.' This is the greatest and first commandment. And a second is like it: 'You shall love your neighbor as yourself.' On these two commandments hang all the law and the prophets."

- Love my neighbors? Including the gossips, the thieves, the perverts? How can I love them like myself?
- Such love comes only if I love God and see myself and my fellow-humans as God does—made in his likeness, creatures whose infinite possibilities are realized only when they know they are loved.

Saturday 23rd August **Matthew 23:1–7**

Then Jesus said to the crowds and to his disciples, "The scribes and the Pharisees sit on Moses' seat; therefore, do whatever they teach you and follow it; but do not do as they do, for they do not practice what they teach. They tie up heavy burdens, hard to bear, and lay them on the shoulders of others; but they themselves are unwilling to lift a finger to move them. They do all their deeds to be seen by others; for they make their phylacteries broad and their fringes long. They love to have the place of honor at banquets and the best seats in the synagogues, and to be greeted with respect in the marketplaces, and to have people call them rabbi."

- "They tie up heavy burdens." Those who have abandoned the practice of religion often talk as though a burden has been lifted from them. They felt it as a weight, a worrying set of obligations.

Jesus is reproaching the Pharisees for making our relationship with God into such a burden, and for parading their religion as a kind of status symbol.

- Lord, may I know you as my joy, my comfort and relief, my secret treasure. This space is sacred. I am happy here.

august 24–30

Something to think and pray about each day this week:

Made for God

I cannot experience God directly. My mind cannot cope with God's infinity. But in various ways I experience the effect of God in my life; for instance, in moments of communion with others, in the joy of being in love, or with real friends, or in company that transports me beyond myself. Or I sense God's touch when I feel empty, incompetent, a failure, unable to make of myself what I want to be. Or when I feel unsettled and long for quiet and peace. In each of these situations, I may feel my incompleteness and be moved by a force beyond myself. St. Augustine said it exactly: "You have made us for yourself, O Lord, and our hearts are restless till they rest in you."

The Presence of God
As I sit here with my book, God is here.
Around me, in my sensations, in my thoughts and deep
within me.
I pause for a moment, and become aware
of God's life-giving presence.

Freedom
I need to close out the noise, to rise above the noise;
The noise that interrupts, that separates,
The noise that isolates.
I need to listen to God again.

Consciousness
Knowing that God loves me unconditionally,
I can afford to be honest about how I am.
How has the last day been, and how do I feel now?
I share my feelings openly with the Lord.

The Word
God speaks to each one of us individually. I need to listen to
what he is saying to me. (Please turn to your scripture on the
following pages. Inspiration points are there should you need
them. When you are ready, return here to continue.)

Conversation
Do I notice myself reacting as I pray with the Word of God?
Do I feel challenged, comforted, angry?
Imagining Jesus sitting or standing by me,
I speak out my feelings, as one trusted friend to another.

Conclusion
Glory be to the Father, and to the Son, and to the Holy Spirit,
As it was in the beginning, is now and ever shall be,
World without end. Amen

Sunday 24th August,
Twenty-first Sunday in Ordinary Time   Matthew 16:13–20

Now when Jesus came into the district of Caesarea Philippi, he asked his disciples, "Who do people say that the Son of Man is?" And they said, "Some say John the Baptist, but others Elijah, and still others Jeremiah or one of the prophets." He said to them, "But who do you say that I am?" Simon Peter answered, "You are the Messiah, the Son of the living God." And Jesus answered him, "Blessed are you, Simon son of Jonah! For flesh and blood has not revealed this to you, but my Father in heaven. And I tell you, you are Peter, and on this rock I will build my church, and the gates of Hades will not prevail against it. I will give you the keys of the kingdom of heaven, and whatever you bind on earth will be bound in heaven, and whatever you loose on earth will be loosed in heaven." Then he sternly ordered the disciples not to tell anyone that he was the Messiah."

- Am I open to Jesus' question "Who do you say that I am?" This text has been used so often for apologetic purposes that it is hard to recapture the drama, the uncertain silence, that must have followed Jesus' question.
- He wondered what they would say, and wonders what I say to the same question. Peter confirmed Jesus' growing sense of his vocation and role.
- Lord, I linger with this question: what are you to me?

Monday 25th August   2 Thessalonians 1:1–5, 11–12

From Paul, Silvanus, and Timothy, to the church of the Thessalonians in God our Father and the Lord Jesus Christ: Grace to you and peace from God our Father and the Lord Jesus Christ. We must always give thanks to God for you, brothers and sisters, as is right, because your faith is growing abundantly, and the love of every one of you for one another is increasing. Therefore we ourselves boast of you among the churches of God for your steadfastness and faith during all your persecutions and the afflictions that you are enduring. This is evidence of the righteous judgment of God, and is intended to make you worthy of the kingdom of God, for which you are also suffering. To this end we always pray for you, asking that our God will make you worthy of his call and will fulfill by his power every good resolve and work of faith, so that the name of our Lord Jesus may be glorified in you, and you in him, according to the grace of our God and the Lord Jesus Christ.

- "Grace to you and peace from God our Father and the Lord Jesus Christ." This prayer is echoed in a greeting used in Eucharistic celebrations.
- The letter gives thanks to God for the community's increase in faith and their patient endurance in the face of persecution, for the sake of the kingdom.
- Once received, faith must be worked out in patient endurance.

Tuesday 26th August   Matthew 23:23–26

Jesus said, "Woe to you, scribes and Pharisees, hypocrites! For you tithe mint, dill, and cummin, and have neglected the weightier matters of the law: justice and mercy and faith. It is these you ought to have practiced without neglecting the others. You blind guides! You strain out a gnat but swallow a camel! "Woe to you, scribes and Pharisees, hypocrites! For you clean the outside of the cup and of the plate, but inside they are full of greed and self-indulgence. You blind Pharisee! First clean the inside of the cup, so that the outside also may become clean."

- When the gentle, loving Jesus raises his voice and blazes forth in anger, he makes me sit up and examine myself, look at the inside of the cup, at my concern for justice and mercy and faith, and at my tendency to greed and self-indulgence.

• Lord, help me to see the dirt, and to clean myself on the inside.

Wednesday 27th August   Matthew 23:2–28

Jesus said, "Woe to you, scribes and Pharisees, hypocrites! For you are like whitewashed tombs, which on the outside look beautiful, but inside they are full of the bones of the dead and of all kinds of filth. So you also on the outside look righteous to others, but inside you are full of hypocrisy and lawlessness."

• Looking good is no trivial matter; it worries a lot of us. Most women say they feel worse about their own looks after reading women's magazines. In the western world, consumers spend billions a year on cosmetics. Boys and girls are spending money to smell and look different before their tenth year.

• Thank you, Lord, for reminding me that looks—including the looks of respectability and righteousness—do not matter. What am I like inside?

Thursday 28th August, St. Augustine   Matthew 23:8–12

Jesus said to the crowds and to his disciples, "But you are not to be called rabbi, for you have one teacher, and you are all students. And call no one your father on earth, for you have one Father—the one in heaven. Nor are you to be called instructors, for you have one instructor, the Messiah. The greatest among you will be your servant. All who exalt themselves will be humbled, and all who humble themselves will be exalted."

• Lord, I have only to see the history of the church to realize how easily these words are forgotten. Churchmen have exalted themselves, looked for titles and exercised leadership by domination rather than service. I need to come back to the memory of you washing your disciples' feet.

- Blessed are those who clean the toilets, put out the garbage, and care for the old and incontinent. We are never as close to God as when we are serving.

Friday 29th August　　　　1 Corinthians 1:17–20

For Christ did not send me to baptize but to proclaim the gospel, and not with eloquent wisdom, so that the cross of Christ might not be emptied of its power. For the message about the cross is foolishness to those who are perishing, but to us who are being saved it is the power of God. For it is written, 'I will destroy the wisdom of the wise, and the discernment of the discerning I will thwart.' Where is the one who is wise? Where is the scribe? Where is the debater of this age? Has not God made foolish the wisdom of the world?

- Paul preached the cross, which to both Jews and non-Jews was sheer foolishness. In the cross there was no political freedom, no eloquence, no wisdom and certainly no respectability.
- Do I choose a Jesus I am comfortable with? Which of God's ways trouble me? "Has not God made foolish the wisdom of the world?"

Saturday 30th August　　　　1 Corinthians 1:26–31

Consider your own call, brothers and sisters: not many of you were wise by human standards, not many were powerful, not many were of noble birth. But God chose what is foolish in the world to shame the wise; God chose what is weak in the world to shame the strong; God chose what is low and despised in the world, things that are not, to reduce to nothing things that are, so that no one might boast in the presence of God. He is the source of your life in Christ Jesus, who became for us wisdom from God, and righteousness and sanctification and redemption, in order that, as it is written, "Let the one who boasts, boast in the Lord."

- Paul tells me to consider my own call. It is central to our faith that each of us is called; we do not initiate our own movement. God calls us into being, and calls us into his presence.
- Do I accept the invitation, or do I resist?

Something to think and pray about each day this week:

The Inner Room

When I come before God in prayer, I ask: Who is this God? He is the mystery supporting all existence, vast and greater than the universe, the source of all. At the same time this Transcendent One is also the most Intimate One, in touch with every atom and molecule, with every energy, thought and desire: so vast and so intimate. No image is adequate to represent God. The name that Moses brought down from Mount Sinai was I AM. This is the God who is our personal God, longing to reveal himself to me in my existence, for he is there. God is calling me into his inner room, and inviting himself into my inner room.

The Presence of God

I pause for a moment, aware that God is here.
I think of how everything around me,
the air I breathe, my whole body,
is tingling with the presence of God.

Freedom

I will ask God's help,
to be free from my own preoccupations,
to be open to God in this time of prayer,
to come to love and serve him more.

Consciousness

In the presence of my loving Creator,
I look honestly at my feelings over the last day,
the highs, the lows and the level ground.
Can I see where the Lord has been present?

The Word

I read the Word of God slowly, a few times over, and I listen to
what God is saying to me. (Please turn to your scripture on the
following pages. Inspiration points are there should you need
them. When you are ready, return here to continue.)

Conversation

Remembering that I am still in God's presence,
I imagine Jesus himself standing or sitting beside me,
and say whatever is on my mind, whatever is in my heart,
speaking as one friend to another.

Conclusion

Glory be to the Father, and to the Son, and to the Holy Spirit,
As it was in the beginning, is now and ever shall be,
World without end. Amen

Sunday 31st August, Twenty-second
Sunday in Ordinary Time   Matthew 16:21–27

From that time on, Jesus began to show his disciples that he must go to Jerusalem and undergo great suffering at the hands of the elders and chief priests and scribes, and be killed, and on the third day be raised. And Peter took him aside and began to rebuke him, saying, "God forbid it, Lord! This must never happen to you." But he turned and said to Peter, "Get behind me, Satan! You are a stumbling block to me; for you are setting your mind not on divine things but on human things." Then Jesus told his disciples, "If any want to become my followers, let them deny themselves and take up their cross and follow me. For those who want to save their life will lose it, and those who lose their life for my sake will find it. For what will it profit them if they gain the whole world but forfeit their life? Or what will they give in return for their life? For the Son of Man is to come with his angels in the glory of his Father, and then he will repay everyone for what has been done."

- Peter has just been congratulated as the rock on which Jesus will build his church. He is comfortable in a theology of grace and glory. Suddenly that rock looks sandy and unsafe.
- Jesus calls Peter abruptly out of his comfort zone into the real world where suffering must be faced.
- Lord, I love to see you in beautiful churches, with music and warm light. Let me recognize you too in pain, loss and insecurity.

Monday 1st September   Luke 4:16–21

When he came to Nazareth, where he had been brought up, he went to the synagogue on the sabbath day, as was his custom. He stood up to read, and the scroll of the prophet Isaiah was given to him. He unrolled the scroll and found the place where it was written: "The Spirit of the Lord is upon me, because he has anointed me to bring good news to the poor. He has sent me to proclaim release to the captives and recovery of sight to the blind, to let the oppressed go free, to proclaim the year of the Lord's favor." And he rolled up the scroll, gave it back to the attendant, and sat down. The eyes of all in the synagogue were fixed on him. Then he began to say to them, "Today this scripture has been fulfilled in your hearing."

- The throwaway details in this passage tell us much about the ordinary life of Jesus. It was his custom to go to the synagogue on the sabbath; though he took issue with details of the Law proclaimed there, he chose to join with his community in the worship of God.
- At the synagogue he was chosen to read to the assembly. The eyes of all in the assembly were fixed on him. It is a moment of grace and promise, as he brings the good news to his own people.
- Lord, this is a scene I would love to have witnessed. Let me unroll it slowly.

Tuesday 2nd September   Luke 4:31–37

He went down to Capernaum, a city in Galilee, and was teaching them on the sabbath. They were astounded at his teaching, because he spoke with authority. In the synagogue there was a man who had the spirit of an unclean demon, and he cried out with a loud voice, "Let us alone! What have you to do with us, Jesus of Nazareth? Have you come to destroy us? I know who you are, the Holy One of God." But Jesus rebuked him, saying, "Be silent, and come out of him!" When the demon had thrown him down before them, he came out of him without having done him any harm. They were all amazed and kept saying to one another, "What kind of utterance is this? For with authority and power he commands the unclean spirits, and out they come!" And a report about him began to reach every place in the region.

- Because of his authority as the "Holy One of God," all evil is ultimately powerless before Jesus. Can I bring the evil that I confront in my life—and in our world—before him?
- How do I feel when I consider these things? Confidence in God? Doubt and fear? Perhaps I should talk this over with Jesus.

Wednesday 3rd September   Luke 4:38–39

After leaving the synagogue Jesus entered Simon's house. Now Simon's mother-in-law was suffering from a high fever, and they asked him about her. Then he stood over her and rebuked the fever, and it left her. Immediately she got up and began to serve them.

- You could see Jesus' life as a struggle against sickness and death. He was a healer, and reached out to cure the pains that disabled people. He wanted them to forget about their bodies and be fit to serve, like Simon Peter's mother-in-law; once her temperature dropped, she got up and prepared food.

Thursday 4th September   Luke 5:4–11

When Jesus had finished speaking, he said to Simon, "Put out into the deep water and let down your nets for a catch." Simon answered, "Master, we have worked all night long but have caught nothing. Yet if you say so, I will let down the nets." When they had done this, they caught so many fish that their nets were beginning to break. So they signaled their partners in the other boat to come and help them. And they came and filled both boats, so that they began to sink. But when Simon Peter saw it, he fell down at Jesus' knees, saying, "Go away from me, Lord, for I am a sinful man!" For he and all who were with him were amazed at the catch of fish that they had taken; and so also were James and John, sons of Zebedee, who were partners with Simon. Then Jesus said to Simon, "Do not be afraid; from now on you will be catching people." When they had brought their boats to shore, they left everything and followed him.

- Lord, I linger on the thought of Simon and the impact you had on him. He was weary after a night's fishing, and might have said: "What do you know about catching fish? You are a carpenter."
- But he responded to that authority in you and resumed fishing. When he hit the shoal of fish, his first reaction is: Go away, Lord, you are out of my league. His second reaction is to leave his boat and livelihood and follow you. It was the start of an extraordinary journey.
- Lord, you are part of my journey. Keep me in your league.

Friday 5th September   Luke 5:33–39

Then the Pharisees and the scribes said to Jesus, "John's disciples, like the disciples of the Pharisees, frequently fast and pray, but your disciples eat and drink." Jesus said to them, "You cannot make wedding guests fast while the bridegroom is with them, can you? The days will come when the bridegroom will be taken away from them, and then they will fast in those days." He also told them a parable: "No one tears a piece from a new garment and sews it on an old garment; otherwise the new will be torn, and the piece from the new will not match the old. And no one puts new wine into old wineskins; otherwise the new wine will burst the skins and will be spilled, and the skins will be destroyed. But new wine must be put into fresh wineskins. And no one after drinking old wine desires new wine, but says, 'The old is good.'"

- Jesus is the bridegroom and this is a time of celebration and joy; this is the time of salvation; God is with his people—Rejoice!
- Am I like the old wineskin, dry and cracked and unprepared for the new wine? Can I change?

Saturday 6th September   Luke 6:1–5

One sabbath while Jesus was going through the grainfields, his disciples plucked some heads of grain, rubbed them in their hands, and ate them. But some of the Pharisees said, "Why are you doing what is not lawful on the sabbath?" Jesus answered, "Have you not read what David did when he and his companions were hungry? He entered the house of God and took and ate the bread of the Presence, which it is not lawful for any but the priests to eat, and gave some to his companions?" Then he said to them, "The Son of Man is lord of the sabbath."

- Lord, what a breath of fresh air you brought to your friends! The Pharisees did not blame them for plucking the ears of corn—the law allowed that to passers-by as long as they did not use a sickle— but for doing that on the sabbath, when the law forbade Jews to winnow or prepare food.
- You pointed to the freedom of spirit in great king David, and encouraged all of us to share it.

Something to think and pray about each day this week:

Looking with love

Calvin says somewhere that each of us is an actor on a stage and God is the audience. The audience is not there to judge the actors, but to enjoy them. This image suggests that God might actually enjoy us, not in any simple sense, of course, but as you enjoy the being of a child even when he is in every way a thorn in your heart. It is another way of suggesting that God looks on us with love: the Prodigal Son's father, scanning the horizon from his window, sees a forlorn, debauched figure slouching towards home, and runs out to meet him, speechless with joy.

The Presence of God

For a few moments, I think of God's veiled presence in things:
in the elements, giving them existence;
in plants, giving them life; in animals, giving them sensation;
and finally, in me, giving me all this and more,
making me a temple, a dwelling-place of the Spirit.

Freedom

God is not foreign to my freedom.
Instead the Spirit breathes life into my most intimate desires,
gently nudging me towards all that is good.
I ask for the grace to let myself be enfolded by the Spirit.

Consciousness

Knowing that God loves me unconditionally,
I look honestly over the last day, its events and my feelings.
Do I have something to be grateful for? Then I give thanks.
Is there something I am sorry for? Then I ask forgiveness.

The Word

I take my time to read the Word of God, slowly, a few times, allowing myself to dwell on anything that strikes me. (Please turn to your scripture on the following pages. Inspiration points are there should you need them. When you are ready, return here to continue.)

Conversation

How has God's Word moved me? Has it left me cold?
Has it consoled me or moved me to act in a new way?
I imagine Jesus standing or sitting beside me,
I turn and share my feelings with him.

Conclusion

Glory be to the Father, and to the Son, and to the Holy Spirit,
As it was in the beginning, is now and ever shall be,
World without end. Amen

Sunday 7th September, Twenty-third
Sunday in Ordinary Time   Matthew 18:15–20

J esus said, "If another member of the church sins against you, go and point out the fault when the two of you are alone. If the member listens to you, you have regained that one. But if you are not listened to, take one or two others along with you, so that every word may be confirmed by the evidence of two or three witnesses. If the member refuses to listen to them, tell it to the church; and if the offender refuses to listen even to the church, let such a one be to you as a Gentile and a tax collector. Truly I tell you, whatever you bind on earth will be bound in heaven, and whatever you loose on earth will be loosed in heaven. Again, truly I tell you, if two of you agree on earth about anything you ask, it will be done for you by my Father in heaven. For where two or three are gathered in my name, I am there among them.

- Lord, this is your way of stopping tell-tales in the church. If I am upset about somebody, then the first person for me to approach is that person, with respect and kindness, no matter who it is.
- Do I run instead to the "authorities," expecting "head office" to come down on my side? Do I write letters of complaint without having voiced my concern to the one I seek to denounce? That is the opposite of Christian behavior.
- Whatever I do when I am upset, Lord, let me do it in charity.

Monday 8th September, Birthday of
the Blessed Virgin Mary   Matthew 1:18–23

N ow the birth of Jesus the Messiah took place in this way. When his mother Mary had been engaged to Joseph, but before they lived together, she was found to be with child from the Holy Spirit. Her husband Joseph, being a righteous man and unwilling to expose her to public disgrace, planned to dismiss her quietly. But just when he had resolved to do this, an angel of the Lord appeared to him in a dream and said, "Joseph, son of David, do not be afraid to take Mary as your wife, for the child conceived in her is from the Holy Spirit. She will bear a son, and you are to name him Jesus, for he will save his people from their sins." All this took place to fulfill what had been spoken by the Lord through the prophet: "Look, the virgin shall conceive and bear a son, and they shall name him Emmanuel," which means, "God is with us."

- What do we know about Joseph? That he loved Mary so much that he suppressed his doubts about her chastity and allowed himself to be regarded as the father of her child, knowing that he wasn't; that he brought up that child as his own; that he taught him his trade; that he loved him; and that Jesus' virile health as an adult is proof of good parenting by his foster-father. Joseph is the obvious patron of adoptive fathers.
- Mary's life is tipped upside down, then Joseph's, then . . .

Tuesday 9th September   Luke 6:12–16

Now during those days he went out to the mountain to pray; and he spent the night in prayer to God. And when day came, he called his disciples and chose twelve of them, whom he also named apostles: Simon, whom he named Peter, and his brother Andrew, and James, and John, and Philip, and Bartholomew, and Matthew, and Thomas, and James son of Alphaeus, and Simon, who was called the Zealot, and Judas son of James, and Judas Iscariot, who became a traitor.

- Jesus is looking beyond the present listeners to a far-off future, when his teaching will change the world. To do this, he called, and he chose twelve men, ordinary men, without influence or special training. What equipped them was the knowledge and love of Jesus.

- Lord, may that be my armament too.

Wednesday 10th September   Luke 6:20–23a

Then Jesus looked up at his disciples and said: "Blessed are you who are poor, for yours is the kingdom of God. Blessed are you who are hungry now, for you will be filled. Blessed are you who weep now, for you will laugh. Blessed are you when people hate you, and when they exclude you, revile you, and defame you on account of the Son of Man. Rejoice in that day and leap for joy, for surely your reward is great in heaven."

- These words are not addressed to people who are waltzing through life without a care. Jesus is speaking to those who know rejection and sorrow.
- His words seem to turn our understanding of "the good life" on its head and give a new definition of happiness. He is painting the inner world of his own heart.

Thursday 11th September   Luke 6:27–31

Jesus said to his disciples, "But I say to you that listen, Love your enemies, do good to those who hate you, bless those who curse you, pray for those who abuse you. If anyone strikes you on the cheek, offer the other also; and from anyone who takes away your coat do not withhold even your shirt. Give to everyone who begs from you; and if anyone takes away your goods, do not ask for them again. Do to others as you would have them do to you.

- Jesus takes us beyond the Beatitudes to set another standard. It is not enough to respond to what happens to us; we must also act—through love, prayer, giving.

- "Do to others as you would have them do to you," has passed into common speech. Can I look at these words again? Can I ask the Lord to help me love my enemies?

Friday 12th September   Luke 6:39–42

He also told them a parable: "Can a blind person guide a blind person? Will not both fall into a pit? A disciple is not above the teacher, but everyone who is fully qualified will be like the teacher. Why do you see the speck in your neighbor's eye, but do not notice the log in your own eye? Or how can you say to your neighbor, 'Friend, let me take out the speck in your eye,' when you yourself do not see the log in your own eye? You hypocrite, first take the log out of your own eye, and then you will see clearly to take the speck out of your neighbor's eye."

- There is humor in Jesus' comment on specks and logs, pricking the pomposity of those who judge rashly. It is another of his "one-liners" that has passed into common speech.
- And it is in speech that we usually rush to judgment. To those who do, Jesus applies the strong judgment: Hypocrite!
- Lord, forgive me for the times when my words are quick and my tongue is sharp.

Saturday 13th September   Luke 6:43–49

Jesus said to the disciples, "Why do you call me 'Lord, Lord,' and do not do what I tell you? I will show you what someone is like who comes to me, hears my words, and acts on them. That one is like a man building a house, who dug deeply and laid the foundation on rock; when a flood arose, the river burst against that house but could not shake it, because it had been well built. But the one who hears and does not act is like a man who built a house on the ground without a foundation. When the river burst against it, immediately it fell, and great was the ruin of that house."

- Even as I write "Lord," I have misgivings. Words come so easily. What you love to see, Lord, is the evidence of love in my life.
- May I go to you, hear your words, and act on them.

Something to think and pray about each day this week:

The Eyes of Faith

Jesus said: "Take up your cross." It is not something you go looking for in faraway places. Sooner or later the Lord hands us a cross, and our job is to recognize it. For each of us there are events that made a difference. No two of us experience the same joyful or sorrowful mysteries. Maybe it was a meeting with a friend, a lover or an enemy. Maybe it was a sickness, or a triumph. We try to see our life through the eyes of faith, with a confidence that God in his Providence can draw good out of the most awful and unwelcome happenings as well as the moments of joy. It is not that we have all the answers, but we have enough to sustain our faith and love. "Faith is the fruit of love, that is, of darkness." It is based on God's faithfulness.

The Presence of God

Jesus waits silent and unseen to come into my heart.
I will respond to His call.
He comes with His infinite power and love
May I be filled with joy in His presence.

Freedom

Everything has the potential to draw forth from me a fuller
love and life.
Yet my desires are often fixed, caught, on illusions of fulfillment.
I ask that God, through my freedom, may orchestrate
my desires in a vibrant loving melody rich in harmony.

Consciousness

How do I find myself today?
Where am I with God? With others?
Do I have something to be grateful for? Then I give thanks.
Is there something I am sorry for? Then I ask forgiveness.

The Word

God speaks to each one of us individually. I need to listen to
what he is saying to me. (Please turn to your scripture on the
following pages. Inspiration points are there should you need
them. When you are ready, return here to continue.)

Conversation

What feelings are rising in me
as I pray and reflect on God's Word?
I imagine Jesus himself sitting or standing beside me,
and open my heart to him.

Conclusion

Glory be to the Father, and to the Son, and to the Holy Spirit,
As it was in the beginning, is now and ever shall be,
World without end. Amen

Sunday 14th September, Triumph of the Holy Cross   John 3:13–17

Jesus said, "And just as Moses lifted up the serpent in the wilderness, so must the Son of Man be lifted up, that whoever believes in him may have eternal life. For God so loved the world that he gave his only Son, so that everyone who believes in him may not perish but may have eternal life. Indeed, God did not send the Son into the world to condemn the world, but in order that the world might be saved through him."

- Jesus says these words to Nicodemus, a Pharisee who came to him at night, searching for answers.
- Jesus' message is not of condemnation, but of God's love and a promise of eternal life. What does all of this mean to me?

Monday 15th September, Our Lady of Sorrows   Luke 2:33–35

And the child's father and mother were amazed at what was being said about him. Then Simeon blessed them and said to his mother Mary, "This child is destined for the falling and the rising of many in Israel, and to be a sign that will be opposed so that the inner thoughts of many will be revealed—and a sword will pierce your own soul too."

- Mary and Joseph were amazed at Simeon's words. They did not just nod their heads and say, "That fits what we expected." Like all mothers, Mary knew that her precious baby was unique.
- But Mary was only gradually discovering what that might mean, in his life and in hers. Let us sit quietly with this scene.

Tuesday 16th September   Luke 7:11–17

Soon afterwards he went to a town called Nain, and his disciples and a large crowd went with him. As he approached the gate of the town, a man who had died was being carried out. He was his mother's only son, and she was a widow; and with her was a large crowd from the town. When the Lord saw her, he had compassion for her and said to her, "Do not weep." Then he came forward and touched the bier, and the bearers stood still. And he said, "Young man, I say to you, rise!" The dead man sat up and began to speak, and Jesus gave him to his mother. Fear seized all of them; and they glorified God, saying, "A great prophet has risen among us!" and "God has looked favorably on his people!" This word about him spread throughout Judea and all the surrounding country.

- This is a scene to relish slowly. Two crowds meet at the gate of the town: the funeral procession, and a large crowd gathered round Jesus. But he is not centered on himself. Instead he is moved with compassion for the forlorn widow.
- That movement of Jesus' heart is what catches me. I know that is during bad moments that I can count on him.

Wednesday 17th September, St. Robert Bellarmine
Matthew 5:17–19

Jesus said, "Do not think that I have come to abolish the law or the prophets; I have come not to abolish but to fulfill. For truly I tell you, until heaven and earth pass away, not one letter, not one stroke of a letter, will pass from the law until all is accomplished. Therefore, whoever breaks one of the least of these commandments, and teaches others to do the same, will be called least in the kingdom of heaven; but whoever does them and teaches them will be called great in the kingdom of heaven."

- Strong words from Jesus about the law. He didn't come to make life softer but deeper.

- What is my own relationship with law and tradition? Am I naturally submissive or automatically rebellious?
- How is Jesus calling me to go deeper?

Thursday 18th September   1 Corinthians 15:1–8

Now I should remind you, brothers and sisters, of the good news that I proclaimed to you, which you in turn received, in which also you stand, through which also you are being saved, if you hold firmly to the message that I proclaimed to you—unless you have come to believe in vain. For I handed on to you as of first importance what I in turn had received: that Christ died for our sins in accordance with the scriptures, and that he was buried, and that he was raised on the third day in accordance with the scriptures, and that he appeared to Cephas, then to the twelve. Then he appeared to more than five hundred brothers and sisters at one time, most of whom are still alive, though some have died. Then he appeared to James, then to all the apostles. Last of all, as to someone untimely born, he appeared also to me.

- Here Paul records one of the earliest testimonies of Christian faith. This is what he himself has received, and passes on; this is firm ground, reaching back to Jesus' life on earth.
- How do I pass on the faith tradition I have received?

Friday 19th September   Luke 8:1–3

Soon afterwards he went on through cities and villages, proclaiming and bringing the good news of the kingdom of God. The twelve were with him, as well as some women who had been cured of evil spirits and infirmities: Mary, called Magdalene, from whom seven demons had gone out, and Joanna, the wife of Herod's steward Chuza, and Susanna, and many others, who provided for them out of their resources.

- This was a remarkable mix of women. Mary Magdalene moved from a dark and troubled past to stand by the cross of Jesus, and witness his resurrection. She is here rubbing shoulders with Joanna whose husband was Herod's financial controller: two women from opposite ends of society.
- What brings these women into harmonious company is the love of Jesus, who likened the kingdom to a great tree in which all sorts of birds build their nests.

Saturday 20th September   Luke 8:4–8

When a great crowd gathered and people from town after town came to him, Jesus said in a parable: "A sower went out to sow his seed; and as he sowed, some fell on the path and was trampled on, and the birds of the air ate it up. Some fell on the rock; and as it grew up, it withered for lack of moisture. Some fell among thorns, and the thorns grew with it and choked it. Some fell into good soil, and when it grew, it produced a hundredfold." As he said this, he called out, "Let anyone with ears to hear listen!"

- The hard path represents the shut mind, that blocks out the word of God. The rocky ground, with a thin layer of soil, is the shallow mind that does not think through the word of God or its consequences, and forgets it when under pressure. The thorny ground means those whose lives are so busy that the things of God get crowded out.
- Lord, I will try to listen with a good heart and produce results.

september 21–27

Something to think and pray about each day this week:

Seeing the Light

At this time of the equinox, in the Northern hemisphere people see the daylight shortening, or while those below the equator see it lengthening. Light is more than just a condition to see by. Sunlight opens the world to us, nourishes our skin and our body, shows us we are still alive. Dylan Thomas' angry poem bids his father "Rage, rage against the dying of the light". Throughout the scriptures God is spoken of as the source of light, living in inaccessible light. Jesus is the light of the world, bringing sight to the sightless. We are to walk as children of the light.

Lord, I treasure your light, and the feeling of the sun on my back. May I never lose my gratitude for the sight of my eyes and the glory of sunlight. I need your light too in the dark hours, when I am baffled by the evil of the world. Be the light of my life.

The Presence of God

I reflect for a moment on God's presence around me and in me.
Creator of the universe, the sun and the moon, the earth,
every molecule, every atom, everything that is:
God is in every beat of my heart. God is with me, now.

Freedom

There are very few people
who realize what God would make of them
if they abandoned themselves into his hands,
and let themselves be formed by his grace. (St. Ignatius)
I ask for the grace to trust myself totally to God's love.

Consciousness

I remind myself that I am in the presence of the Lord.
I will take refuge in His loving heart.
He is my strength in times of weakness.
He is my comforter in times of sorrow.

The Word

I read the Word of God slowly, a few times over, and I listen to
what God is saying to me. (Please turn to your scripture on the
following pages. Inspiration points are there should you need
them. When you are ready, return here to continue.)

Conversation

What is stirring in me as I pray?
Am I consoled, troubled, left cold?
I imagine Jesus himself standing or sitting at my side,
and share my feelings with him.

Conclusion

Glory be to the Father, and to the Son, and to the Holy Spirit,
As it was in the beginning, is now and ever shall be,
World without end. Amen

Sunday 21st September,
Twenty-fifth Sunday in Ordinary Time   Matthew 20:1–16

And Jesus said, "For the kingdom of heaven is like a landowner who went out early in the morning to hire laborers for his vineyard. After agreeing with the laborers for the usual daily wage, he sent them into his vineyard. When he went out about nine o'clock, he saw others standing idle in the marketplace; and he said to them, 'You also go into the vineyard, and I will pay you whatever is right.' So they went. When he went out again about noon and about three o'clock, he did the same. And about five o'clock he went out and found others standing around; and he said to them, 'Why are you standing here idle all day?' They said to him, 'Because no one has hired us.' He said to them, 'You also go into the vineyard.' When evening came, the owner of the vineyard said to his manager, 'Call the laborers and give them their pay, beginning with the last and then going to the first.' When those hired about five o'clock came, each of them received the usual daily wage. Now when the first came, they thought they would receive more; but each of them also received the usual daily wage. And when they received it, they grumbled against the landowner, saying, 'These last worked only one hour, and you have made them equal to us who have borne the burden of the day and the scorching heat.' But he replied to one of them, 'Friend, I am doing you no wrong; did you not agree with me for the usual daily wage? Take what belongs to you and go; I choose to give to this last the same as I give to you. Am I not allowed to do what I choose with what belongs to me? Or are you envious because I am generous?' So the last will be first, and the first will be last."

- Lord, you console me with this story, about your call going out to people at different stages of the day, that is, of their lives. You can always surprise me, both with your challenge to youth, middle age or old age, and with your rewards.

- Your ways are so far above my ways that I cannot grasp the whole pattern. I can simply be grateful that you have said to me now: "You also go into the vineyard." Please keep me on your payroll.

Monday 22nd September   Luke 8:16–18

Jesus said to his disciples, "No one after lighting a lamp hides it under a jar, or puts it under a bed, but puts it on a lampstand, so that those who enter may see the light. For nothing is hidden that will not be disclosed, nor is anything secret that will not become known and come to light. Then pay attention to how you listen; for to those who have, more will be given; and from those who do not have, even what they seem to have will be taken away."

- This is demanding, Lord. I am not comfortable shining before others as an example of Christian living.
- But then I am not much use if I hide because the "light" is your light, not mine. And you point me towards the way I can reveal you: "Pay attention to how you listen."
- What does this mean for me today?

Tuesday 23rd September   Luke 8:19–21

Then his mother and his brothers came to him, but they could not reach him because of the crowd. And he was told, "Your mother and your brothers are standing outside, wanting to see you." But he said to them, "My mother and my brothers are those who hear the word of God and do it."

- Jesus is not disowning his mother, but rather pointing to her greatest glory: that she could say to God's messenger: "Here am I, the servant of the Lord; let it be with me according to your word."

Wednesday 24th September   Luke 9:1–6

Jesus called the twelve together and gave them power and authority over all demons and to cure diseases, and he sent them out to proclaim the kingdom of God and to heal. He said to them, "Take nothing for your journey, no staff, nor bag, nor bread, nor money—not even an extra tunic. Whatever house you enter, stay there, and leave from there. Wherever they do not welcome you, as you are leaving that town shake the dust off your feet as a testimony against them." They departed and went through the villages, bringing the good news and curing diseases everywhere.

- Jesus did not tell the twelve what to say; instead, his instruction was to take nothing and receive hospitality when and as it was offered. There is no mention of sermon notes.
- This passage was an inspiration to Francis of Assisi: he did not want his friars to preach salvation so much as "be" salvation.

Thursday 25th September   Luke 9:7–9

Now Herod the ruler heard about all that had taken place, and he was perplexed, because it was said by some that John had been raised from the dead, by some that Elijah had appeared, and by others that one of the ancient prophets had arisen. Herod said, "John I beheaded; but who is this about whom I hear such things?" And he tried to see him.

- "Herod tried to see Jesus." This urge did not come from openness to God's revelation, but rather from the same idle curiosity Herod was to show during Jesus' passion. But there is also a hint of fear that he may be facing a greater power than he had reckoned.
- Lord, if my religion is just a curiosity or news item, I am better off without it. I long to see you with openness. I desire to come close to you.

Friday 26th September   Ecclesiastes 3:1–8

For everything there is a season, and a time for every matter under heaven: a time to be born, and a time to die; a time to plant, and a time to pluck up what is planted; a time to kill, and a time to heal; a time to break down, and a time to build up; a time to weep, and a time to laugh; a time to mourn, and a time to dance; a time to throw away stones, and a time to gather stones together; a time to embrace, and a time to refrain from embracing; a time to seek, and a time to lose; a time to keep, and a time to throw away; a time to tear, and a time to sew; a time to keep silence, and a time to speak; a time to love, and a time to hate; a time for war, and a time for peace.

- Time is so precious. Lawyers and consultants charge for it, we "waste" it, we "spend" it, we "have" it, we "don't have" it. Each moment passes, to be lost forever.
- The past I can remember, the future I can imagine. Lord, teach me to treasure each moment for these are the only ones I have.

Saturday 27th September,
St. Vincent de Paul   Matthew 9:35–37

Then Jesus went about all the cities and villages, teaching in their synagogues, and proclaiming the good news of the kingdom, and curing every disease and every sickness. When he saw the crowds, he had compassion for them, because they were harassed and helpless, like sheep without a shepherd. Then he said to his disciples, "The harvest is plentiful, but the laborers are few; therefore ask the Lord of the harvest to send out laborers into his harvest."

- Do I know any people who are "harassed and helpless like sheep without a shepherd?" Let me hold them before my mind's eye for a moment.
- Can I now imagine Jesus looking at them? How does he see them? If I feel "harassed and helpless," how does he see me? I ask for the grace to look on the world around me with the compassionate eyes of Jesus.

september 28–october 4

Something to think and pray about each day this week:

Opening Up to Silence

When you want to pray, that is, to raise your mind and heart to God, the place to start is not so much with your mind and heart as with your body. Whether standing, kneeling, sitting or walking, the body should be relaxed and quiet but not sleepy. "If you pray best when lying down," said St. Francis de Sales, "it's your duty to lie down when praying." All right, Francis, then what next? I should become aware of my breathing. Even the simple focus on air going in and out through my nostrils helps to center me, slow me down, and open me to silence.

The Presence of God
I remind myself that, as I sit here now,
God is gazing on me with love and holding me in being.
I pause for a moment and think of this.

Freedom
Lord, grant me the grace to be free from the excesses of this life.
Let me not get caught up with the desire for wealth.
Keep my heart and mind free to love and serve you.

Consciousness
How am I really feeling? Light-hearted? Heavy-hearted?
I may be very much at peace, happy to be here.
Equally, I may be frustrated, worried or angry.
I acknowledge how I really am. It is the real me that the Lord
loves.

The Word
I take my time to read the Word of God, slowly, a few times, allowing myself to dwell on anything that strikes me. (Please turn
to your scripture on the following pages. Inspiration points are
there should you need them. When you are ready, return here
to continue.)

Conversation
Do I notice myself reacting as I pray with the Word of God?
Do I feel challenged, comforted, angry?
Imagining Jesus sitting or standing by me,
I speak out my feelings, as one trusted friend to another.

Conclusion
Glory be to the Father, and to the Son, and to the Holy Spirit,
As it was in the beginning, is now and ever shall be,
World without end. Amen

Sunday 28th September,
Twenty-sixth Sunday in Ordinary Time   Matthew 21:28–32

Jesus said, "What do you think? A man had two sons; he went to the first and said, 'Son, go and work in the vineyard today.' He answered, 'I will not'; but later he changed his mind and went. The father went to the second and said the same; and he answered, 'I go, sir'; but he did not go. Which of the two did the will of his father?" They said, "The first." Jesus said to them, "Truly I tell you, the tax collectors and the prostitutes are going into the kingdom of God ahead of you. For John came to you in the way of righteousness and you did not believe him, but the tax collectors and the prostitutes believed him; and even after you saw it, you did not change your minds and believe him."

- Well, which am I? The smooth but unreliable daddy-pleaser, or the person who, even with a bad grace, does the job?
- The kingdom of heaven is not promised to the charmers, but to those whose life would make no sense if God did not exist.

Monday 29th September,
Sts. Michael, Gabriel, and Raphael   John 1:47–51

When Jesus saw Nathanael coming toward him, he said of him, "Here is truly an Israelite in whom there is no deceit!" Nathanael asked him, "Where did you get to know me?" Jesus answered, "I saw you under the fig tree before Philip called you." Nathanael replied, "Rabbi, you are the Son of God! You are the King of Israel!" Jesus answered, "Do you believe because I told you that I saw you under the fig tree? You will see greater things than these." And he said to him, "Very truly, I tell you, you will see heaven opened and the angels of God ascending and descending upon the Son of Man."

- Lord, I wish you could say of me that I have no guile, and that there is no deceit in my mouth. That would be blessing indeed; help me to earn it.

Tuesday 30th September — Luke 9:51–56

When the days drew near for him to be taken up, Jesus set his face to go to Jerusalem. And he sent messengers ahead of him. On their way they entered a village of the Samaritans to make ready for him; but they did not receive him, because his face was set toward Jerusalem. When his disciples James and John saw it, they said, "Lord, do you want us to command fire to come down from heaven and consume them?" But he turned and rebuked them. Then they went on to another village.

- Here was a bit of standard hostility between a local Samaritan community and some Jewish pilgrims passing by. This may well have been a flash point, where tension broke out, on the route to Jerusalem. This time, Jesus' disciples reacted to the prejudice with spontaneous rage and perhaps some prejudice of their own.
- Lord, it is the flash points that test us. These are the moments that trigger murders and wars. I need to learn this: to face down my rising fury, rein in my indignation and let the inflammatory moment pass.

Wednesday 1st October — Luke 9:57–62

As they were going along the road, someone said to him, "I will follow you wherever you go." And Jesus said to him, "Foxes have holes, and birds of the air have nests; but the Son of Man has nowhere to lay his head." To another he said, "Follow me." But he said, "Lord, first let me go and bury my father." But Jesus said to him, "Let the dead bury their own dead; but as for you, go and proclaim the kingdom of God." Another said, "I will follow you, Lord; but let me first say farewell to those at my home." Jesus said to him, "No one who puts a hand to the plow and looks back is fit for the kingdom of God."

- Our situations may be different but the call is the same: "Follow me," says Jesus.
- Can I take a hard look at my attachments, at anything that blocks me off from giving greater priority to Jesus? Is it material goods, my sense of duty, my relationships?
- Just how deeply have I allowed my faith to penetrate my life?

Thursday 2nd October   Job 19:21–27

"Have pity on me, have pity on me, O you my friends, for the hand of God has touched me! Why do you, like God, pursue me, never satisfied with my flesh? "O that my words were written down! O that they were inscribed in a book! O that with an iron pen and with lead they were engraved on a rock forever! For I know that my Redeemer lives, and that at the last he will stand upon the earth; and after my skin has been thus destroyed, then in my flesh I shall see God, whom I shall see on my side, and my eyes shall behold, and not another. My heart faints within me!"

- Job speaks for every believer who has ever been beaten down by evil and adversity, in great ways or small.
- Lord, as I savor his marvelous affirmation, I pray for all those in despair, who feel their skin destroyed and see no hope. May they too know that their Redeemer lives, and that they will see God.

Friday 3rd October   Psalm 138(139):1–3, 7–10

O LORD, you have searched me and known me. You know when I sit down and when I rise up; you discern my thoughts from far away. You search out my path and my lying down, and are acquainted with all my ways. Where can I go from your spirit? Or where can I flee from your presence? If I ascend to heaven, you are there; if I make my bed in Sheol, you are there.

- Why do these words so comfort me, Lord? What greater consolation can there be than to have somebody know me through and through, and still love me?
- Some of us enjoyed that with our mother or father, but still more with you, my maker and shaper. Do not take your eyes off me. Know me in all my dark corners, and cherish what you know.

Saturday 4th October,
St. Francis of Assisi   Matthew 11:28–30

Jesus said, "Come to me, all you that are weary and are carrying heavy burdens, and I will give you rest. Take my yoke upon you, and learn from me; for I am gentle and humble in heart, and you will find rest for your souls. For my yoke is easy, and my burden is light."

- "Come to me … and I will give you rest." Lord, these lovely words are sometimes linked to a picture of you in pastel shades, in a montage of roses and golden light.
- But it takes strength and courage to remain gentle in face of false accusations and scheming enemies. It is you who are the strong one, not the screamers and war-mongers.

Something to think and pray about each day this week:

A Simple Prayer

Even when our prayer becomes more silent and wordless, as we grow older, the rosary can still help. It still releases our mind, because the telling of the beads becomes quite automatic. There are people, including many in *Sacred Space*, who move from the reciting of the beads into a sort of prayer that no longer needs any thought. It has been called the prayer of simple regard, or the prayer of stupidity, or mystical prayer. Names do not matter. Prayer is a lifting of the mind and heart to God, and for that the rosary is only a springboard. Feel free. It is Our Lady's gift, to be used as it helps us.

The Presence of God

In the silence of my innermost being,
in the fragments of my yearned-for wholeness,
can I hear the whispers of God's presence?
Can I remember when I felt God's nearness?
When we walked together and I let myself be embraced by God's love.

Freedom

I ask for the grace
to let go of my own concerns
and be open to what God is asking of me,
to let myself be guided and formed by my loving Creator.

Consciousness

I exist in a web of relationships—links to nature, people, God.
I trace out these links, giving thanks for the life that flows
through them.
Some links are twisted or broken: I may feel regret, anger,
disappointment.
I pray for the gift of acceptance and forgiveness.

The Word

The word of God comes down to us through the scriptures.
May the Holy Spirit enlighten my mind and my heart to respond to the gospel teachings. (Please turn to your scripture
on the following pages. Inspiration points are there should you
need them. When you are ready, return here to continue.)

Conversation

Remembering that I am still in God's presence,
I imagine Jesus himself standing or sitting beside me,
and say whatever is on my mind, whatever is in my heart,
speaking as one friend to another.

Conclusion

Glory be to the Father, and to the Son, and to the Holy Spirit,
As it was in the beginning, is now and ever shall be,
World without end. Amen

Sunday 5th October, Twenty-seventh
Sunday in Ordinary Time   Philippians 4:8–9

Finally, beloved, whatever is true, whatever is honorable, whatever is just, whatever is pure, whatever is pleasing, whatever is commendable, if there is any excellence and if there is anything worthy of praise, think about these things, and the God of peace will be with you.

- Lord, this is not so easy. I am bombarded with pictures and stories of what is unjust, dishonorable, impure, violent, shoddy and disreputable. This is what fills the journals and screens.
- But I am not being escapist when I linger on people's goodness. The fact is, most of us do our best. It is the purveyors of dirt who are escapist, depressing company. Help me to clean up my mind.

Monday 6th October   Luke 10:30–37

Jesus replied, "A man was going down from Jerusalem to Jericho, and fell into the hands of robbers, who stripped him, beat him, and went away, leaving him half dead. Now by chance a priest was going down that road; and when he saw him, he passed by on the other side. So likewise a Levite, when he came to the place and saw him, passed by on the other side. But a Samaritan while traveling came near him; and when he saw him, he was moved with pity. He went to him and bandaged his wounds, having poured oil and wine on them. Then he put him on his own animal, brought him to an inn, and took care of him. The next day he took out two denarii, gave them to the innkeeper, and said, 'Take care of him; and when I come back, I will repay you whatever more you spend.' Which of these three, do you think, was a neighbor to the man who fell into the hands of the robbers?" He said, "The one who showed him mercy." Jesus said to him, "Go and do likewise."

- The parable struck me hard as a child, and even now, after years of compassion fatigue, it still speaks powerfully: "Go and do likewise."

Tuesday 7th October Luke 10:38–42

Now as they went on their way, Jesus entered a certain village, where a woman named Martha welcomed him into her home. She had a sister named Mary, who sat at the Lord's feet and listened to what he was saying. But Martha was distracted by her many tasks; so she came to him and asked, "Lord, do you not care that my sister has left me to do all the work by myself? Tell her then to help me." But the Lord answered her, "Martha, Martha, you are worried and distracted by many things; there is need of only one thing. Mary has chosen the better part, which will not be taken away from her."

- Jesus was on his way to Jerusalem. He knew what fate awaited him there, and he needed a time of quiet with his friends. Mary sensed this, but Martha, God bless her, wanted to be kind to Jesus in her own way, which meant fussing over a meal.
- Lord, there have been times when I was more in touch with my own habits and emotions than those of the friends who come to me. Give me antennae like Mary's.

Wednesday 8th October Luke 11:1–4

Jesus was praying in a certain place, and after he had finished, one of his disciples said to him, "Lord, teach us to pray, as John taught his disciples." He said to them, "When you pray, say: Father, hallowed be your name. Your kingdom come. Give us each day our daily bread. And forgive us our sins, for we ourselves forgive everyone indebted to us. And do not bring us to the time of trial."

- I call you "Father": Jesus taught me to use this metaphor. I know that you, Lord, are beyond gender and surpass our imagination.
- But I relish the overtones of Father, one who knows and loves me, and whose often mysterious providence is there in everything that befalls me.

Thursday 9th October   Luke 11:5–10

And Jesus said to them, "Suppose one of you has a friend, and you go to him at midnight and say to him, 'Friend, lend me three loaves of bread; for a friend of mine has arrived, and I have nothing to set before him.' And he answers from within, 'Do not bother me; the door has already been locked, and my children are with me in bed; I cannot get up and give you anything.' I tell you, even though he will not get up and give him anything because he is his friend, at least because of his persistence he will get up and give him whatever he needs. So I say to you, Ask, and it will be given you; search, and you will find; knock, and the door will be opened for you. For everyone who asks receives, and everyone who searches finds, and for everyone who knocks, the door will be opened."

- You are no messenger boy, Lord. I hesitate to turn to you with trifles, to bother you with trivia.
- But when a need sears my heart, and I put it to you, then I know you will give to me; perhaps not what I ask, but something that can bring me closer to you.

Friday 10th October   Psalm 110(111):1–6

Praise the LORD! I will give thanks to the LORD with my whole heart, in the company of the upright, in the congregation. Great are the works of the LORD, studied by all who delight in them. Full of honor and majesty is his work, and his righteousness endures forever. He has gained renown by his wonderful deeds; the LORD is gracious and merciful. He provides food for those who fear him; he is ever mindful of his covenant. He has shown his people the power of his works, in giving them the heritage of the nations.

• Who is this remarkable God who has evoked such wonder and love in the people throughout the ages? Majestic and glorious, tender and compassionate.

Saturday 11th October   Luke 11:27–28

While Jesus was speaking, a woman in the crowd raised her voice and said to him, "Blessed is the womb that bore you and the breasts that nursed you!" But he said, "Blessed rather are those who hear the word of God and obey it!"

• Out of this woman's simple faith comes a profound statement of motherhood—the giving of life and nourishment.
• Mary is blessed for her motherhood of Jesus, but much more blessed for hearing the word of God and keeping it.
• How do I hear the Word? Do I give life in the way I follow Jesus?

october 12–18

Something to think and pray about each day this week:

Coming to Attention

This generation has been stimulated more than any generation in history. All day and all night we can be listening or watching, exposing ourselves to the bombardment of words, music and images through all the electronic media. So we do not pray in a vacuum. Our head is full of pictures, tunes and stories. We suffer from what have been called monkey thoughts, clambering all over the place, chattering and distracting us from our centre. One escape from the monkey thoughts is the classical one: focus on how you breathe. Attend to the air bathing your nostrils as you inhale and exhale. Slow down, and repeat a simple mantra like: "Lord, teach me to pray," or "Maranatha," or "Come Holy Spirit."

The Presence of God
God is with me, but more,
God is within me, giving me existence.
Let me dwell for a moment on God's life-giving presence
in my body, my mind, my heart
and in the whole of my life.

Freedom
I ask for the grace to believe
in what I could be and do
if I only allowed God, my loving Creator,
to continue to create me, guide me and shape me.

Consciousness
Knowing that God loves me unconditionally,
I can afford to be honest about how I am.
How has the last day been, and how do I feel now?
I share my feelings openly with the Lord.

The Word
I read the Word of God slowly, a few times over, and I listen to
what God is saying to me. (Please turn to your scripture on the
following pages. Inspiration points are there should you need
them. When you are ready, return here to continue.)

Conversation
How has God's Word moved me? Has it left me cold?
Has it consoled me or moved me to act in a new way?
I imagine Jesus standing or sitting beside me,
I turn and share my feelings with him.

Conclusion
Glory be to the Father, and to the Son, and to the Holy Spirit,
As it was in the beginning, is now and ever shall be,
World without end. Amen

**Sunday 12th October, Twenty-eighth
Sunday in Ordinary Time**   **Philippians 4:12–13**

I know what it is to have little, and I know what it is to have plenty. In any and all circumstances I have learned the secret of being well-fed and of going hungry, of having plenty and of being in need. I can do all things through him who strengthens me.

- Lord, I marvel at the freedom shown by St. Paul. He sat lightly to plenty and to poverty, and could face any sort of trouble—he endured scourging, shipwreck, imprisonment and much more—with peace of soul, because of his trust in your support.
- I would pray for that strength, that trust.

Monday 13th October   **Luke 11:29–32**

When the crowds were increasing, Jesus began to say, "This generation is an evil generation; it asks for a sign, but no sign will be given to it except the sign of Jonah. For just as Jonah became a sign to the people of Nineveh, so the Son of Man will be to this generation. The queen of the South will rise at the judgment with the people of this generation and condemn them, because she came from the ends of the earth to listen to the wisdom of Solomon, and see, something greater than Solomon is here! The people of Nineveh will rise up at the judgment with this generation and condemn it, because they repented at the proclamation of Jonah, and see, something greater than Jonah is here!"

- It is baffling to record that, for a period of thirty years, the Son of Man did not appear to be anything other than a man. From the beginning of his public life, those who did not believe in Jesus' preaching or his miracles discerned nothing of the divine in his features.

- Lord, your warning speaks to me too. I find myself looking for signs and wonders, when the greatest wonder is yourself.

Tuesday 14th October   Luke 11:37–39

While Jesus was speaking, a Pharisee invited him to dine with him; so he went in and took his place at the table. The Pharisee was amazed to see that he did not first wash before dinner. Then the Lord said to him, "Now you Pharisees clean the outside of the cup and of the dish, but inside you are full of greed and wickedness."

- For Pharisees, washing before dinner was a ritual: the water was kept in a special jar, and each washing must use enough water to fill one and a half eggshells. It was poured over the hands, first from finger-tip to wrist, then in the reverse order—and so on. What started as a hygiene response had become a matter of sin.
- Lord, you pointed the Pharisee, and me, back to my inner life, my thoughts and desires. You scold, but always with the aim of change and growth.

Wednesday 15th October,
St. Teresa of Avila   Romans 8:22–27

We know that the whole creation has been groaning in labor pains until now; and not only the creation, but we ourselves, who have the first fruits of the Spirit, groan inwardly while we wait for adoption, the redemption of our bodies. For in hope we were saved. Now hope that is seen is not hope. For who hopes for what is seen? But if we hope for what we do not see, we wait for it with patience. Likewise the Spirit helps us in our weakness; for we do not know how to pray as we ought, but that very Spirit intercedes with sighs too deep for words. And God, who searches the heart, knows what is the mind of the Spirit, because the Spirit intercedes for the saints according to the will of God.

- "The Spirit helps us in our weakness." The Spirit is active, not so much when we are at the height of our powers but when we are in the depths, burdened by weakness. The Christian hope which sustains us is a gift of the Spirit.
- How do I experience hope in my life? Lord, teach me patience with my prayer and my failings.

Thursday 16th October   Luke 11:47–54

Jesus said to the lawyers, "Woe to you! For you build the tombs of the prophets whom your ancestors killed. So you are witnesses and approve of the deeds of your ancestors; for they killed them, and you build their tombs. Therefore also the Wisdom of God said, 'I will send them prophets and apostles, some of whom they will kill and persecute,' so that this generation may be charged with the blood of all the prophets shed since the foundation of the world, from the blood of Abel to the blood of Zechariah, who perished between the altar and the sanctuary. Yes, I tell you, it will be charged against this generation. Woe to you lawyers! For you have taken away the key of knowledge; you did not enter yourselves, and you hindered those who were entering." When he went outside, the scribes and the Pharisees began to be very hostile toward him and to cross-examine him about many things, lying in wait for him, to catch him in something he might say.

- Lord, you were making powerful enemies, and you knew it. You confronted vested interests with extraordinary courage; you knew that you might have to pay a heavy price for their hostility.
- You are also speaking to me. How does a righteous and angry Jesus make me feel? Am I in fear? Do I want to run away? Do I start getting righteous myself?

Friday 17th October   **Luke 12:1–3, 6–7**

Meanwhile, when the crowd gathered by the thousands, so that they trampled on one another, Jesus began to speak first to his disciples, "Beware of the yeast of the Pharisees, that is, their hypocrisy. Nothing is covered up that will not be uncovered, and nothing secret that will not become known. Therefore whatever you have said in the dark will be heard in the light, and what you have whispered behind closed doors will be proclaimed from the housetops. Are not five sparrows sold for two pennies? Yet not one of them is forgotten in God's sight. But even the hairs of your head are all counted. Do not be afraid; you are of more value than many sparrows."

- The more we know about the immensity of the universe, and the intricate laws that govern creation from the movements of the stars to the sub-atomic world, the more unimaginable God becomes.
- Yet Jesus speaks of his Father with tenderness, as one who watches over the fall of a sparrow and counts the hairs on my head. He was surely smiling when he said to his disciples: "You are of more value than many sparrows."

Saturday 18th October, St. Luke   **Luke 10:1–7a**

After this the Lord appointed seventy others and sent them on ahead of him in pairs to every town and place where he himself intended to go. He said to them, "The harvest is plentiful, but the laborers are few; therefore ask the Lord of the harvest to send out laborers into his harvest. Go on your way. See, I am sending you out like lambs into the midst of wolves. Carry no purse, no bag, no sandals; and greet no one on the road. Whatever house you enter, first say, 'Peace to this house!' And if anyone is there who shares in peace, your peace will rest on that person; but if not, it will return to you. Remain in the same house, eating and drinking whatever they provide, for the laborer deserves to be paid."

- Lord, you were sending followers on a mission, so your words here carry weight over the centuries. You sent them in pairs, not as individuals. You told them to travel light and vulnerable, to bring peace, but not to dally with small talk.
- On each of these counts, can I look at my own life today?

Something to think and pray about each day this week:

The Experience of Love

Relish this piece from *The Cloud of Unknowing*, written in the fourteenth century: "Our intense need to understand will always be a powerful stumbling block to our attempts to reach God in simple love, and must always be overcome. For if you do not overcome this need to understand, it will undermine your quest. It will replace the darkness which you have pierced to reach God, with clear images of something which, however good, however beautiful, however Godlike, is not God. So, therefore, never give up your resolve, but beat away at this cloud of unknowing between you and God with that sharp dart of longing love. And so I urge you, go after experience rather than knowledge. On account of pride, knowledge may often deceive you, but this gentle, loving affection will not deceive you. Knowledge tends to breed conceit, but love builds. Knowledge is full of labor, but love, full of rest."

The Presence of God
To be present is to arrive as one is and open up to the other.
At this instant, as I arrive here, God is present waiting for me.
God always arrives before me, desiring to connect with me
even more than my most intimate friend.
I take a moment and greet my loving God.

Freedom
"In these days, God taught me
as a schoolteacher teaches a pupil" (St. Ignatius).
I remind myself that there are things God has to teach me yet,
and ask for the grace to hear them and let them change me.

Consciousness
In the presence of my loving Creator,
I look honestly at my feelings over the last day,
the highs, the lows and the level ground.
Can I see where the Lord has been present?

The Word
I take my time to read the Word of God, slowly, a few times, allowing myself to dwell on anything that strikes me. (Please turn
to your scripture on the following pages. Inspiration points are
there should you need them. When you are ready, return here
to continue.)

Conversation
What feelings are rising in me
as I pray and reflect on God's Word?
I imagine Jesus himself sitting or standing beside me,
and open my heart to him.

Conclusion
Glory be to the Father, and to the Son, and to the Holy Spirit,
As it was in the beginning, is now and ever shall be,
World without end. Amen

Sunday 19th October, Twenty-ninth
Sunday in Ordinary Time   Matthew 22:15–21

Then the Pharisees went and plotted to entrap him in what he said. So they sent their disciples to him, along with the Herodians, saying, "Teacher, we know that you are sincere, and teach the way of God in accordance with truth, and show deference to no one; for you do not regard people with partiality. Tell us, then, what you think. Is it lawful to pay taxes to the emperor, or not?" But Jesus, aware of their malice, said, "Why are you putting me to the test, you hypocrites? Show me the coin used for the tax." And they brought him a denarius. Then he said to them, "Whose head is this, and whose title?" They answered, "The emperor's." Then he said to them, "Give therefore to the emperor the things that are the emperor's, and to God the things that are God's."

- "Whose head is this, and whose title?" People have worked on this reply of Jesus, some hankering for revolution against an oppressive regime, some trying to bolster their conservatism. What is your answer, Lord?
- You hungered and thirsted for justice, and heard the cry of the poor. You also acknowledged that the properly run state is preferable to anarchy or chaos.
- How do I respond to this story?

Monday 20th October   Luke 12:13–21

Someone in the crowd said to Jesus, "Teacher, tell my brother to divide the family inheritance with me." But he said to him, "Friend, who set me to be a judge or arbitrator over you?" And he said to them, "Take care! Be on your guard against all kinds of greed; for one's life does not consist in the abundance of possessions." Then he told them a parable: "The land of a rich man produced abundantly. And he thought to himself, 'What should I do, for I have no place to store my crops?' Then he said, 'I will do this: I will pull down my barns and build larger ones, and there I will store all my grain and my goods.' And I will say to my soul, 'Soul, you have ample goods laid up for many years; relax, eat, drink, be merry.' But God said to him, 'You fool! This very night your life is being demanded of you. And the things you have prepared, whose will they be?' So it is with those who store up treasures for themselves but are not rich toward God."

- The man in the parable doesn't seem a bad man. He seems industrious, and is setting things up nicely for himself, looking forward to an enjoyable life.
- Do I hear Jesus sending alarm bells about "all kinds of greed"? What are those alarms saying to me in my life?

Tuesday 21st October   Luke 12:35–38

Jesus said to his disciples, "Be dressed for action and have your lamps lit; be like those who are waiting for their master to return from the wedding banquet, so that they may open the door for him as soon as he comes and knocks. Blessed are those slaves whom the master finds alert when he comes; truly I tell you, he will fasten his belt and have them sit down to eat, and he will come and serve them. If he comes during the middle of the night, or near dawn, and finds them so, blessed are those slaves."

- How would I like you to find me when you call me, Lord? At peace with you, at peace with my fellows, at peace with myself.
- Let not the sun go down on my anger.

Wednesday 22nd October   Luke 12:45–48

Jesus said, "But if that slave says to himself, 'My master is delayed in coming,' and if he begins to beat the other slaves, men and women, and to eat and drink and get drunk, the master of that slave will come on a day when he does not expect him and at an hour that he does not know. From everyone to whom much has been given, much will be required; and from the one to whom much has been entrusted, even more will be demanded."

- Lord, you are urging me to live in the present, in the Now. Let me not put off what I want to do today. Tomorrow is uncertain, but I have this present moment, and it is only in this moment—not in an uncertain tomorrow—that I can find you.

- This moment is a sort of sacrament, a channel of grace for me. Am I open to receive it, to meet your demands?

Thursday 23rd October   Ephesians 3:15–19

I bow my knees before the Father, from whom every family in heaven and on earth takes its name. I pray that, according to the riches of his glory, he may grant that you may be strengthened in your inner being with power through his Spirit, and that Christ may dwell in your hearts through faith, as you are being rooted and grounded in love. I pray that you may have the power to comprehend, with all the saints, what is the breadth and length and height and depth, and to know the love of Christ that surpasses knowledge, so that you may be filled with all the fullness of God.

- I pray to know something that is unknowable: the breadth and length and height and depth of Christ's love; and that Christ may dwell in my heart through faith, so that I may be rooted and grounded in love.

- Let me sit quietly now. May I "may be filled with all the fullness of God."

Friday 24th October   Ephesians 4:4–6

There is one body and one Spirit, just as you were called to the one hope of your calling, one Lord, one faith, one baptism, one God and Father of all, who is above all and through all and in all.

- This is Paul's vision of unity, though it may be hard to reconcile with the kaleidoscope of superstitions and faiths that confront us today. But we share with the Jews and Moslems a faith in the one true God of Abraham.
- We trust that God is working through all and in all to bring humankind to unity.

Saturday 25th October   Ephesians 4:14–16

We must no longer be children, tossed to and fro and blown about by every wind of doctrine, by people's trickery, by their craftiness in deceitful scheming. But speaking the truth in love, we must grow up in every way into him who is the head, into Christ, from whom the whole body, joined and knitted together by every ligament with which it is equipped, as each part is working properly, promotes the body's growth in building itself up in love.

- "We must no longer be children." Paul points out that we are called to maturity in our faith. We have to be full citizens of this world in which we live, to be fully human as Jesus was.
- We are also called beyond that, to "grow up in every way"; not for the sake of maturity itself but for the sake of unity with Christ and community with each other, in love.
- Is this the path I am taking, or do I have to change direction?

Something to think and pray about each day this week:

Seeking Father and Mother

Six hundred years ago Julian of Norwich tried to express her sense of the love of God in these words: "The love that God most high has for our soul is so great that it surpasses understanding. No created being can comprehend how much, and how sweetly, and how tenderly our maker loves us. As truly as God is our Father, so just as truly is he our Mother. In our Father God Almighty, we have our being; in our merciful Mother we are remade and restored. Our fragmented lives are knit together and made perfect man. And by giving and yielding ourselves, through grace, to the Holy Spirit, we are made whole."

Presence of God

What is present to me is what has a hold on my becoming.
I reflect on the presence of God always there in love,
amidst the many things that have a hold on me.
I pause and pray that I may let God
affect my becoming in this precise moment.

Freedom

If God were trying to tell me something, would I know?
If God were reassuring me or challenging me, would I notice?
I ask for the grace to be free of my own preoccupations
and open to what God may be saying to me.

Consciousness

Knowing that God loves me unconditionally,
I look honestly over the last day, its events and my feelings.
Do I have something to be grateful for? Then I give thanks.
Is there something I am sorry for? Then I ask forgiveness.

The Word

God speaks to each one of us individually. I need to listen to
what he is saying to me. (Please turn to your scripture on the
following pages. Inspiration points are there should you need
them. When you are ready, return here to continue.)

Conversation

What is stirring in me as I pray?
Am I consoled, troubled, left cold?
I imagine Jesus himself standing or sitting at my side,
and share my feelings with him.

Conclusion

Glory be to the Father, and to the Son, and to the Holy Spirit,
As it was in the beginning, is now and ever shall be,
World without end. Amen

Sunday 26th October,
Thirtieth Sunday in Ordinary Time   Matthew 22:34–40

When the Pharisees heard that he had silenced the Sadducees, they gathered together, and one of them, a lawyer, asked him a question to test him. "Teacher, which commandment in the law is the greatest?" He said to him, "'You shall love the Lord your God with all your heart, and with all your soul, and with all your mind.' This is the greatest and first commandment. And a second is like it: 'You shall love your neighbor as yourself.' On these two commandments hang all the law and the prophets."

- Lord, if these two commandments could become my way of life, my religion would be simple and primitive, without arguments or complications.
- Let your words sink deeply into my heart and soul.

Monday 27th October   Luke 13:10–17

Now Jesus was teaching in one of the synagogues on the sabbath. And just then there appeared a woman with a spirit that had crippled her for eighteen years. She was bent over and was quite unable to stand up straight. When Jesus saw her, he called her over and said, "Woman, you are set free from your ailment." When he laid his hands on her, immediately she stood up straight and began praising God. But the leader of the synagogue, indignant because Jesus had cured on the sabbath, kept saying to the crowd, "There are six days on which work ought to be done; come on those days and be cured, and not on the sabbath day." But the Lord answered him and said, "You hypocrites! Does not each of you on the sabbath untie his ox or his donkey from the manger, and lead it away to give it water? And ought not this woman, a daughter of Abraham whom Satan bound for eighteen long years, be set free from this bondage on the sabbath day?" When he said this, all his opponents were put to shame; and the entire crowd was rejoicing at all the wonderful things that he was doing.

- Two things move me in this story: the joy of the woman who for the first time in eighteen years could stand up straight; and the confrontation with the leader of the synagogue who loved systems —the law said that healing was work, so was forbidden on the sabbath—more than people.
- Do I give religious rules priority; use them as an excuse for inaction? Or do I try to do as Jesus does?

Tuesday 28th October,
Sts. Simon and Jude, Apostles   Ephesians 2:19–22

So then you are no longer strangers and aliens, but you are citizens with the saints and also members of the household of God, built upon the foundation of the apostles and prophets, with Christ Jesus himself as the cornerstone. In him the whole structure is joined together and grows into a holy temple in the Lord; in whom you also are built together spiritually into a dwelling place for God.

- "No longer strangers and aliens but you are citizens of the household of God." Lord, let me feel at home with you, ready to find you behind any door I may open, sitting comfortable and ready to listen to me. I belong with you.
- When I am out of the house, you are waiting for me. You know me and my habits, and are happy to have me around.

Wednesday 29th October   Luke 13:22–30

Jesus went through one town and village after another, teaching as he made his way to Jerusalem. Someone asked him, "Lord, will only a few be saved?" He said to them, "Strive to

enter through the narrow door; for many, I tell you, will try to
enter and will not be able. When once the owner of the house has
got up and shut the door, and you begin to stand outside and to
knock at the door, saying, 'Lord, open to us,' then in reply he will
say to you, 'I do not know where you come from.' Then you will
begin to say, 'We ate and drank with you, and you taught in our
streets.' But he will say, 'I do not know where you come from;
go away from me, all you evildoers!' There will be weeping and
gnashing of teeth when you see Abraham and Isaac and Jacob
and all the prophets in the kingdom of God, and you yourselves
thrown out. Then people will come from east and west, from
north and south, and will eat in the kingdom of God. Indeed,
some are last who will be first, and some are first who will be
last."

- Someone asks about salvation, but Jesus turns it all around; it is not
  "how many" are saved, but "how" we are saved. We must work at
  it, we must start now, and we must keep our feet on the ground.
- Lord, lead me through each of these points. How can I improve
  here?

Thursday 30th October   Ephesians 6:18–20

Pray in the Spirit at all times in every prayer and supplication.
To that end keep alert and always persevere in supplication
for all the saints. Pray also for me, so that when I speak, a message
may be given to me to make known with boldness the mystery
of the gospel, for which I am an ambassador in chains. Pray that
I may declare it boldly, as I must speak.

- Even in chains, Paul sees no barrier to being an "ambassador" of
  the gospel. Prayer "in the Spirit" is at the core of his preaching.
- How does prayer feature in my life? Do I make room for the Spirit,
  so that I too receive the "message"?

- Let me sit for a while with the example Paul gives me.

Friday 31st October   Luke 14:1–6

On one occasion when Jesus was going to the house of a leader of the Pharisees to eat a meal on the sabbath, they were watching him closely. Just then, in front of him, there was a man who had dropsy. And Jesus asked the lawyers and Pharisees, "Is it lawful to cure people on the sabbath, or not?" But they were silent. So Jesus took him and healed him, and sent him away. Then he said to them, "If one of you has a child or an ox that has fallen into a well, will you not immediately pull it out on a sabbath day?" And they could not reply to this.

- I am watching you, Lord, but in a different spirit from the Pharisees. They hoped to catch you out in a breach of regulations. I hope to learn more of your spirit.
- The Pharisees were uptight about sabbath regulations. What moved you was different: the suffering of the man with dropsy. It was not rules that touched your heart, but compassion.

Saturday 1st November, Feast of All Saints   Matthew 5:1–6

When Jesus saw the crowds, he went up the mountain; and after he sat down, his disciples came to him. Then he began to speak, and taught them, saying: "Blessed are the poor in spirit, for theirs is the kingdom of heaven. Blessed are those who mourn, for they will be comforted. Blessed are the meek, for they will inherit the earth. Blessed are those who hunger and thirst for righteousness, for they will be filled."

- "Poor in spirit." What does this mean for me, Lord? When I wake up to find somebody has emptied my bank account, should I be singing alleluias?

- No need to go so far. But could I shrug my shoulders thinking: "It's only money." That would be progress, counter-cultural progress.

november 2–8

Something to think and pray about each day this week:

Working our Way

This is a period during which we are reminded of our solidarity with all the dead (on Sunday 2nd), and all the saints (on Saturday the 1st), the uncanonised and maybe the accursed. We are one human family. St. Matthew, listing the pedigree of Jesus, draws attention to the harlot Rahab and the adulterous David and Tamar. What mixture of DNA is in my makeup, linking me perhaps to farmers, poets, kings, criminals, the violent or the victims, the wealthy or the destitute? This is the makeup in which I work out my way to God. I inherited it, I did not choose it. But like a good card-player, I can make much or little of the hand I am dealt. Lord, how am I doing? Help me to improve my play.

The Presence of God

God is with me, but more, God is within me.
Let me dwell for a moment on God's life-giving presence
in my body, in my mind, in my heart,
as I sit here, right now.

Freedom

I need to close out the noise, to rise above the noise;
The noise that interrupts, that separates,
The noise that isolates.
I need to listen to God again.

Consciousness

I remind myself that I am in the presence of the Lord.
I will take refuge in His loving heart.
He is my strength in times of weakness.
He is my comforter in times of sorrow.

The Word

I read the Word of God slowly, a few times over, and I listen to
what God is saying to me. (Please turn to your scripture on the
following pages. Inspiration points are there should you need
them. When you are ready, return here to continue.)

Conversation

Do I notice myself reacting as I pray with the Word of God?
Do I feel challenged, comforted, angry?
Imagining Jesus sitting or standing by me,
I speak out my feelings, as one trusted friend to another.

Conclusion

Glory be to the Father, and to the Son, and to the Holy Spirit,
As it was in the beginning, is now and ever shall be,
World without end. Amen

Sunday 2nd November, Feast of All Souls   Matthew 5:7–12

Jesus said to the crowds, "Blessed are the merciful, for they will receive mercy. Blessed are the pure in heart, for they will see God. Blessed are the peacemakers, for they will be called children of God. Blessed are those who are persecuted for righteousness' sake, for theirs is the kingdom of heaven. Blessed are you when people revile you and persecute you and utter all kinds of evil against you falsely on my account. Rejoice and be glad, for your reward is great in heaven, for in the same way they persecuted the prophets who were before you."

- "The pure in heart will see God." Lord, you have a lot of purging to do on me before I am ready for your presence.
- Maybe I could start today.

Monday 3rd November   Luke 14:12–14

Jesus said also to the one who had invited him, "When you give a luncheon or a dinner, do not invite your friends or your brothers or your relatives or rich neighbors, in case they may invite you in return, and you would be repaid. But when you give a banquet, invite the poor, the crippled, the lame, and the blind. And you will be blessed, because they cannot repay you, for you will be repaid at the resurrection of the righteous."

- Having a meal with family or friends is usually most enjoyable; it is also normal human behavior. But Jesus urges us to go beyond our comfort zone.
- "You will be blessed, because they cannot repay you." This is the generosity that God asks of us, that we give without reward. It is the generosity that increases our capacity to love.
- Where do I start with this?

Tuesday 4th November,
St. Charles Borromeo   **John 10:11–16**

Jesus said to the Pharisees, "I am the good shepherd. The good shepherd lays down his life for the sheep. The hired hand, who is not the shepherd and does not own the sheep, sees the wolf coming and leaves the sheep and runs away–and the wolf snatches them and scatters them. The hired hand runs away because a hired hand does not care for the sheep. I am the good shepherd. I know my own and my own know me, just as the Father knows me and I know the Father. And I lay down my life for the sheep. I have other sheep that do not belong to this fold. I must bring them also, and they will listen to my voice. So there will be one flock, one shepherd."

- "I know my own and my own know me." Good Shepherd, do you know me? It matters so much that I am known as I am, and loved as I am, with a love that persists even when things look bad around me.
- Do I know you? It is a lifelong task, each daily prayer a step in that task, to enter into your heart.

Wednesday 5th November   **Luke 14:25–28**

Now large crowds were traveling with him; and he turned and said to them, "Whoever comes to me and does not hate father and mother, wife and children, brothers and sisters, yes, and even life itself, cannot be my disciple. Whoever does not carry the cross and follow me cannot be my disciple."

- "You either love them or hate them" is a manner of speaking that we hear from time to time, to state a personal preference for one thing over another. Jesus uses a similar style here, to make his point to the crowds.

- "Whoever does not carry the cross and follow me cannot be my disciple." It is the cross that represents the way God's Son died for all humanity.
- Let me sit and think about the cross; what it has meant through the ages; what it means for Christians, for Jews, for Muslims; what it means for me.

Thursday 6th November   Luke 15:1–7

Now all the tax collectors and sinners were coming near to listen to him. And the Pharisees and the scribes were grumbling and saying, "This fellow welcomes sinners and eats with them." So he told them this parable: "Which one of you, having a hundred sheep and losing one of them, does not leave the ninety-nine in the wilderness and go after the one that is lost until he finds it? When he has found it, he lays it on his shoulders and rejoices. And when he comes home, he calls together his friends and neighbors, saying to them, 'Rejoice with me, for I have found my sheep that was lost.' Just so, I tell you, there will be more joy in heaven over one sinner who repents than over ninety-nine righteous persons who need no repentance."

- Jesus' listeners did not have a concept of a God who sought out the lost; rather theirs was a God who turned his back on sinners.
- Jesus' story reassures us that what may be lost now can be found again, and reconciliation achieved.
- How do I respond to those people whom I see as "lost" in some way? How do I respond to my own failings? Have I given up on them or continued to work away at improvements?

Friday 7th November **Psalm 121(122):1–8**

I was glad when they said to me, "Let us go to the house of the LORD!" Our feet are standing within your gates, O Jerusalem. Jerusalem–built as a city that is bound firmly together. To it the tribes go up, the tribes of the LORD, as was decreed for Israel, to give thanks to the name of the LORD. For there the thrones for judgment were set up, the thrones of the house of David.

- Picture the scene: the morning sun reflecting from the golden Dome of the Rock, the most beautiful building in Jerusalem and sacred place for Moslems; a busload of newly arrived, tired pilgrims suddenly silent with emotion. At last, they were in sight of the ultimate goal of pilgrims, the city holy to Jews, Moslems, and Christians.

- Lord, bring peace to your city, and to all the children of Abraham.

Saturday 8th November **Luke 16:9–13**

J esus said to the disciples, "And I tell you, make friends for yourselves by means of dishonest wealth so that when it is gone, they may welcome you into the eternal homes. Whoever is faithful in a very little is faithful also in much; and whoever is dishonest in a very little is dishonest also in much. If then you have not been faithful with the dishonest wealth, who will entrust to you the true riches? And if you have not been faithful with what belongs to another, who will give you what is your own? No slave can serve two masters; for a slave will either hate the one and love the other, or be devoted to the one and despise the other. You cannot serve God and wealth."

- "Whoever is faithful in a very little is faithful also in much." Lord, you invite me to aim at zero tolerance in my heart for dishonesty, half-truths and sly self-indulgence. Thèrése of Lisieux based her *Little Way* on this: "Fidelity is the flower of love, to which nothing is little."

- How do I measure up here? Do I slide away from honest behavior? Do I put "spin" on my actions to conceal what I have done?

Something to think and pray about each day this week:

Making Peace

Armistice Day on 11th November puts me in mind of the stupid wastefulness of war, and the overwhelming joy of peace when arms are laid down. No wonder that the peace-makers earn one of Jesus' Beatitudes; they shall be called children of God (Matthew 5:9). As I move into prayer, I detect rumblings of resentment, or unforgiven injuries, in my heart. That is where wars start. Let me bring them before my eyes in prayer, the people who stir my displeasure. I try to enter into their skin and their heart, and I say to them: go in peace, I have no quarrel with you.

The Presence of God

As I sit here, the beating of my heart,
the ebb and flow of my breathing, the movements of my mind
are all signs of God's ongoing creation of me.
I pause for a moment, and become aware
of this presence of God within me.

Freedom

Lord, grant me the grace to be free from the excesses of this life.
Let me not get caught up with the desire for wealth.
Keep my heart and mind free to love and serve you.

Consciousness

In God's loving presence I unwind the past day,
starting from now and looking back, moment by moment.
I gather in all the goodness and light, in gratitude.
I attend to the shadows and what they say to me,
seeking healing, courage, forgiveness.

The Word

I take my time to read the Word of God, slowly, a few times, allowing myself to dwell on anything that strikes me. (Please turn to your scripture on the following pages. Inspiration points are there should you need them. When you are ready, return here to continue.)

Conversation

Remembering that I am still in God's presence,
I imagine Jesus himself standing or sitting beside me,
and say whatever is on my mind, whatever is in my heart,
speaking as one friend to another.

Conclusion

Glory be to the Father, and to the Son, and to the Holy Spirit,
As it was in the beginning, is now and ever shall be,
World without end. Amen

Sunday 9th November,
Dedication of the Lateran Basilica   John 2:13–16

The Passover of the Jews was near, and Jesus went up to Jerusalem. In the temple he found people selling cattle, sheep, and doves, and the money changers seated at their tables. Making a whip of cords, he drove all of them out of the temple, both the sheep and the cattle. He also poured out the coins of the money changers and overturned their tables. He told those who were selling the doves, "Take these things out of here! Stop making my Father's house a marketplace!"

- In front of this magnificent building in Rome is a statue recalling a vision of Francis of Assisi, showing him as though he and his friar brothers are holding up a crumbling church. It reminds us that the "Church" is not the building, but is God's people.
- Like Francis we are also called to build up God's people.
- What is my role here? Can I do more?

Monday 10th November   Luke 17:3–6

Jesus said to his disciples, "Be on your guard! If another disciple sins, you must rebuke the offender, and if there is repentance, you must forgive. And if the same person sins against you seven times a day, and turns back to you seven times and says, 'I repent,' you must forgive." The apostles said to the Lord, "Increase our faith!" The Lord replied, "If you had faith the size of a mustard seed, you could say to this mulberry tree, 'Be uprooted and planted in the sea,' and it would obey you."

- "If there is repentance, you must forgive." Thank you, Lord. I need this reminder. Forgiveness is not a cover-all blanket, but a reaching out towards the one who repents. Repentance and forgiveness go hand in hand.

- You bid me be discerning, not foolish; but when I forgive, it must be a burying of the hatchet without marking the spot.

Tuesday 11th November   Luke 17:7–10

Jesus said to his disciples, "Who among you would say to your slave who has just come in from plowing or tending sheep in the field, 'Come here at once and take your place at the table'? Would you not rather say to him, 'Prepare supper for me, put on your apron and serve me while I eat and drink; later you may eat and drink'? Do you thank the slave for doing what was commanded? So you also, when you have done all that you were ordered to do, say, 'We are worthless slaves; we have done only what we ought to have done!'"

- "Blessed be God" is no idle prayer. It speaks my confidence in God even when I cannot grasp what God is doing to me. It puts me, as a Christian, in touch with Moslems and with Jews who revere God's will. I struggle against sickness, injustice and evil.
- At the end of the day I may seem to be losing the struggle, but I bless the Lord whose hand is over me.

Wednesday 12th November   Luke 17:11–19

On the way to Jerusalem Jesus was going through the region between Samaria and Galilee. As he entered a village, ten lepers approached him. Keeping their distance, they called out, saying, "Jesus, Master, have mercy on us!" When he saw them, he said to them, "Go and show yourselves to the priests." And as they went, they were made clean. Then one of them, when he saw that he was healed, turned back, praising God with a loud voice. He prostrated himself at Jesus' feet and thanked him. And he was a Samaritan. Then Jesus asked, "Were not ten made clean? But the other nine, where are they? Was none of them found to return and give praise to God except this foreigner?" Then he said to him, "Get up and go on your way; your faith has made you well."

- How long does gratitude last? These lepers were respectful, even fawning, when they were still suffering: "Jesus, Master, have mercy on us." In their misery they joined forces, waiving the old hostility between Jews and Samaritans.

- But when they saw their leprosy healed, and felt themselves whole, nine of them took their blessing for granted and forgot to say, "Thank you."

- Lord, my gratitude often grows cold. Let me count my blessings, never take them for granted.

Thursday 13th November   Luke 17:20–25

Once Jesus was asked by the Pharisees when the kingdom of God was coming, and he answered, "The kingdom of God is not coming with things that can be observed; nor will they say, 'Look, here it is!' or 'There it is!' For, in fact, the kingdom of God is among you." Then he said to the disciples, "The days are coming when you will long to see one of the days of the Son of Man, and you will not see it. They will say to you, 'Look there!' or 'Look here!' Do not go, do not set off in pursuit. For as the lightning flashes and lights up the sky from one side to the other, so will the Son of Man be in his day. But first he must endure much suffering and be rejected by this generation."

- "The kingdom of God is among you." This is the tension of every Christian: to hope that God will intervene and bring about a better world, and at the same time to work and act knowing that it all depends on us.

- Lord, you are warning me not to be distracted by scaremongers and prophets who claim private revelations about the end of the world. It is our world; we have to shape it and care for it with patience and courage.

Friday 14th November   2 John 5b–9

I ask you, not as though I were writing you a new commandment, but one we have had from the beginning, let us love one another. And this is love, that we walk according to his commandments; this is the commandment just as you have heard it from the beginning—you must walk in it. Many deceivers have gone out into the world, those who do not confess that Jesus Christ has come in the flesh; any such person is the deceiver and the antichrist! Be on your guard, so that you do not lose what we have worked for, but may receive a full reward. Everyone who does not abide in the teaching of Christ, but goes beyond it, does not have God; whoever abides in the teaching has both the Father and the Son.

- This letter to an early church encourages its members to remain faithful to Christian life; to "walk" in love, and to "abide in the teaching of Christ."
- Being Christian is being fully human: Christian love and teaching are part of daily life, not "add-ons" or book learning.

Saturday 15th November   Luke 18:1–8

Then Jesus told them a parable about their need to pray always and not to lose heart. He said, "In a certain city there was a judge who neither feared God nor had respect for people. In that city there was a widow who kept coming to him and saying, 'Grant me justice against my opponent.' For a while he refused; but later he said to himself, 'Though I have no fear of God and no respect for anyone, yet because this widow keeps bothering me, I will grant her justice, so that she may not wear me out by continually coming.'" And the Lord said, "Listen to what the unjust judge says. And will not God grant justice to his chosen ones who cry to him day and night? Will he delay long in helping them? I tell you, he will quickly grant justice to them. And yet, when the Son of Man comes, will he find faith on earth?"

- I give thanks, Lord, if I live in a place where the society is fairer than the one the widow knew.
- No matter where or when I live, I still need your words about perseverance in prayer. There have been times when I belabored God and nearly lost heart, overwhelmed by the silence of heaven. Teach me to recognize you in your silence as well as your words.

Something to think and pray about each day this week:

Lady in Waiting

The newspapers fill this month with thoughts of the festive season ahead. Six weeks before the birth, Mary must have been as much preoccupied with thoughts of Christmas as are the retailers who weary us as they count off the days. Joseph was watching her health and activity, trying to temper life's demands on her. Mary grew more and more interior, as expectant mothers do, identifying with the baby-in-waiting, full of hope, and in Mary's case with a sense of being part of a plan beyond her imagining. Lord, do not forget this tiny planet. We still need a Savior, and the hope that he brings. I do not require the glitzy offerings of the marketplace, but I want to be part of your redemptive plan for the world.

The Presence of God
As I sit here, the beating of my heart,
the ebb and flow of my breathing, the movements of my mind
are all signs of God's ongoing creation of me.
I pause for a moment, and become aware
of this presence of God within me.

Freedom
I will ask God's help,
to be free from my own preoccupations,
to be open to God in this time of prayer,
to come to love and serve him more.

Consciousness
Help me, Lord, to be more conscious of your presence.
Teach me to recognize your presence in others.
Fill my heart with gratitude for the times your love
has been shown to me through the care of others.

The Word
I take my time to read the Word of God, slowly, a few times, allowing myself to dwell on anything that strikes me. (Please turn to your scripture on the following pages. Inspiration points are there should you need them. When you are ready, return here to continue.)

Conversation
Remembering that I am still in God's presence,
I imagine Jesus himself standing or sitting beside me,
and say whatever is on my mind, whatever is in my heart,
speaking as one friend to another.

Conclusion
Glory be to the Father, and to the Son, and to the Holy Spirit,
As it was in the beginning, is now and ever shall be,
World without end. Amen

Sunday 16th November,
Thirty-third Sunday in Ordinary Time   Matthew 25:14–30

"For it is as if a man, going on a journey, summoned his slaves and entrusted his property to them; to one he gave five talents, to another two, to another one, to each according to his ability. Then he went away. The one who had received the five talents went off at once and traded with them, and made five more talents. In the same way, the one who had the two talents made two more talents. But the one who had received the one talent went off and dug a hole in the ground and hid his master's money. After a long time the master of those slaves came and settled accounts with them. Then the one who had received the five talents came forward, bringing five more talents, saying, 'Master, you handed over to me five talents; see, I have made five more talents.' His master said to him, 'Well done, good and trustworthy slave; you have been trustworthy in a few things, I will put you in charge of many things; enter into the joy of your master.' And the one with the two talents also came forward . . ."

- This is a difficult parable for the cautious and conservative, who want to keep things as they are, risking nothing and avoiding adventures. Many have gifts for singing, sport, leadership, language, business or whatever, but do not use it, perhaps for fear of failure.
- Am I allowing any of God's gifts to me to rust unseen? Do I fear what might happen to my life if I fully embraced my gifts?

Monday 17th November,
St. Elizabeth of Hungary   Luke 6:31–35

Jesus said to the disciples, "Do to others as you would have them do to you. If you love those who love you, what credit is that to you? For even sinners love those who love them. If you do good to those who do good to you, what credit is that to you?

For even sinners do the same. If you lend to those from whom you hope to receive, what credit is that to you? Even sinners lend to sinners, to receive as much again. But love your enemies, do good, and lend, expecting nothing in return. Your reward will be great, and you will be children of the Most High; for he is kind to the ungrateful and the wicked."

- "Love your enemies." Thank you, Lord, for this calling, to be a child of the Most High, to let your goodness flow through me towards the deserving and the undeserving.

Tuesday 18th November   Luke 19:1–6

Jesus was passing through Jericho, and a man was there named Zacchaeus; he was a chief tax collector and was rich. He was trying to see who Jesus was, but on account of the crowd he could not, because he was short in stature. So he ran ahead and climbed a sycamore tree to see him, because he was going to pass that way. When Jesus came to the place, he looked up and said to him, "Zacchaeus, hurry and come down; for I must stay at your house today." So he hurried down and was happy to welcome him.

- Little Zacchaeus was hated. In that wealthy city he had grown rich by extortion, but he was not happy, and sensed some need for a change in his life.
- If he mingled with the crowd, he would soon be black and blue with sly nudges and kicks. He had good reason to climb out of the reach of the crowd. He aimed to be a curious observer of Jesus, and suddenly found himself called by name.
- Lord give me the confidence to welcome you into my heart.

Wednesday 19th November   Psalm 150:1–6

Praise the Lord! Praise God in his sanctuary; praise him in his mighty firmament! Praise him for his mighty deeds; praise him according to his surpassing greatness! Praise him with trumpet sound; praise him with lute and harp! Praise him with tambourine and dance; praise him with strings and pipe! Praise him with clanging cymbals; praise him with loud clashing cymbals! Let everything that breathes praise the Lord! Praise the Lord!

- There are times when we must give voice to the glory of God, when we put aside our daily concerns and thoughts of our own failings, to Celebrate and praise God our Creator, our Protector, our Savior.
- The psalmist gives us words to start; let us continue.

Thursday 20th November   Luke 19:41–43

As he came near and saw the city, he wept over it, saying, "If you, even you, had only recognized on this day the things that make for peace! But now they are hidden from your eyes. Indeed, the days will come upon you, when your enemies will set up ramparts around you and surround you, and hem you in on every side."

- These were tears of deep sorrow, born of love. Having reached the city, Jesus shows us the depth of his pain over Jerusalem and its failure to recognize his message.
- Each day, my blessings from God are no less than those of Jerusalem. Do I know God's grace and presence in my life?

Friday 21st November   Luke 19:45–48

Then Jesus entered the temple and began to drive out those who were selling things there; and he said, "It is written, 'My house shall be a house of prayer'; but you have made it a den of robbers." Every day he was teaching in the temple. The chief priests, the scribes, and the leaders of the people kept looking for a way to kill him; but they did not find anything they could do, for all the people were spellbound by what they heard.

- So begins the drama of the Passion: Jesus comes into the temple, his "Father's house," this great place of prayer, to purify it for the worship of God alone.
- Those who heard Jesus were spellbound. Can I allow his words to come straight to me, with force and clarity?

Saturday 22nd November   Psalm 143(144):1–2, 9–10

Blessed be the LORD, my rock, who trains my hands for war, and my fingers for battle; my rock and my fortress, my stronghold and my deliverer, my shield, in whom I take refuge, who subdues the peoples under me. I will sing a new song to you, O God; upon a ten-stringed harp I will play to you, the one who gives victory to kings, who rescues his servant David.

- David celebrated God, as his rock, his refuge, his stronghold, his deliverer.
- Can I allow my own images of God to come to the surface? How do I respond to them? with songs of joy? in some other way?

Something to think and pray about each day this week:

A King Stripped Bare

When we call Christ the King, we have to un-think the trappings of royalty, and picture him as Pilate saw him when he asked: Are you a king? He was rejected, in pain, deserted by his followers. He had known fear; he had sweated blood and called on God three times, using the self-same words: Let this chalice pass from me.

Yet Pilate was in awe. Jesus was unafraid now, ready to drain the bitter chalice, but was himself untouched by bitterness. Here was a man who could command the loyalty not so much of the successful and popular, as of the great mass of humankind who also pray daily that God spare them the bitter chalice. If he is a king, it is not as the overclothed icon of Byzantine art, but as the naked, crucified one.

The Presence of God

I pause for a moment
and reflect on God's life-giving presence
in every part of my body, in everything around me,
in the whole of my life.

Freedom

God is not foreign to my freedom.
Instead the Spirit breathes life into my most intimate desires,
gently nudging me towards all that is good.
I ask for the grace to let myself be enfolded by the Spirit.

Consciousness

I exist in a web of relationships—links to nature, people, God.
I trace out these links, giving thanks for the life that flows
through them.
Some links are twisted or broken: I may feel regret, anger,
disappointment.
I pray for the gift of acceptance and forgiveness.

The Word

God speaks to each one of us individually. I need to listen to
what he is saying to me. (Please turn to your scripture on the
following pages. Inspiration points are there should you need
them. When you are ready, return here to continue.)

Conversation

How has God's Word moved me? Has it left me cold?
Has it consoled me or moved me to act in a new way?
I imagine Jesus standing or sitting beside me,
I turn and share my feelings with him.

Conclusion

Glory be to the Father, and to the Son, and to the Holy Spirit,
As it was in the beginning, is now and ever shall be,
World without end. Amen

Sunday 23rd November,
Feast of Christ the King   **Matthew 25:31–40**

"When the Son of Man comes in his glory, and all the angels with him, then he will sit on the throne of his glory. All the nations will be gathered before him, and he will separate people one from another as a shepherd separates the sheep from the goats, and he will put the sheep at his right hand and the goats at the left. Then the king will say to those at his right hand, 'Come, you that are blessed by my Father, inherit the kingdom prepared for you from the foundation of the world; for I was hungry and you gave me food, I was thirsty and you gave me something to drink, I was a stranger and you welcomed me, I was naked and you gave me clothing, I was sick and you took care of me, I was in prison and you visited me.' Then the righteous will answer him, 'Lord, when was it that we saw you hungry and gave you food, or thirsty and gave you something to drink? And when was it that we saw you a stranger and welcomed you, or naked and gave you clothing? And when was it that we saw you sick or in prison and visited you?' And the king will answer them, 'Truly I tell you, just as you did it to one of the least of these who are members of my family, you did it to me.'"

- The Last Judgment, the *Dies Irae*, stirs my heart with fear.
- Yet in the end, Lord, your message is simple, your command easy. You are there beside me in the needy. I have only to reach them to reach you.

Monday 24th November   **Luke 21:1–4**

Jesus looked up and saw rich people putting their gifts into the treasury; he also saw a poor widow put in two small copper coins. He said, "Truly I tell you, this poor widow has put in more than all of them; for all of them have contributed out of their abundance, but she out of her poverty has put in all she had to live on."

- "Clean hands and pure heart and a desire for what is worthwhile": that is a simple and lovely recipe for goodness, a passport to seeing your face, Lord.

Tuesday 25th November   Luke 21:5–11

When some were speaking about the temple, how it was adorned with beautiful stones and gifts dedicated to God, Jesus said, "As for these things that you see, the days will come when not one stone will be left upon another; all will be thrown down." They asked him, "Teacher, when will this be, and what will be the sign that this is about to take place?" And he said, "Beware that you are not led astray; for many will come in my name and say, 'I am he!' and, 'The time is near!' Do not go after them. When you hear of wars and insurrections, do not be terrified; for these things must take place first, but the end will not follow immediately." Then he said to them, "Nation will rise against nation, and kingdom against kingdom; there will be great earthquakes, and in various places famines and plagues; and there will be dreadful portents and great signs from heaven."

- In these last days of the Church's year, we hear Jesus, in Jerusalem, as he faces his own death, foretell crises and great upset facing his followers. Jesus does not minimize or water down the difficulties.
- He himself went on to face the ultimate in crisis and upset. He shows us that the crisis was not the last word. Does that give me hope? How do I respond today?

Wednesday 26th November   Luke 21:12–19

Jesus said to his disciples, "But before all this occurs, they will arrest you and persecute you; they will hand you over to synagogues and prisons, and you will be brought before kings and governors because of my name. This will give you an opportunity to testify. So make up your minds not to prepare your defense in advance; for I will give you words and a wisdom that none of your opponents will be able to withstand or contradict. You will be betrayed even by parents and brothers, by relatives and friends; and they will put some of you to death. You will be hated by all because of my name. But not a hair of your head will perish. By your endurance you will gain your souls."

- "They will arrest you and persecute you . . ." Lord, as you spoke these grim words, you faced your own arrest and betrayal, and the experience of the hatred of your own people.
- In my worst times I remember your promise: "Not a hair of your head will perish. By your endurance you will gain your souls."

Thursday 27th November   Luke 21:25–28

Jesus said to the disciples, "There will be signs in the sun, the moon, and the stars, and on the earth distress among nations confused by the roaring of the sea and the waves. People will faint from fear and foreboding of what is coming upon the world, for the powers of the heavens will be shaken. Then they will see 'the Son of Man coming in a cloud' with power and great glory. Now when these things begin to take place, stand up and raise your heads, because your redemption is drawing near."

- Jesus captures the strong sense of foreboding, of confusion, even of panic that is often with us today.
- Help me Lord, so that I hold firm and look forward, always in the hope that beyond my fear there is a new beginning.

Friday 28th November   Luke 21:29–33

Then Jesus told them a parable: "Look at the fig tree and all the trees; as soon as they sprout leaves you can see for yourselves and know that summer is already near. So also, when you see these things taking place, you know that the kingdom of God is near. Truly I tell you, this generation will not pass away until all things have taken place. Heaven and earth will pass away, but my words will not pass away."

- Lord, you are always telling us to be ready. Something is going to happen.
- Nature astonishes us with new life every spring, and in the same way God will astonish us with a fresh spring in ourselves. Keep that sense of hope awake in me.
- I remember Belloc's lines: "Kings live in palaces and pigs in sties But youth in expectation. Youth is wise."

Saturday 29th November   Luke 21:34–36

Jesus said to his disciples, "Be on guard so that your hearts are not weighed down with dissipation and drunkenness and the worries of this life, and that day catch you unexpectedly, like a trap. For it will come upon all who live on the face of the whole earth. Be alert at all times, praying that you may have the strength to escape all these things that will take place, and to stand before the Son of Man."

- As we dip towards the end of the year, the liturgy reminds us of the end of the world. We struggle to merge our scientific knowledge of the universe from the time of the Big Bang, with what the Lord is telling us about the end of time.
- Always he is warning us to be alert, praying for strength.

Sacred Space

Sacred Space: The Prayer Books (over 50,000 copies sold) are prayer guides inspired by the very popular, successful, interactive website, www.sacredspace.ie. Both the books and the site offer a way to reflect and pray each day of the year; both present a time to quietly connect with God and a space to be spiritually nourished, healed, challenged, and transformed.

Advent begins December 2, 2007!

Sacred Space For Advent and the Christmas Season 2007-2008

Jesuit Communication Centre

The first annual edition of *Sacred Space for Advent and the Christmas Season 2007-2008* is an ideal way to pray and reflect during this often-hectic time of year. Building on the popularity of the website www.sacredspace.ie and the successful series of *Sacred Space* prayer books, *Sacred Space for Advent* includes readings, reflection questions, and prayer starters for each day of the Advent season. This small, take-along resource is ideal for anyone, whether you already visit the site, use the annual *Sacred Space* prayer books, or are simply searching for an on-the-go way to pray during Advent.
ISBN: 9781594711398 / 96 pages / 4" x 6.25" / $2.25

Ash Wednesday is February 6, 2008!

Sacred Space for Lent 2008

Sacred Space for Lent 2008 includes readings, reflection questions, and prayer starters for each day of the Lenten season. If you already visit the site, use the annual *Sacred Space* prayer books, or are simply searching for a fresh way to pray for Lent, you'll be glad you found *Sacred Space for Lent*.
ISBN: 9781594711602 / 128 pages / 4" x 6.25" / $2.25

Coming Fall 2008
• • • SACRED SPACE THE PRAYER BOOK 2009 • • •

ave maria press®

Available from your bookstore or from
ave maria press / Notre Dame, IN 46556
www.avemariapress.com / Ph: 800-282-1865
A Ministry of the Indiana Province of Holy Cross

Keycode: F0A0807000O